Thanks to God
and the Revolution

Roger N. Lancaster

THANKS TO GOD AND THE REVOLUTION

Popular Religion and Class Consciousness in the New Nicaragua

COLUMBIA UNIVERSITY PRESS

NEW YORK   1988

COLUMBIA UNIVERSITY PRESS
New York   Guildford, Surrey
Copyright (c) 1988 Columbia University Press

LIBRARY OF CONGRESS
Library of Congress Cataloging-in-Publication Data

Lancaster, Roger N.
Thanks to God and the revolution : popular religion and class
consciousness in the new Nicaragua / Roger N. Lancaster.
p.   cm.
Bibliography: p.
Includes index.
ISBN 0-231-06730-5
ISBN 0-231-06731-3 (pbk)
1. Christianity—Nicaragua. 2. Social classes—Nicaragua—
History—20th century. 3. Communism and religion—History—
20th century. 4. Nicaragua—Politics and government—1979– I. Title.
BR625.N5L35 1988
277.285'082—dc19   88-4960
                                                                  CIP

Printed in the United States of America

Casebound editions of Columbia University Press books are Smyth-sewn
and printed on permanent and durable acid-free paper

A los niños de los barrios populares,
"los hijos de Sandino" y el futuro de Nicaragua
—y especialmente a E., L. y W.

Contents

Acknowledgments

At Berkeley it has been my privilege to work with the professors whose influences appear and reappear throughout this book. Some of those professors include Burton Benedict, Stanley Brandes, Elizabeth Colson, George De Vos, and William Shack. The moral support of Gerald Berreman, Robert Blauner, and Jack Potter proved invaluable in the preparation and execution of my fieldwork; their enthusiasm fueled my own, and their suggestions have been of no small significance in the production of this manuscript. I should especially thank Nancy Scheper-Hughes, adviser to this project, teacher of several years, and friend of long acquaintance. Her seminars, classes, and reading courses have stimulated my own intellectual development, and her example has set a high standard of commitment to both humanism and social science.

Thanks are also in order to Richard Adams and Michael Taussig, who showed interest in my work, and whose lengthy discussions proved very helpful in the final preparation of this book. An earlier draft of this manuscript was read by an interested friend, Joe Morris, and much of this material was also productively discussed with David Goldman. Their suggestions have allowed me revisions and refinements that I hope will make the finished manuscript more accessible to a nonanthropological audience. Of course, I have not incorporated all of the recommendations of either scholars or friends, and the observations and analysis contained in this finished product are uniquely my own; I take responsibility for any errors.

My findings are based on three periods of participant-observation fieldwork in Managua's working-class barrios: December 1984–January 1985, May–December 1985, and May–June 1986.

Funding for fieldwork in a revolutionary milieu was not easy to obtain, and I have lost track of exactly how many foundations rejected my proposals. I am therefore particularly indebted to those sources of funds that actually came through. Research was funded by a travel grant from the Center for Latin American Studies and the Tinker Foundation, a Graduate Humanities Research Grant from the Regents of the University of California, and three separate small grants from the Lowie Funds of the Department of Anthropology at Berkeley. Write-up and revisions were later supported by a generous stipend from the Institute for the Study of Social Change, located at the Berkeley campus.

Thanks are also in order to relevant institutions in the host country: to the government of Nicaragua, for permitting my research to be carried out in an absolutely open, unconstrained, and unconditional manner, and to the *Centro Ecuménico Antonio Valdivieso*, whose members were accessible to my questions and who introduced me to some of the base community workers quoted herein.

They say an acknowledgment is a scratch where it itches. There are personal as well as academic itches, and I should thank my mother, father, and sister for their moral and emotional support. From the age that I was two or three and throughout my early childhood, my mother used to read to my sister and me from the King James version of the Bible every night before bedtime. I well remember asking, every two or three sentences, "What does that mean," and soliciting commentary and explanation, until eventually I was as versed in the Bible—and King James English—as other children might be in Mother Goose or Grimm's fairy tales. Traces of this early moral and intellectual training are not at all absent in my work. And the moral support of grandparents, aunts, uncles, and cousins far too numerous to mention has buoyed me up through various difficulties.

The largest debts are those that are personal *and* intellectual. I would never have finished this task without the patient assistance of Philip Pincus: who was there, who endured three bouts of dengue in the field, and who always kept an open yet critical perspective as this project evolved. Many of the chapters in this book grew out of innumerable conversations with Philip. It is because of his questions, comments, criticisms, and demands for clarification that much of what is best in my work took shape.

My greatest debt of all is to the kind and hospitable people of those *barrios populares* in Managua, with whom I worked, ate, and lived during my fieldwork. Following a wise anthropological tradition, my informants must remain anonymous; I can not mention anyone by name here. Moreover, to protect the privacy and anonymity of my subjects, the names of persons and even barrios which appear in this book are fictitious.

Whether offering me a cup of coffee in the early morning, sharing a glass of *chicha* in the afternoon heat, or sitting and talking with me inside the front porch while an inevitable tropical rain beat hard on the tin roof overhead, the workers of Nicaragua opened up their homes and their hearts to me. To you, subjects, informants, *compañeros*, and *compadres*, I will be forever grateful. You have affirmed my faith that the common people, *el pueblo sencillo*, have the consciousness, the will, and the ability to become actors in their own drama, the subjects of their own history. This book is for you, in the hopes of peace.

PROLOGUE
Theses on a Philosophy of Central American History[1]

PLAZA

In the Plaza of the Revolution, off to one side, stands the ruined Cathedral of Managua. Its insides were shaken out, its hull cracked, by the 1972 earthquake that destroyed Managua and shook the Somoza dynasty beyond repair. Now an assortment of grass, weeds, and vines grows inside the church, among sun-bleached murals that depict the lives of saints. In this manner, the old colonial structure offers an appropriate testimony to the Old Church, the Old Religion: a Church of Spain, of European conquistadores, of brown silent peasants receiving mass from white priests who are always talking, talking, talking. This was also the Church of the occasional activist priest, who dedicated himself to protecting the Indians, or advocacy of the poor, or the salvation of the peasants as a class; the Church of occasional insurrection. Ultimately, too, it was the Church of the Poor, and the wafers and words it offered were the only redemption available to all those who labored five hundred years in poverty and oppression.

On the other side of the Plaza, as boldly juxtaposed as design could allow, is Carlos Fonseca's grave with its eternal flame. Carlos Fonseca Amador, founder and major theorist of the FSLN; "Jefe de la Revolución," "of the dead that never die," just as it is written on the tomb, underneath the flame that never goes out. The stone also says, though it is not written there, "You are the light of the world."

ECHO

When political events are held in the Plaza of the Revolution, wedged in between the eternal flame of Carlos Fonseca and the ancient ruined church, an eerie effect is created. The church walls facing the Plaza are always freshly decorated with revolutionary banners and slogans for such festive occasions: the new face on an old edifice. (The opposite walls are always left unretouched.) In such moments, before the event proper is underway, the church itself, dull and gray with age, often seems distinctly uncomfortable with its new veneer of bright colors and loud slogans. But when the broadcast system is hooked up, and the electrical speakers in the Plaza are placed on strategic light poles; when the crowds of thousands are gathered and chanting and the rhetoric of revolution is on its most striking display, then a curious transformation seems to occur within the walls of the old cathedral. Timed to such close temporal proximity that many never notice it at all, the church *delivers up its echo of each and every word broadcast in the plaza.*

In these milliseconds that transpire between the spoken word and its echo in the ruins—and who can stand before us and say with certainty which of the two is more real?—fit perfectly a five hundred year history of Nicaragua. In these twinklings of impossibly compressed time, all the voices of a half-millennium cry out in polysemic cacophony, and the cracked walls of the church appear in a half-noticed moment: iridescent.

The Old haunts the New. The Old contains the New. The Old invigorates the New. And in the synchronicity of these moments, the Old pushes by means of the New toward its own transcendence and self-negation—

HISTORY

—So do not think for one minute that the Old is just some construct invented by the New, some symbol deployed in a moment of pitched battle with great adversaries. No. The Old is more real than the New. Since the Conquest, twenty generations have labored without ceasing in the mines, plantations, and factories of the oppressor. What has the mere present that could stand against such a mighty and terrible fact? The New cannot bend the Old to its whims. Just the reverse is true.

"Father Valdivieso[2] dies defending the indigenous, not just once, but each moment in Nicaraguan history, along with Sandino, and Fonseca. There is not enough room in heaven for all the martyrs, so they stay on the land, wandering and inspiring it forever."

TRAP DOOR

"History is progressive, they will tell you, grandson of mine, in the schools of the oppressors. They will tell you that History is a succession of good things, stacked one atop the other. And perhaps that is the ways it is, for them. But this is not true, for us. History is sameness. Christ is forever being killed by the Roman soldiers, here in the hills of Nicaragua, just as he was killed in the Bible five hundred years ago. And even now, at this moment, María is giving birth to Christ in the countryside, and his disciples are already walking the earth waiting for him. And the same Roman soldiers are already at the hill, waiting to kill him.

"What is History, then, you want to know? History is a series of trap doors through which the people are always falling, into ever grimmer systems of exploitation, until the savior comes with his army of saints, and brings the apocalypse that changes Heaven and Earth and Man."

CHE GUEVARA

His eyes were as a flame of fire.
—Revelation 19:12.

There is a Hill that is called both Myth and History; it is shaped like a skull. All around that Hill swarm the multitudes of humanity, who go about their disconnected lives: eating, drinking, sleeping, making love. The noise of their activity sounds from afar like swarms of gnats.

And now atop that Hill two enormous statues have appeared. The left one is Mosaic in cast: a great grey beard, bushy brows, a high ridged forehead—but no, that is not Moses; the lionous head is that of Marx. The other figure has made his simultaneous appearance: a younger man, wearing a crown of thorns, carrying a great wooden cross. These statues are made of granite, and yet they move, slowly, for the stone is miraculous granite. They cast their fiery eyes about, scanning the multitude. And wherever they look, the terrain becomes momentarily illuminated, and wherever a section of the crowd is illuminated, the people become motionless for a moment, and stand transfixed in the eyes of these two giants who stand on the Hill that is called Myth and History. When the gaze passes on to other sections of the great crowd, however, everyone, once frozen, resumes their disjointed and disconnected motions.

The two statues are not only moving their heads about and changing their positions, they are growing, growing, larger, larger. It seems that soon they will loom even larger than the Hill itself. Eventually, they happen to pass their spotlight gazes not outward onto the multitude, but directly across and onto each other. Each thereby becomes frozen in the gaze of the other; and each continues to grow larger and larger in this position.

And in the intersection of their fiery stares, a marvellous thing happens. The air shimmers for a moment, a new space opens up and discloses there a new image, supported in the air itself. He suggests aspects of both the previous statues, but he wears guerrilla fatigues, and turns his eyes upward in an attitude that is both beatific and violent.

And the crowd that could become neither Marx nor Jesus; this is a thing that it can become.

IDOLS

Howl, ye inhabitants of Maktesh,[3] for all the merchant people are cut down; all they that bear silver are cut off. And it shall come to pass at that time that I will search Jerusalem with candles, and punish the men that are settled on their lees: that say in their heart, The Lord will not do good, neither will he do evil.
—Zephaniah 1:11–12

Your missionaries, whether they be Catholic or Protestant, have always said the same thing about us: that we make images of God out of stone and wood, that we make God in the image of Man. But in the Bible itself, it says that Man is made in God's image, so what is the big difference here? We know that God exists because Man looks like Him; We are our only testimony to His existence. So it is only natural that we should make images of ourselves to remind us of God.

It is you who worship an abstract god who have committed idolatry. Jehovah is not an imaginary number. Yahweh is not some intellectualized reflection upon the infinite. You have invented an idol to the abstract and called it a god! But it is perhaps appropriate that a civilization without life should invent a lifeless deity.

"But the one true God exists in the face of those who are suffering, in the sweat of our oppression, in the muscle and sinew of our work. He stoops down to us, through his Son, to animate us in our struggle against the centuries old oppressor. God is in the people, and in their struggle against the slavery of the Egyptian, the Roman, and the Yankee. His salvation is the salvation of the poor, and how mightily He will punish the oppressors of the poor on that terrible day of reckoning!"

CALENDAR

It is right that Walter Benjamin should emphasize the calendrical aspects of class consciousness, calling our attention to the cyclical and repetitive nature of holy days.

This is not some peculiarity of Jewish religion. "A holiday is a day for remembrance." And what does it remember? The Old Calendar is a simple mnemonic device to the deepest and most profound sense of class consciousness. This is not class consciousness in the laudable but restricted sense evinced when workers are able to calculate their labor's relative worth on the existing market, and thus know what the union should be asking for in this year's negotiations. It is more primitive than that. It is a class consciousness with the depth of what others would call "racial memory," or "primordial sentiments." It calls up memories of the ancestors, and connects the present to the past. It embodies the most profound sense of peoplehood that the poor can attain. We relive the birth, the crucifixion, the resurrection; we remember the state of the poor in the first century, struggling under the yoke of Roman imperialism; our own state of affairs is clarified and interpreted to us through the scripture, the holiday, the mass. And this is the significance that salvation takes: it is the redemption of the past through the present; this is why the return of the messiah resurrects the dead themselves . . .

I wish to go further. This messianic vision of history, which is diametrically opposite the progressive telling of history, actually arrests the flow of time and achieves a universal present. The time of the now is structurally identical with the time of Christ. Everything on the present historical plane is mirrored in the constellation of things two thousand years ago. Ideas leap from the Bible, then, into the mouths and deeds of present actors. By the same script that Herod sent out soldiers to kill all the male infants in the land, Somoza, helpless before History, willed the Guardia Nacional to indiscriminately cut the throats of Managua's boys and adolescent males. *"Herod!"* the people cried in recognition, which was simultaneously a recognition of themselves as the trans-historic poor. The Bible thus ceases being a mere text contextualized, and for revolutionary believers becomes the contextualizing text of present-day activity: a script, a guide, a promise. And it is especially the messianic promise of salvation.

There is a celebrated painting by Paul Klee, in which a transparent cross is superimposed over a non-Christian mythological setting; this theme reappears in various of Klee's paintings. It is exactly like that. The myth of Christ displaces and supplants all other previous mythologies; it is as though they, too, were awaiting the arrival of the true messiah. Similarly, the orienting myth of class consciousness, which is the kernel of the religion of the poor, subverts all other myth and bends all present, past, and future reality to its concerns.

The New Calendar—with its revolutionary holidays—likewise both supplants and absorbs the Old one. It marks neither the eternal suffering of oppression, nor the perpetual victory of the adversary, which are the cyclical themes that serve to keep class consciousness alive; rather, the New Calendar marks the eternal triumph of revolt and revolution, and calls up remembrance of great sacrifices in the past in order to point to the protracted sacrifices that will be necessary now and in the future for the success of the revolution. The New Calendar thus stands in exactly the same relation to the Old Calendar as messianic to legal Judaism; as Christianity to Judaism; as Liberation Catholicism to the Old Religion. For, as Benjamin reminds us, to cling to the letter of tradition, without the "prophetic vision" implied therein, is to reduce the past to a cipher—what the priests of the New Theology call, and what Marxism has always called, escapist religion. And the New Religion both explodes and redeems the Old one through the historical trampoline of prophetic vision.

REDEMPTION

Again, this sense is equally present in Marxism and Christian communism, with epiphenomenal differences. The ostensibly "irreligious" Soviet cinema has produced the most arresting image of this religious and traditional aspect of socialism, but, naturally, with peculiarly Russian characteristics. In the film *Siberiad*, a tiny village is threatened with destruction from an uncontrolled oil fire. Only by turning the village graveyard into a firebreak, and thus destroying the graveyard, can the village be saved. The painful decision is taken; the razing of the graveyard begins. And against the background of bulldozers, fire, and destruction that constitute technological progress, the ancestors themselves *emerge from their graves* and walk among the living, embracing them and reassuring them of their decision. This is simultaneously the saddest and the most joyous moment in modern cinema. It depicts the communion of the dead with the living, the past with the present. Like Benjamin's, it is a *revolutionary* nostaligia.[4] The tradition can only be saved by its total destruction and reconstitution in new forms; and while there is no immediate route off the path of progress-through-development, socialism—as a more "conservative" system—can provide the means for containing the most socially destructive and anomic aspects of material progress. (Under capitalist development, the devil himself swallows up tradition, the past and all its contents.)

CLASS STRUGGLES

It is this selfsame desire for communion with the dead oppressed, this selfsame desire to dynamite the very continuum of history, that manifests itself in the proletariat when class struggle is at its decisive hour. This is what caused Marx to pen his famous line: "The history of all hitherto existing society is the history of class struggles." What follows is an exhortation and a reminder of the terrible charge of the modern proletariat: to redeem a ten thousand year history of oppression. This is Marxism at its most mythic, the single image most capable of motivating the masses of poor.

Now if anything follows from Marxism as historical or anthropological practice, it is that such a universal history of the poor cannot be *written*. The dialectic is milieu-specific. Every oppressed class is on its own, as it were, without any help from history not of its own making. Every social formation remains trapped in its own historical dialectic.

Marxism as political practice springs that trap. Whereas anthropological and historical Marxism *differentiates*, the Marxism of political movement *assimilates*. The will to power of the proletariat seeks out those junctures of the past—any past—that bear any resemblance whatsoever to its own situation, and animates them with its own desires. It writes its universal history *post factum.* The world-historical poor; the trans-historical class struggle; the universal dialectic, and the redemption of history: these exist, then, only in the fevered dreams of the conscious proletariat. But that is real enough to be real. And more real indeed than all the attempts of academic historicism to achieve accuracy.

LIBERATION THEOLOGY

He hath shewed the strength of his arm; he hath scattered the proud in the imagination of their hearts. He hath put down the mighty from their seats, and exalted them of low degree. He hath filled the hungry with good things; and the rich he hath sent empty away.
—Luke 1:51–63

Liberation theology knows that the salvation of the poor is the common project of two faiths, Marxism and Christianity. And the theology of liberation itself emerges at the moment of contact between the Old Religion and Marxism. But the religion of hope is not thus merely some mechanical "new syncretism" of each, blending two old faiths to make a new one, as one might graft two trees together to make one. Rather, it only makes explicit what was implicit in the Old Religion. There is nothing "radical" about it. It sees itself as the most traditional and conservative version of Christianity, and takes the communism of the original church as its central message. This is its image of the past: an unbroken chain of oppression, running right up to the present. The Bible chronicles that history and future of the poor, on their long march to God and communism. The original message of Christ was revolution. If that message was lost, suppressed, or driven underground, it is the sacred charge of the orthodox to revive it.

TO JUDGE THE QUICK AND THE DEAD

There are those who are always touting this or that particular movement as "different" from its predecessors, and always looking for "socialism with a human face." These well-wishers always offer their tepid support to revolutionary governments and movements in Third World countries at the beginning, only to withdraw even that once those governments have become consolidated and their policies apparent. Many of these same people are welcoming liberation theology as a "liberalizing" influence on revolutionary movements on the Latin American continent. They are mistaken. They do not understand that every redemption is also a day of reckoning, that every salvation is also a judgment day: by the same motion that Christ redeems the poor, he condemns the rich to eternal torment. They have imagined the theology of liberation as a "progressive" vision, when in fact it is a messianic one, tormented by demons and motivated by dreams in which the progressives have long since stopped believing. The Jehovah of the Poor is not—nor should he be—the kindly grandfather of American secular Christianity, Santa Claus-like, bearing gifts for all. He is the wrath of the people incarnate. There is no tolerance in him.

> Think not that I am come to send peace on earth: I come not to send peace, but a sword. (Matthew 10:34)

> And he shall rule them with a rod of iron: and he treadeth the winepress of the fierceness and the wrath of Almighty God. (Revelation 19:15)

Thanks to God
and the Revolution

INTRODUCTION
Seeing Nicaragua

CONTEXT

On my first day in Nicaragua I had been seated late into the night with a working-class family, talking politics and drinking the national drink, *pinol.* Nicaraguans so identify themselves with this beverage that they sometimes refer to themselves collectively as *pinol-latas* (literally, *"pinol* cans"; the *pinol*-drinkers). *Pinol* is an odd-tasting concoction to most North American palates; its key ingredient is ground toasted corn, to which is sometimes added oats and rice, likewise toasted and ground. (The smell of *pinol* being prepared in a large clay pot over an open fire is unmistakable and unforgettable.) These grains produce a robust if unfamiliar drink, somewhat muddy-looking to my eye; the grain powders ultimately settle as a thick sediment at the bottom of one's glass.

Over our *pinol,* then, we had been discussing Nicaraguan–North American relations, and what appears to most Nicaraguans to be a decidedly perplexing phenomenon: Reagan's continuing popularity in the United States and his reelection to a second term, in the absence of apparent coercion. "What could be wrong with these crazy gringos?" my hosts wanted to know, "Don't they know what he's doing to Nicaragua and to all the Third World?" I was thus initiated early on into the highly politicized environment in which I would be conducting fieldwork: "political" topics were rarely absent from any day's discussions or interviews, and, even when formally absent, were never very far away.

We discussed the sorts of things that Nicaraguans invariably discuss on their first encounters with North Americans: the Sandinista revolution and its immediate popular benefits—for this family, those benefits included childhood disease innoculations (and several members proudly showed me their smallpox vaccination scars), free health care, subsidized basic foods, and home electricity and running water. Our conversation eventually turned to what I was to later learn is a very typical question asked by Nicaraguans upon first meeting foreigners or strangers, in much the same way that a North American might ask, "And where were you born?" or "Where are you from?" This question, similarly, is designed to locate the person in his social milieu, but Nicaraguans determine that milieu not by a physical geography but by a spiritual one. "And what is your religion?" Everyone waited for a response.

This question was later to become for me an easy entrée into the belief structure of the people. I cannot count how many conversations or interviews I subsequently opened with this question, which rarely failed to evoke active interest in my research. But on my first night in Nicaragua I scarcely knew the lay of the land, and the question raised some trepidation on my part. "I am an atheist," I answered in all sincerity, though hesitantly, having decided ahead of time to be absolutely frank on such topics. Puzzled heads turned to each other in consultation, and the mother discussed this finding with her eldest daughter for a moment. I was myself by now nearing the bottom of my glass of *pinol*, and confronting the disturbing ambiguity it always leaves me: whether to eat or to drink this not-quite-solid, not-quite-liquid precipitant. I was asked for further clarification. "Is an atheist a Protestant of sorts, or what?" I expanded, explaining that I did not believe in the existence of God. "You mean you're an agnostic," two people simultaneously offered. "No," I explained, "an agnostic is someone who is uncertain about whether God exists or not, someone who isn't sure. I am an atheist, a much firmer position, which means that I believe God doesn't exist."

The family was visibly surprised by this unequivocal response, and I was becoming somewhat uneasy. In the light of later knowledge, it seems improbable that my informants were entirely unfamiliar with the term *"ateo."* It is more likely that they were scarcely able to credit their ears with what they had just heard, for a confession of *ateísmo* is a more improbable thing in Nicaragua. "We will take you to mass right away," the mother quite calmly announced, and that was the end of it for the night. However, this family would not rest until it had seen me off to the first available mass, in the nearest popular church—and every day for almost a week my hosts reminded me not to forget our appointment in church.

Thus began my encounter with religion in Nicaragua—and I shall call it "religion" here, in the anthropological tradition, although many of my informants, in their own tradition of liberation theology, insist that what they practice is not "religion" at all, which would be at best a trivialization and at worst a falsification of sacred texts, but rather *faith*, defined as a true version and profound actuation of scriptures in daily life. Indeed, it was this conversation (and others like it) and the chain of events it set in motion that eventually compelled me to focus my study on popular religion and class consciousness in Nicaraguan society. As I was to later learn, my informants had considered a profession of atheism neither as a simple belief (or absence of it) nor as an affirmation of humanism—an angle which I was always trying to communicate—but rather, as a confession of despair: an all-encompassing despair with social and political as well as religious connotations. To be godless, for almost all Nicaraguans, even many who call themselves materialists or Marxists, is to be directionless, centerless, lost. This strong sense is not so qualitatively different from the experience of religion in what we are accustomed to think of as the more "conservative" segments of North American society, except that in Nicaragua it baptizes a radically different political and social practice. And it was precisely this point that drew me, again and again, willy-nilly, to consider the intersection of popular religion and class consciousness in Nicaragua's revolutionary milieu.

I will confess that my confrontation with Nicaraguan religion originally produced in me an intellectual dissonance. It is not that I am unfamiliar with strong religious feeling. I grew up in a poor rural Southern community, and was there reared to be a Baptist preacher. My path to atheism was not an easy one lightly taken, and it was certainly *not* one uninformed by strong religious experience in a working-class context. Nonetheless, religion and belief in God had long appeared to me in the terms of classical Marxian humanism: as *prima facie* evidence of alienation, and moreover as inherently alienating—and this conviction was all the greater for being tempered by direct experience with the phenomenon. Yet, here was a case in which the exact opposite relationship between religion and alienation was claimed, and moreover appeared to actually hold: religion and belief in God evinced a profound absence of alienation and acted as a means of overcoming it. If, then, my study was originally and generally conceived as a study of cultural processes in the Nicaraguan revolution, in practice it became more specifically concerned with precisely that aspect of these cultural transformations for which I was least able to account, and which in fact gave me the most intellectual dissonance, given my state of knowledge and theoretical perspective.

I recount this by way of giving the reader a sense of my general motives in this study. I will not claim an "absence of subjectivity" here, any more than I would claim to lack a personality, or to be cut adrift from my own experiences or social relations. It seems to me that such claims are issued so as to better conceal the operation of bias, interests, and motives in a study, and to give anthropology a "scientistic" veneer of "objectivity" or to evade the implicit social responsibilities of the investigator to his subjects. I see anthropology, rather, as an "intersubjective" practice, wherein the subjectivity of the people under study is understood by honest but no less subjective observers.[1] Observation, then, is never (and can never be) a "passive" act; it is further complicated when it is observation in turn observed by the subjects of study—and my informants were always reminding me that they, too, were watching me, learning about my beliefs, and assuming a give-and-take in our relations. Commonly, my informants would ask me: "And what are you writing in your notes about us today?" and then proceed to offer suggestions on the interpretation of their own culture and practices. I remain indebted to my subjects for this active and most legitimate interest in my work. Far from being inhibited by this type of interest, I was often able to refine and sometimes completely revise my models.

Anthropology, then, is really what precipitates from the intersection of many gazes, and we can no more deny the role of interest and motive, both personal and social, in the production of knowledge than we could take the ethnographer out of the ethnography, the observer out of his observations, or all these out of their social contexts. This relationship is raised to the level of self-consciousness in the type of anthropology called "reflexive" or "critical."

In keeping with the spirit of this type of anthropology, I confess, then, that I remain an atheist. I say this not out of gaudy exhibitionism (which is indeed a danger in self-reflexive social science) but in order to be as honest with my readers as I was with my informants, many of whom may have other feelings on the topic and should be put on notice that my intention is a sociological and not theological analysis of religion. In a sense, this analysis of religion (as a sociological and not spiritual phenomenon) requires a methodological atheism. What I have seen in Nicaragua has greatly altered my assessment of both religion and theism; I might even describe myself as "religious" in the social-political sense herein developed. However, while what I have seen has shaken my assumptions about religious belief and practice to their very foundation, nothing that I have seen compels me to believe in the existence of a deity. But after all, this basic situation is not so different from that which normally confronts any anthropologist who studies a culture to which he does not belong. We are always studying beliefs we can never really share, and it is precisely this "outsider" perspective of participant-observation in a study of the Cultural Other that defines the anthropological approach. I hope that my treatment doesn't offend believers; I would like to think that there is much here with which they can agree. And as part of my general method, I have in fact outlined various of the major ideas contained in this book for some of my informants, who have generally agreed, at least sociologically, with most of my points.

If "seeing" is a social practice, constrained by all sorts of personal, psychological, social, and political criteria, then "seeing Nicaragua," for a North American, is a particularly charged process. Our histories are intertwined; the history of Nicaragua has long been the history of U.S. intervention. This litany of intervention exploded most dramatically in 1855 when William Walker's filibusters, a group of private U.S. mercenaries operating with the tacit approval of their government, invaded Nicaragua, on the pretext of helping to consolidate a Liberal government there, but in fact for the purpose of annexing Nicaragua as a new slave-holding state in the United States. Slavery had actually been outlawed in Nicaragua since 1822; undaunted, Walker declared himself president of Nicaragua, and then declared slavery to be reinstituted. Failing to conquer Nicaragua, Walker eventually withdrew his troops. But ever the optimist, he later reinvaded the country, and was eventually captured and put to death.

The United States Marines proper landed in Nicaragua a half dozen times since the Walker episode, and have occupied that country for a grand total of more than twenty years (leaving behind a number of English words, North American names, and the national sport, baseball). After interfering for more than a decade in a protracted civil war, U.S. military forces eventually withdrew for the last time in 1933, having organized, trained, armed, and supplied the national police force that the marines were to leave in their wake, the Guardía Nacional. Anastasio Somoza, the head of that national guard, made his effective control over the country official by seizing power in 1936, and it was again the United States that kept him—and for years to come, his family—in power with substantial military and economic aid.

When the Somoza dynasty was in its final days during the Sandinista revolution of 1979, U.S. helicopters were poised on Nicaragua's borders to intervene; their intervention was stayed, according to Nicaraguans retelling their own history, by a historical fact, and by an accident—which bears some explaining, as this was perhaps the only significant juncture in modern Nicaraguan history when the United States did *not* militarily intervene. The historical fact was the failure of American intervention in Vietnam, which had created widespread skepticism of similar military interventions in other places: the so-called "Vietnam syndrome." The accident was the national guard's ill-timed assassination of ABC news correspondent Billy Stewart, an event captured on film by his assistant, hiding nearby. There was nothing unusual about the assassination, except that it was an American journalist who was killed; except that it was captured on film; and except that it was seen by TV viewers in the United States. But it is at the convergence of such accidents of history and twists of fate that real history is made. The revolution proceeded, for a time, without direct U.S. intervention.[2]

And now we are intervening again. Briefly, there was a period of relatively good relations between Washington and the new government in Managua. Having been forced by circumstance not to intervene in the revolution, the Carter administration decided that Nicaragua was to be a showcase and a test of its human rights-oriented foreign policy. Economic aid was planned, some of which was actually sent, to help the country recuperate from the devastating effects of the full-scale civil war that had brought the Sandinistas to power. All of this ended when the Reagan administration took office, and the CIA quickly began recruiting, organizing, supplying, and arming expatriate national guardsmen into a fighting force of counterrevolutionaries: *la contra.* The contra landed on Nicaraguan territory in 1981, and has since that time been waging a "dirty war" against the Sandinista government and the Nicaraguan people. Its pattern of attacks on unarmed civilians, its systematic destruction of educational and medical facilities, its international narcotics trafficking, and a general pattern of terror against the Nicaraguan civilian population has been well-documented by international observers and human rights organizations.

It would do no good to pretend otherwise, then: the experience of the North American visitor in Nicaragua is already conditioned by what Condominas calls "the colonial preterrain" (1973). This is equally true whether that visitor be a political observer, journalist, tourist, student, or anthropologist (Lancaster 1986). This was driven home to me with painful force one day, when I was walking through a playground in Managua where a dozen or so pre-school age children were playing. The sight of an obviously foreign stranger caught their attention, and they ran to me, to begin asking questions. Was I carrying pens? They badly needed pens. Paper? There was a national shortage of paper. How much did my watch cost? "Where are you from?" one boy finally asked. When I told him the United States, another boy looked at me and said in a manner that was quiet, deliberate, and sad, "It is because of you[3] that we have a war."

Even in less extreme cases, the preterrain is inescapable. The anthropologist invariably comes from an affluent, powerful, colonial country, even if he is not himself rich or powerful. His base of operations, the university, includes among its many functions that of advising power: in a consulting role with government policy, or in its training role for officials of the multinational corporations. He studies poor and typically powerless people living in poor, powerless, colonized countries. And what is the nature of such a discourse, structured as it is by the colonial and neocolonial context, generated, as it is, at these extreme junctures in the flow of economic and political power in the world? Anthropology invariably generates knowledge of Third World populations that is consumed by whoever wishes to read it in the metropole countries. The danger here is of the anthropologist becoming an instrument in the neocolonial process, whereby information follows the same route as labor power and resources: extracted from the peripheries and transferred to the metropoles, for the benefit of the latter and to the detriment of the former. Even with theoretically critical or reflexive mechanisms built into one's method, there is the real danger of generating knowledge harmful to the subjects of one's study, and the danger is ever-present in the inherent structure of anthropological investigation in the real world (see Berreman 1981a:72–126, especially 84, 91; Condominas 1973:4; Du Bois 1944, 1960:xiv–xv).

Sides there inevitably are, and these appear all the sharper in "hot spots" of global conflict like Central America, where the sides are well-known to all and the conflicts are violent and out in the open. Faced with such a politically charged milieu, then, one may choose any number of theoretical and practical perspectives. The perspective of colonial apologism and self-conscious managerialism (see Malinowski 1947:138–150; Evans-Pritchard 1952:109–129) have not fared well in recent decades; nowadays, few anthropologists would credit these as respectable academic approaches.

The current options more often revolve around attempts at evading such issues, such sides. A positively confident "helping" perspective is commonly invoked: applied anthropology. Taking a piecemeal and superficial approach to the problems of powerlessness and maldistribution—for instance, in the field of medicine—"helping" anthropology offers itself as a Florence Nightingale to the poor and oppressed: it will tarry here on this problem, this patient, before moving on to other problems, other patients, wringing its hands and offering its advice to whoever will listen. Taussig has referred to this as "liberal reform-mongering" (1978).

The real danger of this approach lies not so much in its obvious lack of efficacy—which may actually be its redeeming characteristic—but in its revival of essentially managerial techniques of observation. It is from the outset attached to organs of policy and management. It considers this or that aspect of the social life as "a problem," and offers its recommendations for "solutions"—to organizations and agencies like the World Health Organization, local governments, the Agency for International Development, the World Bank, or the International Monetary Fund. There is no assurance in this form of practice that knowledge generated with the aid and consent of subjects will not be turned into a weapon against the very people it ostensibly intends to assist—indeed, it is almost a certainty that such knowledge will constitute itself as oppressive power, for "assistance" is already one of the powerful managerial techniques in the repertoire of fully developed neocolonialism.

Another response to the problem of issues and sides is evasion. One may try to sidestep issues like power, stratification and oppression by pursuing the most esoteric of all possible information, in the process more or less deliberately obliterating the lines and webs that intricately connect one's informants to a class, a nation-state, a world market economy. This way invariably leads to obscurantism and distortion; it may be beautifully written, literate, and even, in a sense, humanistic, but it involves an automatic default of both intellectual curiosity and social responsibility. Or one could write directly on the topics of neocolonialism, power, and stratification, but do so in such an embellished or obscure theoretical manner as to render the information conveyed unintelligible or nearly unintelligible to all but highly trained specialists. Or, finally, one could pursue an obsessive methodological precision to the exclusion of and as a substitute for dealing with the social issues one confronts in fieldwork. (C. Wright Mills treated many of these evasions in his treatise, *The Sociological Imagination* (1959), which remains timely today.)

The problem lies in the preexisting sets of social relations which the anthropologists finds impervious to either good intentions or evasions. In this preterrain, anthropological observation is inherently problematic. The only way to avoid becoming irrevocably enmeshed in the hidden and not-so-hidden implications of those relations is to confront them from the outset, and to integrate the issues of power and stratification into the study design proper. This method is not foolproof. It carries dangers of its own. But the method that is aware of and sensitive to issues of power and stratification, and is dedicated to the pursuit of the informant's point of view— that is, the point of view of the poor, the powerless, and oppressed— is not as likely to harm its subjects, and may even ultimately bring about some good. It is less likely to bring about harm because this is precisely the type of method, the type of knowledge, that power elites typically neither need themselves nor want widely available. For what has such a method to say to power, other than that it rules by systematic injustice? What can it tell of the world economic system, except to document exploitation and maldistribution? But this method's reason for existing is not to engage in some dialogue, no matter how scolding, with established power; nor is it a mediator that lies between wealth and poverty, demanding concessions from the former on behalf of the latter. Rather, it is a peculiar type of practice: a discourse between the anthropologist and his subjects, the latter of whom are always in the process of discovering and developing their *own* power and counter-power. If elites care to listen in, they are not likely to hear anything that will give them great comfort. And this type of knowledge may actually bring about some good if it helps the global poor acquire a clearer picture of themselves in their own self-initiated processes.

Now I am not dogmatic enough about this—or any other—form of social science investigation to assert that it is foolproof, that no form of harm can follow from it, and that it invariably yields good results. On the contrary, my claim is minimal: that it is less likely to result in harm, and may actually result in some good. I would paraphrase and rephrase Orwell's famous "Why I Write," then. The world economic system and its concomitant conflicts and dislocations exist, independently of the social scientist, his political orientation, his theoretical methods, or his propensity to treat them directly. It is foolish to imagine that we can avoid writing about such topics in an age like our own. "Everyone writes about them in one guise or another. It is simply a question of which side one takes and what approach one follows." And far from obscuring one's vantage as a social investigator, a self-conscious political commitment to the cause of the poor can *illuminate* issues. The more one is conscious of what Orwell acknowledges as "political bias," the more one can act politically without sacrificing either aesthetic integrity or intellectual standards (Orwell 1968:5–6)—and, I would add, likewise: the more one can pursue intellectual standards without sacrificing political commitments.

My practical claims are also minimal here because, while it is possible that social science *might* take some part in the social transformations of wealth and power underway in the world today, it is improbable that that role will be or can be very significant. The notion that social science has or should have some sort of "leadership" role, or even close consultation role, in radical movements is deeply seated in radical social science, despite all practical evidence to the contrary. This notion appears to be derived from some broader premise that natural leadership follows or should follow from one's ability to analyze: an unselfconscious blending of the meritocratic and techocratic impulses that define so much of legitimation procedure in the late twentieth century.[4] Actually, the role of ideology is and will be much greater, as I hope to document in what follows; the role of social science will probably ever be after the fact, indirect and attenuated precisely because, unlike ideology, it lacks genuine chiliastic vision; it will not take the leaps of faith or make the assertions of hope that provide the real intellect of radical political movements. Moreover, methodologically, social science is typically *intellectually* radical in a manner which frequently gets in the way of political radicalism; it is always probing, turning paradigms inside out, deconstructing what we mean when we say such words as "class," "power," or "freedom" and engaging in interminable debates over the nature of its own existence. It is not that these are bad things to do; in fact, they are necessary preconditions for the existence of genuine social science proper. But neither are they very practical, nor can they excite masses of people. No, ideology is much better suited for that task: intellectually conservative and politically radical, it can hold sway over movements in precisely the way that cultures hold sway over societies. And dressed up as either "science" or "religion," ideology exerts an appeal in social-political movements that social science could never hope to emulate, although it may accurately describe the action of that ideology over masses, the conditions that lead to their radicalization, the pre-existing beliefs that make possible and condition their radicalization, etc.

Some will spot here two "dangers." The first "danger" involves probing the fragile powers of the poor and making potentially sensitive information available to established power. This is indeed a danger. That "anthropology as snooping" (Strathern 1979) has on occasion lapsed into "anthropology as spying" (Berreman 1968; Horowitz 1967; Wolf and Jorgensen 1970) is well known. More to the point, Foucault (1979:170–230) has deciphered the power relationship implicit in the act of one-way observation, and has forever exploded any blind faith we might have in the notion that "Truth" is somehow outside, above, or opposed to "Power." No one can any longer feign naivete or innocence about such matters.

The choice of Nicaraguan society as a subject matter both heightens and minimizes this risk. On the one hand, most anything may be deemed a "political" or "sensitive" topic. On the other hand, this information is already continually available to power, as Nicaragua has been under intense scrutiny by a veritable army of journalists for some time now. Under conditions like these, personal judgments become critical, and I have exercised them where I have deemed them warranted. The anthropologist's first responsibility is to act in a manner that reduces risk to his or her host population. And lapsing into silence is the only ethical strategy when speaking truth to power endangers one's hosts.

The other "danger" is of a different sort: that in describing the action of something, we will also denude it of its "pretensions"; that in understanding the *appeal* of religion or ideology, we also deny or negate its *reality*. This, again, is to confuse categories of analysis. Most people are not positivists about what they believe. It is precisely here that ideology and social science operate in entirely different spheres. Belief is more potent than mere analysis; and indeed, it is at its most potent precisely when it generates forms of analysis that make the underlying belief untestable and unquestionable. For instance, it would be hard to demonstrate to a Western student, even with excellent examples and impeccable logic, the shortcomings of the concept "progress," precisely because it has advanced beyond the realm of belief or ideology and generated a system of analysis, positivist science, which not only justifies it, but whose entire existence turns on the image of progress: knowledge is seen as unfolding in a more or less orderly progression through the mechanisms of trial and error, in the same manner as technology, economic development, species, or weapons systems. Likewise, the belief systems and ideologies of revolutionary movements quickly generate forms of exegesis that prove the infallibility of sacred texts, despite whatever apparent counterexamples. This is true of Christianity, and it is true of Bolshevism. It is also true of liberation theology and *Sandinismo* as well. To point this out is not to deny anything of the "truth" of these belief systems, because that truth is outside and beyond the realm of empirical or positivist investigation as such; rather, we are concerned with defining a very different level of truth: the social truths that beliefs represent.

If we imagine otherwise, it is because we are using incorrect or inadequate conceptions of "ideology" from the outset. Mannheim, for instance, essentially sees ideology as synonymous with "false consciousness" (1936, passim), but this misses the point. How could ideology be "false" from the interior point of view of its practitioners? It will not be seen as false except in moments of revolutionary transformation, when it is in fact being replaced by a *new* ideology. The relationship of ideology to truth, then, is of a different sort. Verifiable by its own rules, and vital precisely because it is not subject to scientific standards of evaluation, ideology speaks truths of a nonempirical order. It is social truth, group truth, that ideology embodies. We may therefore document the practice, ontology or divergences of Christianity as ideology and analysis without ever diminishing the social truth it embodies. Moreover, such investigation may actually be seen as *demonstrating* the existence of that type of social truth—in a manner verifying the belief as a social practice, at least in its context and its time. The words of Durkheim, a deeply religious atheist, are worth repeating here:

> The reasons with which the faithful justify (religions) may be, and generally are, erroneous; but the true reasons do not cease to exist, and it is the duty of science to discover them.
>
> In reality, then, there are no religions (or ideologies—RNL) which are false. All are true in their own fashion; all answer, though in different ways, to the given conditions of human existence. . . .
>
> Religious representations are collective representations which express collective realities. (1965/1915:14–15, 22)

LOCATION

This book is based on participant-observation in five poor and working class barrios of eastern Managua. These barrios largely conform to a single broad type that may be described as follows: people urbanized at any point within the last generation or two, drawn from small towns and rural areas from which they were displaced by the growth of the capitalist agriculture sector. Eastern Managua has been the site of religious proselytizing for two decades, by both revolutionary Christians and Protestant fundamentalists: long enough that these phenomena can be securely studied as part of the revolutionary process.

The factor that draws our theoretical interest to these neighborhoods stems from the revolution itself. The Nicaraguan revolution broke a long-standing trend in revolutionary movements that have consistently come to power on the strength of their rural, not urban, support. (See for instance, Wolf 1969). Unlike the Chinese, Cuban, or Vietnamese revolutions, the Sandinista revolution was made by a combination of rural-based guerrilla warfare and critically timed *popular urban insurrections.* These urban insurrections successfully projected Sandinista political and military power into the heart of Nicaragua's cities. "City," then, was not synonymous with "enemy" or potential enemy in the fashion of more rural-based revolutions. This was in fact the first time since the Russian October Revolution (which was actually urban-centered and lacked strong rural roots) that *urban insurrection* has played a strategic role in a socialist revolution (see Petras 1980). Urban consciousness in Nicaragua, then, is a particularly appropriate subject. The barrios under study here not only all participated in those crucial insurrections, but some of them were among the most militant barrios in the country.

Certain questions spawned this study, then, and implicitly pervade it. Under what conditions and owing to what circumstances did urban neighborhoods come to be strategic participants in the Sandinista revolution? What is it about the consciousness of these sectors of the population that disposed them to participate in the revolution, and how is it different from other urban populations that have eschewed revolutionary movements? And what is the place of these neighborhoods in the new revolutionary state?

The social field of my investigations encompassed three distinct barrio types. My most extensive experience and where I lived was in what I shall designate a "middle working-class" barrio, Erasmus Jiménez. On the whole, it was distinctly "popular"—and the majority of its residents classified themselves as *los pobres* (the poor)—although it did contain a small middle-class element. Yet it was by no means the most "popular" barrio in the area. Virtually no one in this neighborhood could be described as economically marginal. Many of its residents were skilled or semiskilled workers, and some were "white collar." Only a few could be classed as unskilled labor, and an emphasis on mobility through education[5] and political activism was very evident. Specific occupations ran a gamut that included small shopkeepers, artisans, petty functionaries, mechanics, soldiers, police, secretarial and clerical workers, factory workers, and a few day laborers. This barrio's residents began aspiring to lower civil service positions under the Somoza regime, and has, in effect, catapulted itself into those sorts of positions in and through the revolution. About three-quarters of the households in this barrio have TV sets, and virtually all own radios. The physical environment is quite pleasant if poor: adjoining, gaily painted conrete houses line concrete walks that are kept well-shaded and cool in the tropical heat by mango, coconut, banana, and other tropical trees.

The other barrios in my field of experience and observation lay on or near the boundaries of the above one, in all directions. Barrio Rigoberto and Barrio Peru may be typed "lower working class." Their residents were visibly poorer than the residents of the previous barrio, and occupations tended markedly more in the direction of manual and relatively unskilled labor. What artisanship existed here tended to be in lower-return fields of endeavor (repair as opposed to manufacture, for instance), and some of the residents could be described as "economically marginal," although this was rare. While nearly all the households in these barrios owned radios, only a third or so owned TV's. As in the preceding barrio, many residents believe in social mobility through education and activism, although fewer seem to actually achieve this end, or, at any rate, fewer achieve it as impressively as in the former. The physical environments also showed marked differences from that of the middle working class: some of the houses in these two barrios were concrete, but most were wood; the walks were unpaved dirt, not concrete, and quickly turned to mud after a rain; the outdoor lights usually did not work at night.

The final type I shall designate "economically marginal" (*los marginados*), and likewise includes two barrios: Sergio Altamirano and Catalonia. Including refugees from *contra* terror and families fleeing the ongoing rural dislocation of the war in Nicaragua's northern and mountainous provinces, the residents of these barrios are the most recent immigrants to Managua from the countryside. They are typically engaged on or just outside the peripheries of integrated or productive economic activity. Unskilled or semiskilled manual labor represents the peak of the occupational scale here. Many are unemployed or only sporadically employed. What artisan or entrepreneurial activity exists also tends toward the very low-return and unproductive categories, such as selling water in the marketplace, or vending *carbón* (a cheap variety of charcoal) in the community. A television is rare indeed in these *repartos*, although about half the households possess radios. The physical environments of these barrios were visibly the poorest of all. While houses in other barrios were cojoining, the houses here were individual, and made of wood, with dirt floors. Almost every house sports large cracks in the walls where boards often fail to meet. In the dry season the wind constantly blows dirt through these houses; in the rainy season rain blows through the cracks or falls in through holes in the roof. Running water is not yet connected to individual houses but to a central water source on the block, and nightlights are altogether absent on the interior of the barrio, although they do line the streets that define the boundaries of these barrios.

My methods of investigation were participant-observation and interviewing. I ultimately developed close relationships with several households in each barrio type; these acted as my primary informants. I had considered using standardized questionnaires, followed by word association exercises, and finally thematic perception tests in order to solicit standardized and statistically comparable responses, but discontinued that method after a few weeks experience in the communities. Scientific surveying and empirical methods of this sort ultimately did not promise to get at the meaning structure of religious practice any better than extended interviewing and daily observation. In practice, it proved far more productive to conduct daily conversations with my informants, in which we discussed topics and events as they arose: international relations, biblical verses, religious practices, illnesses, and deaths. Moreover, questionnaire surveys seemed like the kind of practice that would put me at a greater social distance from my informants, rather than draw me closer to them, and for the kind of study I was conducting free discussion and trust were essential. Perhaps most decisive, however, was my reflection on the sort of atmosphere I would create for myself employing such positivist-empiricist methods: a gringo, wandering around with papers and forms, asking a lot of questions and writing things down. Although people are quite accustomed to the sight of foreign visitors in most of Managua, and in many parts of Nicaragua generally, anything about visitors that suggests officiousness and social distance immediately generates quiet speculation and gossip that the visitor is acting as a CIA agent and collecting information to be used against the people. So partly out of preference, and partly out of necessity, I settled for qualitative over quantitative methods.

CONCEPTS

This is a study, first, of religious processes in present-day Nicaraguan society, and specifically in the poor neighborhoods of Managua. It is, therefore, an ethnography of a social revolution that is still in progress, and of the religious and ideological processes underway in that revolution. It is also a study of the human responses generated by the world economic system, which is to say, a study of political power and class consciousness. And this is, after all, how Nicaraguans themselves tell the simultaneous story of their religious experience, their national history and their class project, if one bothers to listen.

Apart from notable exceptions,[6] social revolution has not normally constituted a proper subject matter for anthropological investigation. Indeed, from the inception of modern ethnographic techniques, the discipline as much as possible eschewed the very concept of change and defined its subject matter in terms of the traditional, the nonmodern, and the primitive. Anthropology in effect has tried to operate "outside of history"—or, at any rate, to situate its informants outside of history (Fabian 1983); that was the nature of its humane art and its radical counterpoint to modern civilization.

But, in fact, anthropologists have from the very beginning studied people who were already in the process of social changes induced by contact with colonialism, international markets, and even the anthropologists themselves. It is just that at first such changes were relegated to the farthest margins of the investigation proper, to the status of distressed afterthought. Change among the Trobriands appears in Malinowski's classic ethnography, then, only in brief references. The book's first sentence alludes to the recent extinction of some of the coastal populations in the South Sea Islands; the last sentence warns that "time is short for Ethnology" (1961:1, 518).[7] In between lies the timeless whole of Trobriand society, the magic of the kula: as though suspended in non-time between two chips of time.

Malinowski's sparse and sorrowful citations here are not at all atypical. Classical ethnography deliberately brushed against the grain of historical change. It would prune back all the distracting phenomena that marked a society's tragic entry into the modern world. Its emphasis was on "reconstructing" the conditions of the past, in resuscitating the *traditional* life that was no longer really so (Mead 1939:266–277). In a sense, ethnography was the endeavor to *save* tradition—if only ethnographically—before the terrible and disrupting onslaught of modernity.

Later anthropology has become increasingly timeful as opposed to timeless, and increasingly centered on the process of *social change* as a proper subject of focus. This was inevitable as the subject of study shifted from primitives to peasants and even proletariats, and as the process of modernization made primitives into peasants and peasants into proletariats. History was forced upon anthropologists even as it was forced upon anthropology's subjects. Robert Redfield's own intellectual career spans something of this shift in emphasis; his final essay concludes, "The peasant and the anthropologist are both changing" (1960:77).

How does the social life progressively differentiate and stratify, in the interaction between traditional forms and the modern market-place? More importantly, how are these changes perceived by the subjects under study? The emphasis of this anthropology is less to reconstruct a pristine past (although tradition may remain its real obsession), and more to approximate the mechanisms of change in and through the cultural logic of the people under study. It is here specifically that Marxism has become relevant to anthropology, and many of the anthropological studies of social change, straightfor-wardly or not, employ one variant or another of Marxist analysis.

Abner Cohen provides a useful definition of this new anthropol-ogy, one that integrates the old anthropology's interest in custom or tradition with the new conditions of modernity faced by tradi-tional people everywhere.

> Social change is essentially a change in the forms, distribution and exercise of power and the struggle for it, and social anthropology is concerned mainly with the role of custom in this change. Social anthropology is thus essentially a branch of political science and is chiefly concerned with unfolding the political implications of cus-tom under various structural conditions. (1969:212–213)

Cohen's study traces the impact of new market conditions on eth-nicity in Nigeria. Other authors have considered the impact of eco-nomic conditions on social class and class consciousness. June Nash's (1979b) ethnography analyzes the traditional and communitarian roots of working class consciousness among Bolivian tin miners. Michael Taussig (1980) elaborates a symbolic analysis of class consciousness among plantation workers in Colombia and tin miners in Bolivia: how the stuff of tradition and modernity coexist and clash in two rural proletariats' cultural perception of the marketplace and its effects. In a similar vein, Jean Comaroff (1985) traces out the material of class consciousness and resistance to colonialism in South Africa's dissenting Churches of Zion. Finally, Aihwa Ong (1987) discerns in the outbreaks of spirit-possession among Malay women workers the proliferation of countertactics, microprotests, and covert resistance: most essentially, the popular mobilization of fragments from the traditional moral economy against work discipline in the modern capitalist factory.

While studies of class consciousness, even militant class consciousness, have become more common in the anthropological literature, the tacitly understood *result* of class consciousness—revolution—has not been well-studied by anthropology. The relationship between *culture and revolution* remains largely unexplored. There are a variety of reasons for this absence. Revolutionary regimes are not necessarily interested in being studied, and may well resist scrutiny by outsiders from Western states. In particular, when they invite study it is not likely to be of the anthropological sort. At least one of the attempts at doing anthropology in a revolutionary state was terminated for political reasons: Oscar Lewis' study of culture in the Cuban Revolution was abruptly ended when his findings apparently contradicted the official view of culture under the new system (see Lewis, Lewis and Rigdon, 1977–78).

At the other end of the world, funding organizations may not grant priority to research in revolutionary countries during revolutionary periods. The reasons are multiplex: more often than not, the perceived ideological danger of such topics is the primary consideration. Not the least of such reasons, however, is the potential reaction of host populations—quite apart from the possible reactions of host governments or counterrevolutionary organizations in the country. And anthropology in a revolutionary setting does present certain special difficulties. June Nash describes being under effective siege for several days as a potentially suspect North American during one of Bolivia's periodic insurrections (1979a). In the end, the anthropologist himself may prefer a tranquil and relatively unproblematic social setting—although in the real world these are increasingly scarce.

Overall, a variety of conducive factors exist in the case of Nicaragua. Travel is unrestricted between the United States and Nicaragua. The Nicaraguan government does not attempt to discourage social science research, and in fact tries to encourage it. The Nicaraguan people are largely friendly and open to North American guests. The bulk of restrictions involve implicit ideological prohibitions at the North American end, and the implicit difficulty of securing funding for research that potentially challenges the stereo-types presently constructed about the nature of Nicaraguan society.

I have drawn on a number of theoretical currents to describe my findings in Nicaragua. I consider this work "Marxist" in the sense that it recognizes the primacy of social class (and class conflict) in the production of consciousness, culture, and religion. It is also, however, expressly a critique of Marx's famous aphorism on religion as opiate, and will reconsider Marx's explicit and implicit under-standing of religion as embodied in his theory of alienation. At the same time, I have found it useful to refine my description of class/religious processes by using a number of Weberian concepts: nota-bly, the opposition and coexistence of practical magic and ethical religion (1963), as well as the dialectic between tradition and ration-alization (1947, 1958, 1971). In the work of Lukács (1971) and those who followed, such Weberian concepts have long been articulated into Marxism.

This study has been much influenced by my discovery, coeta-neous with my fieldwork, of the work of Walter Benjamin and Georges Sorel. Both Marxists, each was interested in a general area of special relevance to this study, and I have drawn consistently on their par-adigms. Georges Sorel, whose work largely antedates World War I and the Bolshevik Revolution, accurately anticipated the impor-tance of 'myth' in solidarizing militant class consciousness and in motivating socialist revolution (1950, 1976). Walter Benjamin, a lit-erary critic and social theorist loosely associated with the Frankfurt school, wrote during the fascist period on the importance of tradi-tion and religion in class consciousness (1968, 1977, 1978, 1979). Like Sorel, and no doubt influenced by Sorel (see Lowy 1985:46–47), he detailed the negative consequences of the "myth of progress" for class consciousness and social revolution; each believed that the working class could be revolutionary only to the extent that it aban-doned bourgeois faith in the image of progress. Sorel and Benjamin, then, clarify for us not just certain concepts relevant in understand-ing religion and class, but more importantly, religion and revolution.

In a sense, my study breaks with certain anthropological tradi-tions: its subject matter, social revolution, is relatively unique for the discipline, and many of my theoretical concepts are conse-quently drawn from nonanthropological literature. And clearly, I have been inclined more toward interpretive and theoretical findings (es-pecially the implications for Marxist theory) than toward the descriptive and empirical methods of standard ethnography. Of course, liberation theology in Nicaragua is most decidedly a "religious revitalization movement," and religious revitalization movements have been deemed appropriate subject matter for anthropology ever since the discipline first began studying the anomic effects of colonialism and modernization on and in dominated peoples.[8] And, in the sense that social revolution more generally speaking is also a revitalization movement (Wallace, 1970), it, too, decidedly falls under the rubric of anthropological investigation.

But in another sense, my study is more "classical" than much of the current anthropology in existence: I attempt broad generalizations relevant to the whole of society and its direction, rather than detailed close work on small areas of culture, much in the spirit of "old" ethnography. And while I constantly treat "political" topics, I do so in the manner of political anthropology rather than political science proper, which is to say, I keep culture and custom in the forefront of investigation; I base my conclusions on participant-observation fieldwork, rather than archival research; and I avoid generating the long strings of organizational acronyms that dominate many of the political science studies on Nicaragua. Likewise, while much of this study examines religion, it is in no sense theological: my conclusions are drawn from what I have learned in the barrios, not on biblical texts or theological exegesis.

Finally, I should say a word about the nature of my data, my impressions, and their replicability. I am not convinced that an observer similar to myself would have necessarily drawn the same conclusions about the nature of popular religion in Nicaragua had he visited that country in a distinctly nonrevolutionary period. It may well be that such an observer, like some of the early Sandinistas, would have concluded that the traditional popular religion exerted a largely stabilizing influence on the society on behalf of the old regime. And no doubt at that moment in history, it did—while at the same time welling up a largely unconscious popular revolt that could later take expressly revolutionary and conscious form.

Nor can I be absolutely certain that all of my social-political observations about liberation theology or evangelical Protestantism will hold in the future, although I am certain of them for the time being. As scenarios unfold, internal social relations and the alignment of forces shift. It may be that tomorrow a new constellation of forces will emerge—improbably, that the evangelical masses will take up the counterrevolutionary cause; that either the Popular Church or the official church will cease to exist; or (as some have speculated), that the Popular Church and the evangelical church will fuse to become a new church of the poor.

The point is not to hedge my bets, but rather to say that ethnography and analysis are always products of their moment in history. In this case, they are products more specifically of a moment in the Nicaraguan revolution, as seen, recalled, and assembled by this particular craftsman. While any number of the particulars as depicted in this book may well undergo substantial revision, alteration or rapid change, the major premise of this book, I trust, will not. The major premise, simply put, is this: not only is religion not inimical to revolution, as was Marx's impression and as has been the stated position of many revolutionary movements since, but revolution in fact *requires* religion—both rational and irrational—in a manner that is inherent in class solidarity, revolutionary mobilization, and social reconstruction. The Nicaraguan revolution throws a particularly illuminating light on the relationships between class, revolution, and religion: revealing, first, because of the directness of these relationships in the Nicaraguan experience, where religion has been most directly and explicitly appropriated to revolutionary ends. Second, as the Nicaraguan revolution is yet young, and still in a sense *unfolding*, we may witness aspects of all three major motions still in play: class consciousness, revolutionary mobilization, and the process of revolutionary reconstruction.

I

RELIGION
IN A
REVOLUTIONARY
MILIEU

The story is told of an automaton constructed in such a way that it could play a winning game of chess, answering each move of an opponent with a countermove. A puppet in Turkish attire and with a hookah in its mouth sat before a chessboard placed on a large table. A system of mirrors created the illusion that this table was transparent from all sides. Actually, a little hunchback who was an expert chess player sat inside and guided the puppet's hands by means of strings. One can imagine a philosophical counterpart to this device. The puppet called "historical materialism" is to win all the time. It can easily be a match for anyone if it enlists the services of theology, which today, as we know, is wizened and has to keep out of sight.

—*Walter Benjamin*
from "Theses on the Philosophy of History"

As long as there are no myths accepted by the masses, one may go on talking of revolts indefinitely, without ever provoking any revolutionary movement. . . . A myth cannot be refuted, since it is, at bottom, identical with the convictions of a group, being the expression of these convictions in the language of movement; and it is, in consequence, unanalysable into parts which could be placed on the plane of historical descriptions.

—Georges Sorel
from Reflections on Violence, *49–50*

The spirit of the Lord God is upon me; because the Lord hath annointed me to preach good tidings unto the meek; he hath sent me to bind up the broken-hearted, to proclaim liberty to the captives, and the opening of the prison to them that are bound; to proclaim the acceptable year of the Lord, and the day of vengeance of our God; to comfort all that mourn . . .

—Isaiah 61:1, 2

———

Go to now, ye rich men, weep and howl for your miseries that shall come upon you. Your riches are corrupted, and your garments are motheaten. Your gold and silver is cankered; and the rust of them shall be a witness against you, and shall eat your flesh as it were fire. Ye have heaped treasure together for the last days. Behold, the hire of the laborers who have reaped down your fields, which is kept back by fraud, crieth; and the cries of them which have reaped are entered into the ears of the Lord of sabaoth. Ye have lived in pleasure on earth, and have been wanton; ye have nourished your hearts, as in a day of slaughter. Ye have condemned the just; and he doth not resist you.

—James 5:1–6

CHAPTER ONE

The Religion of Tradition: The Popular Religion

But many that are first shall be last; and the last shall be first.

—Matthew 19:30

Generalizations are possible, and one may find threads of meaning that unite the various religious currents in Nicaraguan culture. But religion in Nicaragua is not a simple or unitary phenomenon. Apart from the well-known schism[1] between the conservative church hierarchy and the revolutionary Popular Church, any number of additional currents and sub-currents may be identified within actually practiced Catholicism: influences that tend to follow the variegated lines of region, ethnicity, and social strata and status. And when the vigorous new phenomenon of Protestant fundamentalism is accounted for, the picture becomes all the more complex.

The major diverging currents of religious belief in Nicaragua correspond to socioeconomic strata, so much so that we can almost assign distinct religious outlooks to various social classes, and even to marked sub-categories within those classes. Almost invariably, elites (in both urban and rural contexts) adhere to a traditional *and*— what is more important—a *conservative* Catholicism which posits spiritual and moral authority in the established offices of the Church and, at least in principle (though certainly not in practice), carefully marks the distinction between political and spiritual realms.[2] Even more specifically, these elites remain loyal to the *highest* offices in the Church, which are at present (and for the forseeable future) distinctly nonrevolutionary. This outlook—whose theology is called "escapist" by its liberation critics (see Miranda 1982:12–17)—could be readily summarized by the prominent billboards on display in Managua quoting Pope John Paul II on his trip to Nicaragua: "This people hungers and thirsts for God." The Pope's phrase cogently summarizes the response of class and religious elites in Nicaragua to the demands of the poor: Where material hunger and thirst are all too evident, the Conservative Church does not counsel political action, but rather recommends purely spiritual solutions. Or, as the Pope admonished the same restive crowd in Managua when it began chanting "We want peace," "The path to peace is through the Church."

Increasingly, as one moves away from the elite end of the class spectrum and toward the disadvantaged end, Catholicism undergoes a series of marked transformations, culminating at some point in a clear ideological break. It is not that a radicalized poor in Nicaragua have abandoned the Church, or, as the Conservative Church more frequently implies, abandoned the spiritual realm; rather, it is that a radically different *interpretation* of the Church and of the spiritual realm defines religion in the popular classes. Many there adhere to the revolutionary doctrine of liberation theology in one form or another. They have more or less systematically broken with the Conservative Church of the religious hierarchy and now follow a movement called the "Popular Church," based on the teachings of liberation theology.

The basic situation is well-known, and a substantial literature already exists on the development of what is effectively a politicized two-Church schism, not just in Nicaragua, but throughout Latin America. What became apparent to me in my fieldwork in Managua was that, important though this Popular-Conservative Church opposition may be, it fails to cover the entirety of religious practice in Nicaragua, even if we restrict ourselves to Catholicism. A yet-distinct third sphere of religious activity exists, predating the development of a breach in the Church and laying the basic groundwork for that schism.

POPULAR CLASSES, POPULAR RELIGION

What is treated in this chapter is sometimes called "folk religion" in the anthropological literature, and that name is perhaps as accurate as what I shall designate the "popular religion." Redfield's folk-urban continuum, from which the concept of "folk religion" is drawn, is still useful precisely because it treats culture simultaneously as a whole *and* as a system of parts: integrated at some levels, and divided by social class at others. Like the rest of culture in stratified societies, then, religion assumes two major poles based on the hierarchical relationships that obtain between elites and masses. In traditional Latin American societies, as in all societies sharing something like a "peasant mode of production" (Marx 1963:123), those poles roughly correspond to *urban elites* and *rural folk*. Thus, while sharing a common cultural rubric (in this case, Catholicism), elites and folk participate in greatly differentiated *aspects* of that culture.

These opposite poles in the folk-urban continuum are not only differentiated, they also dynamically interact and constantly give rise to new syntheses of the cultural totality based on these interactions. One may thereby speak of a cultural opposition and dialectic in such settings, between the "great tradition" of urban elites and the "little tradition" of rural peasants (Kroeber 1948:280–286; Redfield 1930, 1941, 1955, 1960). These cultural poles, especially on the religious ground, can also alternately situate, frame and interpret the class struggle between elites and popular classes.

Elite traditions differ from folk ones, first of all, to the extent that they represent esoteric specializations of knowledge. Where they are not imposed from without (by force, invasion, colonization), "great traditions" are in fact *rationalized* and *systematized* versions of the folk culture. These "great traditions" are always imparted through a lengthy educational process and involve specialization in esoteric knowledge inaccessible to the common folk.

From the point of view of elites, the "great tradition" provides both a legitimation and an instrument of their rule—and it is important to remember that religious elites are continuous if not identical with class elites in peasant-based economies.[3] Naturally, the message of elite religion is always likely to proclaim the justness and wisdom of the ruling class, or, at any rate, the futility of resisting it. Or, where less immediately politicized, the great religions are likely to offer an "escapist" focus on the hereafter rather than the here-and-now. In the practice of thereby administering the spiritual needs of the poor, religious elites can act as powerful agents of social control and stabilizers of social situations riddled with class conflict.

The "little tradition" of the common folk is typically ministered to by specialists trained in the elite tradition. Yet the popular practice and the common people's interpretation of that practice can never correspond exactly to the elite version. Before all else, popular belief and practice will almost always remain closer to the practical concerns of uneducated people, and are more likely to tend in the direction of what Weber calls "practical magic" rather than "ethical, rational religion" proper (1963:32–45). But the ethical element is never entirely absent at the popular end of the continuum, and where it makes its appearance, it is ever likely to acquire interpretations not necessarily in harmony with the interests of elites (see for instance Bakhtin 1984; also Nelson 1986). From the point of view of these non-elites, the practice of religion—which is eminently "popular" from their point of view, even where contact with the religious bureaucratic apparatus brings them into a dynamic interaction with elites—may be seen in any number of its shades: it may be a means of manipulating nature and the supernatural; it may be seen as a means of manipulating elites; it may act as an instrument of social and economic leveling at the lowest level of social organization, the immediate community (Wolf 1955:458, 460; 1957; and 1959:216; see also Vogt 1976, and Smith 1977). In its own quasi-ethical sphere, popular religion may foster and consolidate the class consciousness of the poor by embodying in the rich all that is evil and full of vice, while at the same time interpreting in the poor all that is just and good and finds favor with God. Even a purely "escapist" religion may achieve the effect of producing a powerful, if restrained, class consciousness through its very escapism and indirection, so long as the poor can find an interpretation that offers redemption for those who suffer in this life and punishment for their oppressors in the next life. It is a step, but it is not such a giant step, from a traditional religion thus conceived to a revolutionary God of the Poor.

At least in part out of this pressure for a different type of utility meeting distinctly popular needs, periodic innovations and divergences will arise at the base of religious or cultural practice. These innovations may involve the magical exigencies of peasants pursuing practical ends, and elaborating rituals to achieve those ends (Redfield 1955:14, 17–18). Or they may involve the need for radical salvation that we encounter in urban proletariats, as well as wherever peasants are being proletarianized (Weber 1963:95, 101). These innovations may be revolutionary, reformist, or neither in nature, depending on political, social, and economic factors distinct from the sphere of religion and ideology proper. In either case, what is at first marginal to sanctioned religious practice and spurned by elites *may* provide a source for the periodic revitalization and change in the entire tradition of a society.

What I will designate "popular religion" is not substantially different from what Redfield would designate "folk religion." I mean to designate essentially the same process, whereby the poor assume interpretations and meanings of religion from their own point of view, as distinct from the elites with whom they share a general system of meaning. I call the category "popular" rather than "folk" because "folk" usually specifies a peasantry and I am concerned with the religious beliefs and practices of *all* the popular classes, especially urban ones, and not just the classical peasantry. The clean terminology of sociological stratification models proves difficult to apply with any rigor on the field of Nicaraguan society, and perhaps Redfield's most of all. Nicaragua's mass of *campesinos* proper more accurately resembles a "rural proletariat" (Mintz 1953, 1978) in many parts of the country than a classical peasantry, at least in terms of its economic activity (Rudolph 1982:75–77; Collins et al. 1986:268). This process of rural proletarianization is not a recent phenomenon; it began in the 1870s with the spread of coffee plantations, and was accelerated by the cotton boom of the 1950s, and again, by the spread of cattle ranching in the 1960s. Rural proletariats, however, rarely achieve exactly the sort of outlook acquired by industrial proletariats, and Nicaragua's mass of landless *campesinos* and day laborers was no different: away from the atomizing effects of city life and the work schedule of the factory, Nicaragua's rural proletariat lost the exact economic function of a peasantry while retaining much of its cultural outlook.

At the same time, virtually no strictly defined urban proletariat exists, and paradoxically I have often felt the most appropriate label for Managua's poor is "urban peasants" (Roberts 1978). Most of the city's residents have only recently migrated from rural parts of the country, and the rural roots are very evident in the language, beliefs, and cultural practices of the people. Most of Managua's poor population maintains close personal and family ties to their small town or province of origin. If a classical peasantry scarcely exists on the economic terrain, this is more than offset by a very widespread and persistant sense of peasant *culture* in Nicaragua, evident in both the city and country. One might be justified, then, to simply use the term "folk religion," as long as one understood its peculiar conditions in Nicaraguan society.

Nicaraguans themselves designate as "los pobres" (the poor) the mass of working and lower class people, without regard to occupational distinction or one's location in rural or urban sectors. Thereby about 85 percent of the country's population could fit more or less comfortably into this category, "the poor." Having adapted a Latin Marxist terminology for popular usage, ordinary Nicaraguans also quite casually refer to the collective entity of the poor as "the popular classes." I have kept with this latter terminology in describing the religious belief and practice of the poor as the "popular religion." This usage, more so than the term "folk religion," is in keeping with the strong emphasis on social class that everywhere manifests itself in Nicaraguan society and which has put in wide usage such terms as "popular classes," "the popular accent," "popular church," "popular revolution." And indeed, the *fiestas* that celebrate Nicaragua's patron saints, who figure so prominently in the popular religion, are often called *"fiestas populares,"* and the saints themselves are sometimes referred to as *"los santos populares."*

The traditional "popular religion," as I will discuss it, is *not* structurally identical to the revolutionary Popular *Church*, which is treated in the next two chapters, although there is a large area of overlap between them—much greater than the overlap between popular religion and the Conservative Church of the religious hierarchy and elite classes. We may even see the Popular Church as an outgrowth from or subset of the popular religion: rationalized and systematized, to be sure, but with a proletarian or popular rationality, not an elite one (see Weber, 1963: 97, 101). Even less *apparent* overlap exists between the popular religion and the most genuinely *new* religion of evangelical Protestantism, although at least some of the ideological basis for conversion preexists in the popular religion itself (see chapter 4).

The popular religion is, at any rate, where an understanding of religion in Nicaragua must begin: it is the traditional religious practice of the masses of the people, and it precedes the more modern manifestations of religious practice, both temporally and logically. The traditional beliefs of the people are shaped and codified, consciously and unconsciously, in the popular religious practice. Indeed, it is in the *santos populares* and the *fiestas patronales* that we seek out what Bakhtin (1984:145–195) called the language of the people, what Gramsci (1971:348) called the "good sense" of the people, and what Bourdieu (1977:72–95) calls the essential structures of the *habitus*. To interpret those symbols, to read those messages, is to read the consciousness of the popular classes, as typically and traditionally constituted; it is also to discover the starting point of popular consciousness that, in this case, provided the springboard for a systematic and revoutionary class consciousness. The popular religion, then, is the first building block of all that follows.

THE SACRED AUTHORITY STRUCTURE

As in much of traditional Catholicism in Latin America, the major preoccupation of the Nicaraguan popular religion was and is with the saints, especially the patron saints of the various cities and provinces in Nicaragua. The burgeoning house of saints represents the crucial link in an elaborate chain of divine command. The saints act as intermediaries between the godhead and the bulk of humanity. If God the Father, Son, and Holy Ghost are purely and wholly divine, and the bulk of humanity wholly profane, then how shall the two interact? How should base humanity go about approaching the divine when seeking cures and favors? It is here that the popular religion throws out its bridge over that chasm between this profane world and that sacred one, and approaches that purely sacred one through an intermediary category, mingling the human and the divine: the saints. The saints are dead humans who have achieved a special sacred status by living especially exemplary lives. And it is they who are approached for cures and special favors.

The saints divide the world and their responsibilities toward the world along two axes, one vertical, the other horizontal. On the vertical one, we see the range from the purely sacred to the purely profane: the Holy Trinity is purely sacred. The Virgin Mary is the saint that most closely approximates that divine status, and in the popular mind she is touched by divinity herself: for bearing the son of God, and remaining free of "original sin." Next, distinctly after Mary, range the remaining New Testament saints, then the patron saints, and finally, at the bottom of this axis, humanity itself. Along the horizontal dimension, the saints divide among themselves responsibility for specific locations—and it is here that, practically speaking, the saints are invested with their overriding importance, for the saints are not just the general link between God and man, but rather, it is the *patron saints* who forge the *specific* links to *specific* locations and regions.

This elaborate chain of command—the divine, the saintly, the human—both establishes and represents the authority structure of the traditional religion. It also establishes an authority structure in popular consciousness more generally. Indeed, from the popular point of view, we may now add a fourth link in the chain of command, a little lower than the saints, a little higher than ordinary folk: the priests. In Nicaragua, the priests garner authority precisely to the extent that they live a life appropriate for one seeking saintly status; they thereby inherit a little of the divine authority that is passed along down the chain of command. They expend their authority to the extent that they deviate from this ideal in the pursuit of the rewards of this world, especially money and sex. It quickly became apparent in my observations of several Nicaraguan communities that the priests do not easily or passively inherit the authority of their office; asceticism, restraint, and a life of service to the poor were the traits that clearly defined a good, godly priest. Any hint that a priest did not really care much about the lives of his poor parishoners, or that he was "womanizing" on the sly, or that he was "in it for the money"—and people would point to glaring examples of each of these—proved sufficient to raise the spectre of a powerful anti-clericalism. Whose opinion the people will respect on ethical and practical issues, then, and why, will be strongly informed by these images of piety, self-denial, and sacrifice that invest saints, priests— or even, on occasion, ordinary people—with sacred authority.

It is important to remember here that the average Nicaraguan does not exact of himself these standards of behavior—at least not under the reign of the popular religion. The role of the ordinary person is to be as good a Christian as possible; to keep the religious observances; to see to it that the children are baptized (and, if possible, confirmed) into the Church; to avoid the mortal sins; and if lax, then not to be *too* lax. It is not so much the role of ordinary people to *represent* the religious ideals, then, as to *endorse* and *recognize* them.

A very elderly woman was dancing in the procession for San Jeronimo in Masaya, "paying a promise," as it is called, to the saint for his cure of someone in her family during an illness. She was clearly a devoted follower of the Saint Doctor, and expressed fervent religiosity and great seriousness in her every motion in the dance. But the crowd was very large, and the cobbled streets of Masaya are very narrow, and it so happened that every time the band would strike up or stop playing the saint's processional song, the crush of people would accidentally push into the old woman, or someone would step on her toes. And invariably, upon being accidentally shoved or stepped on by the crowd, she would emit the loud exclamation, "*Ay, jodido!*" This mild vulgarity, undoubtedly the most commonly employed exclamatory in Nicaraguan Spanish, is difficult to translate, as no strict equivalent exists in English. Loosely, it connotes annoyance, distraction, or bother. One might say that it reflects a clear preoccupation with the theme that one is being taken advantage of: in personal interactions, in business dealings, in the marketplace, or in any sphere of life. Closely related to the idea of *aprovecharse* (to be used or taken advantage of), it might be loosely rendered, "Oh, screwed again!" Its real force lies somewhere between "Oh, screwed" and "Oh, fucked."

This incident exemplifies well something of the religious demeanor of ordinary people in Nicaragua, in evidence even at a solemn religious occasion. Mild vulgarities, though not strong obscenities, come very easily to the lips of most people. It might well be said that Nicaraguans are a religious people, even a righteous people, but no one would say that they are a *pious* people. Real piety is for the pious few in charge of ministering to the spiritual needs of the very human masses—or, similarly, those in charge of political leadership.

Now some will immediately see in this hierarchy of piety and purity an implicit if crude reflection of the class hierarchy, and a means of positioning some (priests) vested with conservative interests over others (the popular classes) whose real interests are presumed to be otherwise. This may be deduced from the fact that both class and religious structures may be represented as *hierarchies,* and graded along a series of superior and inferior positions. And indeed, this *is* at least *one* of the possible correspondences of the material and spiritual hierarchies—and one constantly encouraged by the tendency of elites to monopolize religious offices, especially at the higher levels of the religious bureaucracies. Religious elites derived from class elites will always try to translate the power of the class elites into religious authority. But this remains only one of several possible correspondences, for all hierarchies are not invariably the same. A *representational* hierarchy (of purity and piety) is not necessarily the same thing as a *class* hierarchy (of power or property), nor need it inherently represent one. On the contrary, while such a representational hierarchy *may* embody the lines of class power, vesting them with legitimation and sacred authority, it may also represent the totality of the poor, its "higher" levels corresponding to the "higher," "more profound," or "more abstract" levels of its interests and social integration. And this correspondence will always find resurgence and renewal at the lower end of the class scale, away from the interpretive influences of the theological seminaries, cardinals, and popes

The cult of the patron saints, then, may well appropriate the language of the patron-client relation (see Forman 1975:216–217), but it is at the same time a *subversion* of that language: one's loyalty is at least theoretically contingent on the saint's fulfillment of his obligations to the people, and the saint's authority ultimately rests on the execution of his role as benefactor of the poor. Jesus Christ himself is often referred to as a saint (*Santo Cristo*), and is sometimes treated much like a patron saint by the poor: entreated for favors, engaged in bargains, manipulated for worldly ends. The patron saint, like Christ himself, is a more powerful patron, allied with the poor and ultimately superior to the patrons of this world.

Thus, while the sacred-profane continuum may well correspond to, represent, and reinforce the elite-popular continuum, it may also—perhaps simultaneously or polysemically, and perhaps situationally—represent an embodiment of social principles and conducts quite antithetical to the interests of the powerful class, and certainly in opposition to its excesses. This antithesis is the popular religion at its most active; it defines those points in its structure at which the popular religion most closely approximates the status of a *radical* religion. When a poor peasant who has never heard of liberation theology expresses his conviction that the rich are doomed to punishment in the afterlife for the sins they have committed against the poor in this one, he has clearly set the ball rolling that might culminate in a systematically revolutionary religion or ideology.

Yet even at its minimalist and most "conservative" conceptualization, as measured from the standpoint of revolutionary religion proper, the authority structure of the popular religion is always a two-way street: to be effective it must exact demands not only on the appropriate comportment of the poor, but on the rich as well. This is implicit in the nature of the bond between a faith and its followers. The church is primarily an institution of "authority," and not force; to preserve its authority it cannot afford to stray too far from certain reasonable limits, for it is ultimately in the hands of the poor to either bestow or withhold divine authority. And a church hierarchy which insists on baptizing and blessing practices, persons, or ideas that diverge too radically from the more popular conceptions of sacred authority that dominate belief at the base of that church—that hierarchy risks rupture, schism, and ultimately extinction of its own offices.

Upper and lower classes, then, may converge on the terrain of certain symbols, beliefs, and authority structures, only to diverge on their interpretations of these. And religious practice is clearly a sphere in which class conflict and compromise are brought to bear.

Throughout Latin America, it is well known, many popular saints are actually based on pre-Columbian deities who were absorbed into the post-conquest Church under new names and as patron saints of the same locations served or inhabited by those pre-Catholic deities (Brenner 1929). Thus, from the very beginnings of modernity in the New World, one sees a dynamic—a struggle and a synthesis—between elites and masses in religion that plays itself out first on the grounds of an opposition between the colonial and the indigenous (and will later play itself out on the grounds of social class proper). The Spanish elites were able to impose their religion and convert the indigenous as part of the colonizing routine, but the indigenous were also able to affect their will, to some degree, on the shape of the resulting religion. And indeed, that was the road that Catholicism had long traveled: spreading throughout Europe as well, it likewise absorbed elements of pre-Christian religion under the rubric of a highly flexible Christianity.

In some cases in the New World, the colonial religion was more or less immediately subverted by the indigenous, through the personages of certain Spanish priests, to oppose the excesses of colonialism and hamper the effectiveness of colonial exploitation—so much so that the curbing of religious power in the New World was ultimately necessary for the expansion and consolidation of colonial power proper. Christianity in Latin America thus embodies from the beginning a class conflict as well as a cultural conflict. Christianization was an aspect of colonial domination, and the initial imposition was clearly carried out by nothing less than brute military force. But domination baptized by authority is always a two-way street, and sometimes the interests of the colonized were remarkably well articulated through the established Church.

Curiously, though, this syncretized aspect of the popular religion seems less evident in Nicaragua than in parts of Mexico and Central America where the indigenous roots of culture are more evident. Unlike a number of other predominantly mestizoized cultures in Latin America, the remnants of indigenous practices do not often appear on the surfaces of Nicaraguan culture. One cannot normally buy magic potions in the marketplace, and little remains of an indigenous herbal medical system. Similarly, few of Nicaragua's patron saints appear to be Christianized indigenous deities. In fact, most of Nicaragua's patron saints seem to have made their appearance relatively late: The festivals for Santo Domingo in Managua, for instance, have been practiced only since 1885. (Many festivals in Latin America have much earlier origins.) Most of the popular saints seem to have appeared in that general time frame, and to represent much later adaptations of Catholicism made by mestizoized peasants and workers rather than by the conquered indigenous.

But other aspects of Nicaraguan popular religious practice correspond quite well to similar Latin American versions of Catholicism, and to peasant/popular religious practices generally. On the surface, we see a concern with the magical and the practical, especially how to affect cures. If one reads the "material" of popular practice closely enough, however, one can also discern the outlines of an ethical sub-religion in development. This ethical sub-religion is always contextualized by more "mundane" concerns (health, good luck, well-being, personal favors), to be sure; it never ranges very far from the grip of magical manipulation, and it lacks a clearly systemetized or rationalized basis. But in the absence of these refinements, the popular religion nonetheless promotes an ethical or ideological system that roughly, if unselfconsciously, corresponds to the social interests of the popular classes, and which already suggests a possibility and a direction of departure from the religion of the elites.

THE COMING AND GOING OF
SANTO DOMINGO

The fiestas held in honor of Santo Domingo, Managua's patron saint, provide an excellent case study and make a good place to investigate the symbols and meanings of the popular religion. Of relatively long-standing tradition, the holiday's public procession and festivities are highly charged symbolically and formally ritualized. By virtue of their location in the capital city, Santo Domingo's fiestas are clearly the largest in scale and participation of all the religious celebrations held in Nicaragua (apart from Purísima, which is not a centrally located celebration, but rather simultaneously held at household and neighborhood levels across the entire country). Moreover, Santo Domingo closely resembles popular fiestas held in cities and departments throughout the populous western third of Nicaragua.

These fiestas occur annually and in two parts. August 1 is the Arrival of Santo Domingo; August 10 his Departure. Most of the year, a small representation of the saint no more than a foot high "lives," as the people say, in a small church in the hills outside Managua. On the first of August, this tiny statue (affectionately called by the diminutive nicknames, "Mingo," and "Minguito"), is carried by a dozen or so men in a long procession from his usual resting place to the church that bears his name in Managua. On the tenth, the saint is returned to the small church where he usually "lives." His transport in either direction is a massive, festive occasion that traverses a 15-kilometer route and takes most of the day to complete. No more than a few dozen to a few hundred people march or dance the entire procession—part of which is undertaken in the full heat of a tropical day, and which often passes through a tropical shower or two—but tens of thousands participate by going part of the route, or by lining the streets along the way as actively involved spectators. The excitement of the participants and their undertakings stands in striking contrast to the singularly unimpressive-looking image of the saint himself: tiny and encased in a small glass tube, the image is dwarfed and often rendered quite invisible by the float of flowers on which it rests.

From the time the procession of celebrants reaches Managua (around 9:30 in the morning), the total crowd size in the vicinity of the saint becomes enormous. Segments of the crowd, numbering in the hundreds and even thousands, frequently spill over into the fields and open-air spaces that have dotted much of Managua since the 1972 earthquake. And the procession acquires, on the outskirts of the capital city, a rowdy, ribald atmosphere which at times feels like a near-riot. In this atmosphere of throngs and alcohol, there are the inevitable occasional fistfights—sparked by an accidental push, a heave of the crowd, a harsh word—and these fights produce waves of motion in the crowd much like the crisscrossing action of wind on a wheat field: some run to see the fight, while others too close at hand run to get away from the violence.

By and large, the atmosphere is friendly enough, though, and the fealty of the celebrants real enough. The crowd intermittently emits the chant/response, "*Viva Santo Domingo!*" "*Viva el doctor de los pobres!*" Very little printed matter exists on Santo Domingo de Guzman; my informants tell me that he was an herbal doctor who ministered to the poor of Managua and the surrounding countryside in the last century. Perhaps that he was an *herbal* and not a medical doctor is significant in two ways: first, herbal medicine, as a cheap form of practice, would have been within the reach of the poor, thence situating Domingo's practice from the very beginning as a form of "popular medicine"; second, this emphasis on herbalism may indeed be the distant harkening of mestizoized peasants and workers to an indigenous past that is only dimly recalled. The Saint Doctor now continues making periodic appearances to the poor, especially women, to recommend specific herbal cures for their children's illnesses. It is worth reiterating that, like most aspects of the popular religion, the procession for Santo Domingo is a distinctly *popular* occurrence; the procession snakes its way through predominantly poor and working class barrios, and the celebrants and observers are almost entirely drawn from among *los pobres.*

Fidelity to and reverence toward Santo Domingo are acted out through a variety of impressive costumes and ritual behaviors, which are simultaneously deemed religious and entertaining: religious because the people insist they represent unspecified religious ideas, and because many of the participants have contracted cures and favors from the saint by promising to appear at the fiesta in such disguises and ritualized roles. And these disguises and rituals are also entertaining in the true sense of spectacle and display. They command audience attention and approval, and are designed to bring a sense of levity and festivity to the proceedings. Punctuated by the explosion of firecrackers and bathed in alcohol, most holidays are simultaneously and without contradiction both religious and entertaining events.

Among the most popular figures to appear in the procession are *las vacas* (the cows), who alternately dance with and charge the crowd. It is generally adolescent boys or young men who come disguised as the cows. This costume centers on the dried skull of a long-horned cow, usually painted, and worn at the pelvic level. From the horned skull in front, a large metal loop encircles the youth in back, extending as far as three feet behind, like an oblongated hoop skirt rung. From that loop hangs a large cloth skirt, usually brown, that reaches almost to the ground and suggests the body of the cow. This whole apparatus, skull in front, body trailing behind, is in turn supported and stabilized by two relatively inconspicuous straps, each of which crosses one shoulder and attaches at the back of the cow's head as well as near the rear of the metal hoop in back.

The operators of these cow disguises are almost universally male and young (late teens and early twenties), and the horns protrude most pointedly from the youth's groin. At least one of the youths I observed seems to have consciously recognized the phallic implications of this arrangement and had painted several crude but very recognizable erect penes on his skirt. Again, these cows perform the "dance of the cows," which is to alternately dance with and charge at the crowd. It is with a thrust of the hips and pelvis and a raising of the horns that these cows participate in the festivities, threatening other male revelers and, when possible, "goring" them from behind, otherwise charging their genitalia. The scene around the cows, always dominated by boys and young men, could be characterized as an atmosphere of real excitement verging on the hysterical. With a charge or threatening gesture, the cows send the audience running and dodging. Laughing but alert to further charges, the youths then return to the arena of the cow, and the game continues. The near-hysteria of this ritual is not entirely symbolic; injuries are rare, but they do occur, and over the course of the day a couple of dozen people may require treatment by medics as a result of the actions of overzealous cows.

On two occasions I saw the male domination of this ritual altered. On the first, an excited woman in cow costume charged threateningly through the crowd, an attack which evoked stares of disbelief and a few hostile remarks about her impropriety. The second was more elaborate and stylized, and was accepted by observers with rapt attention as a legitimate feminine version of the male practice. In her cow outfit, this second woman was dancing with two people, a man and a woman, very slowly and very gently. She would turn to the man first and rotate her hips, bringing one of the horns slowly up to the man's groin. As he backed away, dancing, she pursued him, slowly, until touching his crotch with the right horn. Then, she would repeat the same teasing and suggestive motions on her other side with the woman, also barely touching her crotch, with the left horn.

Another of the costumes is a figure sometimes known as "El Toro" (the bull), but more usually called "El Diablo" (the Devil). There are many fewer Devils at the procession than cows, and unlike the cows, who are usually played by young men, the Devil is typically played by an older man. He is indeed an impressive sight: usually a sizable and robust man, preferably with an enormous belly, he wears but a loincloth around his waist and is covered from head to foot in shiny black grease. (Nicaraguans typically envision the Devil as black rather than red.) Sometimes, he is covered with oily tinsel to suggest coarse, greasy hair. On his head, he wears a headpiece from which protrude two large, long bull horns. This is a most effective representation, and I have seen numerous small children cowering in fright at the sight of these Devils. The Devils alternately march and dance in the vicinity of the saint's procession, carrying long sticks or spears. Small children are sometimes painted black or red to suggest miniaturized Devils of much this same mold.

Some men and boys cover themselves with black grease to suggest Indians—and *negro* may refer not only to blacks, but also to very dark-skinned Indians. Curiously, they wear the feathered head-dresses and shoe-polish war paint designs of Hollywood movie Indians, rather than the costumes of any indigenous tribe whose customs and dress have long since been forgotten. Like the Devil, they carry long, wooden spears; similarly, they sometimes dress their children in the same attire; and likewise, they sometimes collect money for charity by dancing, in this case "tribal dances," and then passing a can around for donations afterward.

La Gigantona, or, the Giantess, is perhaps the most popular and impressive of the disguises present in honor of Santo Domingo. The Giant Woman is a large marionette figure, hollow from the waist down. She is operated and carried from the inside by a sturdy youth, who remains concealed behind the skirts of the Giant Woman with only his feet visible, which appear to belong to the woman herself. Clothed in bright colors and cheerily made-up, the Giant Woman towers over all other celebrants at an average height of about twelve feet, with "breasts" that sometimes reach two feet in length. This popular figure also puts in regular appearances at other holidays— "wherever the people are happy," "to express the happiness of the people." However, she is perhaps most prominent (and numerous) at the fiesta for Santo Domingo. In this fiesta, as on other occasions where I witnessed her, she danced with various boys and men; very occasionally, she would rush the crowd, head slightly lowered, in a manner not unlike the cows.

Finally, any number of youths engage in a type of petty delinquency that has become part of the standard ritual for Santo Domingo. If there are several dozen cows present, a few dozen each of assorted Devils and Indians, and only a dozen or so of the impressive *Gigantonas,* then all of these numbers are dwarfed by the sheer scale on which the petty delinquencies and prankstering of youth are carried out. In some form or other, *thousands* of Managua's youth participate in a "greasing" game—which undoubtedly originated from the large quantities of grease used in the Devil and Indian costumes. Armed with rags or bunches of grass that have been soaked in grease or automotive oil, and with their own faces and clothes well-smeared, these youth range over the crowd of celebrants, greasy-handed, smearing the faces or backs of other participants. This greasing becomes infectious, and spreads by way of older boys to younger children and, not at all infrequently, to adults; from males eventually to females, and back again; from one end of the procession to another.

When grease is short, some boy will invariably slide underneath a nearby car, remove the oil drain plug, and fill the rag afresh with oil, involuntarily donated by some unknown benefactor wealthy enough to own a car. Many spectators arm themselves with sticks and limbs to ward off greasing, but this actually seems to attract it by making it more of a challenge. The greasing game may be a relatively recent innovation in the festivities (like the Hollywood Indian tribe costumes), although it has been practiced now for several years: long enough that recent immigrants to the city and young adults think of it as traditional. Some of the older participants disapprove of these antics, in much the same way that adults here express their disapproval of the standardized petty vandalisms associated with Halloween; others accept them as a natural if annoying part of the festivities. And clearly, even if this is an innovation of recent decades, it is not at all out of keeping with the ribald atmosphere or other symbolic manipulations of the holiday.

RITUALS OF INVERSION AND REVERSAL: THE WORLD TURNED UPSIDE DOWN

Now symbolically, what is one to make of all this apparent chaos? How are we to "read" the "messages" encoded in the Arrival and Departure of Santo Domingo? In the case of this sort of practice, it is not enough to simply *ask* the participants what this or that means, for, as we shall see, the very efficacy of the popular religion rests on its operation at subconscious levels. Obviously symbolic creatures appear, dance, charge; the crowd interacts with them; but as in a dream, the event is experienced in its totality as a visceral phenomenon, whose meaning may be intuited, but rarely directly "read" by the participants. If one asks, then, "What does this represent?" one is invariably told simply "a cow," "a devil," "a large woman," or if one asks, "What does it mean?" the response is usually "It is just traditional," "It is sacred," "It is for fun," or "It is just how we do things."

But semiotically, any event with the long history of *la fiesta de Santo Domingo*, celebrated on such a large scale and subject to continuous innovation and change, *must* be embodying certain ideas, representing certain social meanings, communicating certain messages, even if these are all kept subconscious and prevocal. All that is at issue is the appropriate "reading" of those messages in the proper context of their communication.

In the first place, who is Santo Domingo? Above all else he is a *benefactor of the poor*. As a doctor in his earthly life, he eschewed the monetary rewards and material gratification of his profession and class status, and pursued instead a life of service to the poor. He stooped down from his class position in order to lift up the poor and oppressed. (This is perfectly consistent with the image of Saint Doctors deployed throughout Nicaragua, except that Santo Domingo actually was an herbal doctor in real life, whereas others appear to have become "doctors" *after* achieving sainthood.) Thus, on the terrain of social class he reenacts the spiritual message of Christianity: God stooping down from his perfection to lift man out of sin and want; and in his supernatural status as saint, Santo Domingo again does exactly the same thing.

And the cult of Santo Domingo is most emphatically a cult of the poor; it is the poor who turn out in throngs to celebrate his annual arrival and departure. Palma (1985) has noted that Domingo is distinctly a "popular" saint, always making his appearances in "popular" places (street and farm) rather than the "elite" spaces of the enclosed official church. Whatever else it is, the myth and symbol surrounding Santo Domingo constitutes a conversation whose subject is *the poor*.

What is the nature of that discourse, generated out of the people about themselves, through the particular person of a saint? In every respect, the fiesta for Santo Domingo bears marked similarities to European and Latin American religious processions that have been treated as rituals of inversion and reversal: i.e., rituals that metonymically and metaphorically represent "a world turned upside down," and act out themes of revolt and overturn (see Bakhtin 1984; Davis 1978). Along a variety of dimensions, every symbol in play in the fiesta for Santo Domingo represents a *reversal* or *inversion*, a world turned upside down, an established order challenged by its own contradictions. Domesticated and usually docile animals turn on and charge their human masters. Specifically, female animals charge male humans. Women tower over adult men, who appear as mere infants beside them, and likewise rebel against male authority. Youth run amok, blackening their elders' faces and engaging in acts of petty vandalism against property. Primitive Indians reemerge from a vanquished history, and walk about the streets to assert their challenge to civilization. And in the anarchy, the Devil himself is loosed, and his minions scurry about: seemingly out of place in a procession designed to commemorate the life of a saint, but very much in keeping with the nature of that commemoration, which is the metaphoric device of trangression, inversion, and revolt.

The theme of "dirt" is very much in evidence here: if "dirt" is "matter out of place" (Douglas 1966:7, 35–36), then most of these symbolic manipulations challenge the organization of the established order precisely by *dirtying* it. The greasing game in particular embodies this aspect of "dirt," and I have heard it on various occasions referred to as "dirtying." And "dirt" in Nicaragua is also a metaphor for sex, which is likewise "out of place" in public discourse. All of these undertakings are tinged with a libidinally charged atmosphere of sexual anarchy. Along one grid, genders are symbolically reversed: the Giant Woman may be seen in terms of transvestic ritual, and, likewise, male actors represent themselves as female cows. It is not unheard of for *cochones*[5] to appear at this procession in transvestic or semi-transvestic apparel, flirting with other men along the way. Along another grid, polymorphous sexual drives are symbolically acted out in public through, for instance, the very phallic horns of the cows.

Without developing the idea, Palma (1985) has called the procession and its symbolic personages "The Rebellion of Woman," and perhaps she is alluding to the anthropological literature on rituals of inversion and overturn. Such rituals most typically stress reversals of gender, and these have been interpreted as radical commentaries on the nature of sexual stratification. It is clear that the fiesta speaks more than incidentally through the symbology of male-female oppositions—but not to the exclusion of human-animal, civilized-primitive, old-young, and even divine-diabolic relations. I would assert that no particular set of oppositions here can be seen as the 'privileged' or unifying set. Indeed, while most of these oppositional relations clearly entail metonymic aspects (in which the part stands for the whole, e.g., female subordination for domination in general), I would argue that their *metaphoric* aspects (in which one thing stands for another, e.g., females for the popular classes) are more compelling. The one opposition not distinctly "mentioned" through these personages is the privileged and unifying set that all metaphorically address, and around which the whole symbology of the proceedings is organized, if we recall who Santo Domingo is (*"el santo de los pobres"*) and what he represents (divine aid for the poor): that is, the elite-popular opposition.

It is, then, through metaphor and indirection that Santo Domingo addresses the *real* subject of the revolt of the poor against the social order. A religious practice ostensibly "about" magical cures and saintly favors, acted out through a variety of puzzling idioms and symbols, is actually "about" popular revolt, a perpetual inverting of the class order and a leveling of invidious social distinctions. It is the lower overturning the higher, the world turned upside down, that these proceedings illustrate. In the dialectical play of subject-object, the proceedings around Santo Domingo capture the image of *perpetual revolt*. The ideological distance between the traditional, popular religion and the new, revolutionary theology of liberation, then, is much less than it might appear to be at first glance.

It will not do at all to see liberation theology as a current that suddenly and inexplicably sprang into existence, without precedent or tradition, or that was perhaps imported by priests with foreign ideas. More than one liberation priest has remarked "I knew nothing about the Bible and true Christianity until the peasants taught me" (Carney 1985). Much of the interpretation of biblical texts embodied in liberation theology is derived from the informal meetings of Christian base communities, where peasants and workers read and study the Bible and evolve their own interpretation of the scriptures, free of the inhibiting direction of high church officials. These "new" interpretations are typically shorn of the magical and ritualized aspects of the old religion, but beneath the surface is more than is immediately apparent of the traditional popular religion.

What is less clear is whether one should view the popular practice, ultimately, as a socially stabilizing one, or as one that mobilizes social forces and ideas that threaten the established order. One current of functionalist anthropological interpretation would stress the cathartic aspects of these symbolic inversions. "Acting out" revolt, in this model, diminishes the endemic pressures on and conflicts in the social system by affording people the periodic release of a brief rule-breaking spree, only to reunite them again more forcefully with the rules of social order.[6]

The Marxist equivalent of this functionalist assessment might find in the parallel between Santo Domingo stooping down to help the poor and God stooping down to help the poor a certain implicit class paternalism. How could the poor be imaging themselves in any radical or potentially radical manner if that image is mediated from the outset by figures such as saints, who are often derived from members of the middle and upper classes? Is this not a failure to perceive and act on the class reality *as its own realm?* And aren't these fetishes of religion, like the fetishism of commodities, exactly what Marx had in mind by "alienation?"

This latter objection, I think, is misled by the phantasm of some form of "pure" or "unmediated" class consciousness which is presumed to be possible on a large scale. For how could such an "unmediated" class consciousness be achieved on a mass scale without the systematic destruction of every shred of preexisting culture that would serve to situate, contextualize or interpret class position? In effect, without severing the people from their past? Recent history shows that, far from providing the springboard for radical movements, the razing of traditional culture renders class consciousness impossible, and instead leads to a pliant and depoliticized state in which the routine mechanisms of commodity production can bring about a widespread fetishism of commodities, and a concomitant reproduction, *ad infinitum*, of the nonrevolutionary proletariat.

Another interpretation would stress that these periodic rituals of transgression keep alive the image of revolt in the social imagination of the poor, and advocates of this interpretation can point to a long history of the synergistic relationship between the symbols and trappings of such rituals and radical political movements (Bakhtin 1984; Davis 1978). Both perspectives here address salient issues, and, in practice, either effect—stabilization or destabilization—could inhere in these rituals, depending on a variety of other social, political, and economic factors not immediately tied to the rituals themselves. The most that one could say is that, when revolt is not imminent, these periodic discharges of libidinous and rebellious energy may well serve to pacify the masses of the poor, but that, at the same time, they do keep alive the image of revolt and rebellion.

The main point that distinguishes the popular religion of tradition from the revolutionary religion of hope, then, is emphatically *not* that one invariably acts to stabilize the class order and the other to destabilize it. Rather, each operates as a "religion of the poor," and each is capable of sparking radical political activity; the one acts through indirection, evasion, and elaborate metaphor—tactics appropriate for a subreligion not necessarily aware of its status as such, and which must keep its more political content symbolically "underground"; the other acts directly as a class-conscious and class-based religion with an undisguised awareness of itself as such. In short, the real difference is between the *indirection* or *implicitness* of the popular religion and the *direction* or *explicitness* of the revolutionary religion. Similar symbols and ideas are in play, but the popular religion embodies itself as a metaphoric and magical com-

mentary on social class, while the revolutionary religion is embodied as a straightforward and rationalized commentary on and analysis of social class.

A TEST CASE

Fortunately, in the field of Santo Domingo's fiestas, we have an appropriate test case for this thesis. If Santo Domingo falls securely
under the rubric of "popular religion" as we have described it (i.e.,
implicitly radical), then attempts at making his political message
explicit should be unsuccessful, for they would challenge the primarily metaphorical form of the popular practice. We can "test" this
with two examples.

The Popular *Church* of liberation theology occasionally tries to
"politicize" the festivities of Santo Domingo. During my fieldwork,
it attempted to hold a left-wing celebration of Santo Domingo's Eve
on July 31, separate from the traditional celebrations and featuring
a variety of popular musical bands. This event was not well-at-
tended, while the traditional Santo Domingo's Eve celebrations attracted thousands, despite their competition with well-liked musical entertainment. The attempts of the Popular Church in this field
were poorly envisioned: in the first place, the events around Santo
Domingo are already "political," but in the second place and equally
importantly, it is a politics that operates on a subtle, unselfconscious and metaphoric level. It will not do to simply try and replace
the magic of the bulls and the Giant Women with the appeal of a
Nicaraguan rock band singing political lyrics. Although both have
their place, both do not have the *same* place. To underscore the political content of the popular religion is to negate the form of that
practice and to transform it into something else, whereby it loses
its appeal as popular religion. These efforts of the Popular Church
to "politicize" Santo Domingo, then, necessarily represented a contradiction of forms.

A more impressive case revolves around the recent history of the
Gigantona in the festivities. The present ritual of the Giant Woman,
as I have described it, is only a fragment of the ritual as it was practiced until very recently. Before the revolution, the *Gigantona* was
ritually accompanied by a number of *Cabezones* (or *Cabezudos*), Big-
Heads. The Big-Heads were played by young, preferably barely pre-
adolescent boys, wearing giant masks that covered their entire heads
and represented much older adult males. These dwarf-like figures of
men with misshapenly large heads would approach the Giant Woman,

and offer her 20 córdobas to dance. While dancing, the Big-Head would recite poetry in keeping with the atmosphere of parody and jest: sardonic and often risque verses on relations between men and women; or sometimes even merely vulgar couplets whose culmination was the allusion to private body parts (the anus, penis, vagina) or acts (excretion, urination, passing gas). For instance, the following verse is typical of its category:

> *Una vieja y un viejo*
> *Se metieron dentro de un pozo;*
> *La vieja le decía,*
> *Ay, qué viejo tan baboso.*

> *An old woman and an old man*
> *Fell down inside a well;*
> *Said the old woman to him,*
> *Oh, what a stupid old man!*

Two more examples will suffice; all of these were recounted to me by observers and participants old enough to recall with some clarity the verses in play.

> *Las chicas de este tiempo*
> *No saben pegar un botón,*
> *Pero al novio le dicen*
> *Ay; amorcito te espero en el portón.*

> *The girls of this day and age*
> *Don't know how to sew on a button,*
> *But to their boyfriends they say,*
> *Oh, my love; I'll wait for you at the gate.*

> *Una vieja se sentó*
> *Encima de una tomatera.*
> *Los tomates salieron bailando*
> *Al compás de su pedorrera.*

> *An old lady sat down*
> *On top of a bowl of tomatoes.*
> *The tomatoes came out dancing*
> *To the beat of her farts.*

It is significant to note, in what transpires, that the Big-Heads represented the only personages in Santo Domingo's proceedings endowed with the gift of speech. Their role was commentary: on the proceedings; on male-female relations; on the foibles of life. Their perspective was ironic, satirical and sardonic, and much of the amusement they provided was the shock of vulgar public discourse: it was the rules of public discourse that they violated, linguistic transgression that they afforded. And every year provided an entirely new opportunity for verbal experimentation and accomplishment in this flexible ritual, for new compositions appeared at every fiesta, and none appear to have acquired permanent status there.

In 1979, just after the Triumph of July 19 (which is how Nicaraguans refer to the culmination of the Sandinista Revolution that overthrew the Somoza regime), the role of the *Cabezones* began to transform itself. Spontaneously, the Big-Heads began offering anti-imperialist, anti-Somoza, and anti-capitalist verses. Eventually, the majority of their compositions were straightforwardly political in nature, and at that moment the Big-Heads simply disappeared from the fiestas. Since 1983 the Giant Women have roamed and danced the streets unaccompanied by their former stylized suitors, the Big-Heads.

Now it was neither by governmental nor religious pressure that the Big-Heads changed their verses; this was a spontaneous development engineered at the lowest levels by the youthful composers and participants, many of whom had been manning barricades, hurling Molotov cocktails, or wielding guns only months before in the battles for Nicaragua's cities. It was only a natural development: the Big-Heads talk about what people—especially male youth—talk about or want to hear talked about. The revolution "gave the poor their voice," as is often said, and it seemed perfectly in keeping with the overturn of the established order—as embodied in both the revolution and the proceedings for Santo Domingo—for the Big-Heads to begin saying things that had been taboo only a short time ago. And the atmosphere of Managua in 1979 and the immediately subsequent years was so politicized that it would be difficult to imagine *not* talking about the imperialists, the national guard, the capitalists, and the like. But in passing from the vehicle of indirect and symbolic political commentary to direct political commentary, the Big-Heads also undermined the basis for their own existence in the popular religion. Theirs was no longer a discourse of revolt through the indirection of symbolic transgression, but a message of revolution that had self-consciously assembled itself. So likewise, neither by governmental nor religious decree, nor by any other conscious decision, but by a silent functional exigency, the Big-Heads fell mute and disappeared from the scene. They had evolved beyond the point of the popular religion proper, had transcended its bounds, and were no longer at home there. And so they ceased to exist.

TRADITION AND REVOLUTION: LEVELING

It is worth mentioning here that Masaya, whose reputation precedes it as the most traditionally religious town in the western corridor of Nicaragua, was also a militant stronghold during the 1979 revolution. This large agricultural town of Indian farmers spends a good portion of every year preparing and celebrating a half-dozen or so distinct local religious observances, some of which are several days in duration. During the insurrection, Masaya led the way; arming themselves with whatever they could find, its citizens drove Somoza's national guard from the city and executed the guard's regional director stationed there. In Monimbó, the indigenous barrio, people took up what proved to be effective bows and arrows, no doubt reflecting on their Indian status in much the same way that the depiction of Santo Domingo's Hollywood Indians reflects on the pre-Columbian heritage as well.

This sort of correspondence between traditionalism and revolution need not confuse us, if we keep in mind that the traditional religion already embodies a strong if indirect class consciousness. More pointedly, the traditional popular religion invariably contains an assortment of social leveling mechanisms, which may be primarily symbolic, or material, or both simultaneously. These leveling mechanisms may take the form of messages symbolically communicated, as through the personages in the fiesta for Santo Domingo; or their impact may be materially felt, as in the cost levied against affluent members of the community in sponsoring such elaborate ritual displays. Anthropology has long been aware of this latter "leveling" aspect of popular religion: it is difficult for one to get ahead of one's neighbors in an economic sense if affluence imposes an incumbent obligation to sponsor the community's lavish religious displays.

Foster's (1965, 1972) original thesis on envy and "limited good" might well be called a conservative theory of peasant conservatism. It attempts to explain peasants' resistance to economic development and modernization in terms of their traditional world view. Peasants, the theory maintains, believe good things (wealth, well-being, health) to be in perpetually short supply and hence limited in availability; the more one person has, the less others will have. The natural outcome of this ideology is envy and, not incidentally, resistance to the capitalist innovations which (in Foster's view) might greatly increase the store of wealth for all: accumulation of capital, rational reinvestment, and differential reward targeted to differential rate of production. This paradigm has been roundly critiqued from every imaginable angle—and yet it remains compelling: traditional people do exhibit a high degree of "envy" in their attitudes toward wealth,[8] and traditional religious practices the world over seek to redress imbalances in economic distribution by means of lavish ceremonial expenditures and the periodic leveling of wealth.[9] While we might account for the basic world view as "an expectation of reciprocity" (Gregory 1975) rather than "the idea of limited good," it seems inescapable that envy and leveling are crucial underpinnings of economic and religious traditionalism. One might see these "conservative" phenomena as "obstacles" from the point of view of liberal theories of capitalist development—and surely this traditionalism is an obstacle from the standpoint of the entrepreneur who would like to avail himself of cheap labor and increase his profits (Weber 1958:58–62). But from the point of view of socialism such phenomena carry radical implications indeed (see, for instance, Aberl 1962; Taussig 1987:393–412): they already constitute a real bulwark against capitalist accumulation and exploitation, and they provide a moral paradigm that might readily be mobilized within a newly articulated class consciousness. Further yet, they already suggest a working model for revolutionary redistribution.

One may still see this aspect of the popular religion at work in Nicaragua today: *mayordomos* are responsible for many of the religious celebrations undertaken for the patron saints, especially in rural communities. Such sponsorship means temporary economic ruin for the "big men" (*hombres grandes*) compelled, as a result of their good fortune, to fund these fiestas. The celebration of *Purísima*, a week long holiday celebrating the Virgin Mary's purity, provides much the same effect on a smaller neighborhood scale. In the popular barrios, it is considered incumbent upon the relatively more prosperous members of the community to "throw a Purísima," and to do so in the right style. "The right style" means generously giving away large quantities of gifts to one's neighbors and friends: gifts such as drinks, sweets, fruits, and toys, along with an accompanying sponsorship of lavish fireworks displays and religious icons commemorating the Virgin Mary. In December 1985, to throw a Purísima in style in Managua required the expenditure of more than 100,000 córdobas, or, at the then-current rate of exchange, better than $130. This may be put into perspective when we realize that the average income for a worker in Managua at the same time was around 24,000 córdobas a month, or about $30.

Two observations follow: poorer members of the community will disproportionately benefit from these seasonal expenditures, typically being on the receiving end of these gift distributions, and will only rarely expend money themselves. At the same time, throwing a Purísima has the effect on those who have been more prosperous during the preceding year of effectively wiping out their savings and eliminating any material advantage they might be accumulating over their neighbors. The annual celebration of the Virgin Mary's purity, then, is not coincidentally also the approach of a great leveling device that vigorously levels the economic distinctions that have accumulated in a community over the year.

One may refuse to throw a Purísima that lies within one's means, but at some risk: consistent refusal will label oneself *pinche,* a particularly dreaded derogative, signifying "stingy."[10] A "stingy" person in a popular barrio is first subjected to gentle and friendly prodding by his immediate neighbors. If this proves futile, he will become the subject of increasingly hostile gossip. If this, too, proves ineffective, the gossip continues but takes on an increasingly *public* and often confrontational character. Few who wish to continue getting along with their neighbors will pursue this path any further. While entrepreneurial activity exists in the poor neighborhoods, it is already seen as suspect (in contrast to "honest" or "manly" labor with one's hands—that is, "work that makes one sweat"). Rational savings and investment by an entrepreneurially minded resident are seen as much more direct threats to the community, and that perception is expressed through hostile labeling, gossip, and confrontation: that neighbor is stingy; he is selfish, he is trying to take advantage of people, depriving them of their due. Rational capitalist business activity, then—more so than petty corruption, price-gouging, or vending shoddy products, all of which evoke substantial hostility in their own right—*necessarily marginates* its participants from the traditional-minded community of origin.

Purísima is a festive occasion. At the same time, it is tense, and much of the envy and class resentment that lies barely subterranean all year threatens to come to the surface: "this neighbor is being *pinche*"; "that neighbor has given me nothing, though we have lived beside him for years, and he is always borrowing things, even though he makes more money that we do"; "and just look at them, devout and pious now in front of the Virgin Mary, but how do they act the rest of the year?"

In this manner, the "tradition" embedded in the popular religion is a dynamic, not a static, process, and embodies a social relation. That social relation is *leveling*. It signifies more specifically that one's property is not exactly one's own, that property entails obligation, and that the demands of the group take precedence over the whims of the individual in disposing his property.

Such leveling practices and the accompanying consciousness they entail have often been treated as "peasant conservatism" in the anthropological literature (Redfield, 1960; Foster, 1965, 1972; see also Erasmus, 1961, 1968; and Banfield, 1958). To the extent that these practices "conserve" a degree of social equilibrium in the most traditional communities, they are indeed "conservative." They clearly hamper capitalist development by impeding rationalized planning and accumulation. If capitalism is a "progressive" vision, the popular religion is conversely a "conservative" one, for it values tradition over change, fixed means-ends relations over manipulable ones, leveling over open-ended competition, and reciprocity over exploitation. This image and practice of leveling, so central to popular religion, is conservative, and it is decidedly normative, but it is not reactionary. And it is here that the popular religion lays the groundwork for socialism's appeal to peasants and the recently proletarianized poor of Latin America: the perpetual working of these leveling mechanisms is the touchstone of the traditional religious practice, the image of a stable society its image of social good. The image of socialism that exerts its greatest appeal to peasants and workers is much the same: a great, final leveling of the social classes, whereby the rich are cast down and the poor lifted up, and which anticipates a society characterized by its stability and timelessness.

In the next chapter we will explore in more detail how the specifically "conservative" imagery of traditional religious belief may be mobilized in revolution—in this case it is synthesized as a "new religion," but one that bears the stamp of an old one.

CHAPTER TWO
The Religion of Hope: The Popular Church

And I saw a new heaven and a new earth: for the first heaven and the first earth were passed away; and there was no more sea. . . .

And I heard a great voice out of heaven saying, Behold, the tabernacle of God is with men, and he will dwell with them, and they shall be his people, and God himself will be with them, and be their God.

And God shall wipe away all tears from their eyes; and there shall be no more death, neither sorrow, nor crying, neither shall there be any more pain: for the former things are passed away.

And he that sat upon the throne said, Behold, I make all things new.

—(Revelation 21:1, 2–6)

Liberation theology is a diverse and variegated movement, evident throughout most of Latin America, and encompassing many tendencies, interpretations, and theories.[1] There is no reason to suppose that what holds true of this movement in Nicaragua will necessarily hold true in Brazil, or Colombia, or Mexico, each with its own distinct traditions and social conditions.

What most generally distinguishes the practice of liberation theology in Nicaragua from its equivalents in countries like Brazil is its strong anticlerical sensibility and content. In Brazil, whole segments of the upper ecclesiastical bureaucracy have assimilated and propagated the message of "Christ the Liberator." In Nicaragua, the upper church hierarchy has singularly resisted such radical reinterpretations of Christianity and sees such movements at the base of

Christendom as constituting a clear challenge to ecclesiastical authority. Thus, the base community movement in Nicaragua grew up "in an almost clandestine manner" within the church, and ultimately evolved into a loosely defined Popular Church of base communities, affiliating congregations and priests organized parallel to and in conflict with the offices of the established church. Its message from the beginning was democratic, populist, and anti-ecclesiastical, and, indeed, its critique of the church hierarchy attains the status of a crucial doctrine in the movement.

In the end, the theology of liberation may prove to be as diverse as Catholicism more generally, and subject to the same range of local interpretations and doctrinal elaborations as any other international religious practice. Even within Managua itself, divergences of interpretation exist. For instance, a few of my informants speak kindly of the "preferential option for the poor" enunciated by the Latin American Bishops' conference at Medellín in 1968 and at Puebla in 1979 (Berryman 1987:42–44). This is particularly true of the trained officials who staff the bureaucratic apparatus of the Popular Church. Most base community activists in the working-class barrios, on the other hand, become apopleptic at the very mention of this phrase. "Our faith is not 'preferential,' nor is its message 'optional.' " explained one informant. "This preferential option business is a theology of *liberalism*, and it has nothing to do with liberation. It is a tool of the religious hierarchy."

I will not try here to be exhaustive on so large a subject as liberation theology in Latin America, nor to typologize its various currents and sub-currents. Nor, for that matter, will I discuss in much detail doctrinal religion out of the theological texts, except where those texts throw light on what I have observed of popular theology in Managua's barrios. Rather, I will develop my interpretation of liberation theology, as I have observed it in operation in Nicaragua, at the level of working-class communities in eastern Managua, especially in Rigoberto and Peru. These *barrios populares* are where the revolutionary religion is most widely believed and practiced, and where the movement takes its most militant form.

LIBERATION THEOLOGY AND REVOLUTIONARY IDEOLOGY

Liberation theology provides the closest thing to an overarching ideology of the Sandinista Revolution and its subsequent reconstruction of Nicaraguan society. It may be true that the *guiding* theory behind government in Nicaragua is a locally modified Leninism.[2] Or, one might prefer to call that guiding ideology *Sandinismo*, a term which defines the guerrilla strategy of Sandino, as modified by the Leninist interpretations of Carlos Fonseca and subsequent leaders of the FSLN (Borge et al. 1982; Instituto de Estudio del Sandinismo 1983; Sandinista Leaders 1985). But even if we distinguish between "overarching" and "guiding" ideologies, it is important to remember two things.

First, Sandinism, Marxism, and Leninism in Nicaragua quickly absorb the symbols and metaphors of locally received Christianity, even to the point that in practice it becomes difficult to distinguish "religious" from "political" belief proper. This is especially true the closer one moves to the community level. Perhaps this was not always the case, and perhaps—as some have suggested—the original view of Christianity taken by the Sandinistas was "tactical" rather than "strategic" (see discussion in Randall 1983:29, 175–177). That is, the Sandinista leadership's original approach to the Church seems to have been instrumental and pragmatic: it foresaw a tactical and temporary alliance of Christianity with Marxism rather than a strategic and permanent one.[3] At the present, however, and at the level of popular belief and practice, that relationship is not merely tactical; indeed, it transcends even the notion of a strategic alliance. Rather, the two are organically related and at the point of fusing to achieve the *identity* of (a certain sort of) Christianity with Marxism/Sandinism (see, for instance, O'Brien 1986).

Second, of the various rationalized and systematic ideological currents deployed in and by the process of revolution, it is liberation theology (or the teachings of the Popular Church) that has gained the widest following in Nicaragua. All else (Sandinism, Marxism, Leninism) is largely articulated *through* and *by* liberation theology, and, in effect, relegated to dependent status: parasitic systems living in the body of the revolutionary Christ, or, perhaps, branches of a tree whose roots ultimately lie in the teachings of the Bible. This is difficult for a non-Nicaraguan to understand, but it is vital to understanding ideology in the new state. *Secular* actions are very typically given *religious* rationales and cast in religious language, especially when ordinary people discuss these things among themselves. Christianity is thus the master plan around which other plans and blueprints are organized.

For instance, I have heard neighborhood militants explaining that collectivization is an appropriate national policy because, after all, the early church was a collectivist institution (see Acts 2:44–54). Thus, collectivization of the farming economy only replicates the teachings of Christ, and moreover, collectivism is the only form of economic activity expressly approved in the Bible.

On any number of occasions I have been presented with the following basic argument; this was its most systematic presentation:

They say that the Soviet Union is an atheist country, but this is just a lie that the reactionaries tell. Look at what the Soviet Union has done for us: it sends us food, medicine, technical aid, and arms to defend ourselves. Now look at what the United States does to us: it sends us nothing but oppression, dictatorship, death, and destruction. No, the liars have it all wrong. The Soviet Union is a good and godly country, trying to develop a system of social justice. It lives and acts by a conception of God more pious than all the teachings of the church hierarchy. It is a Good Samaritan country that comes to the aid of the poor countries of the world. It is the United States that is the atheist country! It acts in a clearly godless manner. It behaves exactly like the thieves and bandits in the story of the Good Samaritan.

At the more doctrinal level, an article in *Amanacer*[4] strains to bring the essentially secular pronouncements of Sandino under the rubric of revolutionary Christianity (Girardi 1985:30–35). In a similar vein, the Mexican theologan José Miranda has attempted to reduce Marxism to Christianity (1980). In these examples, both popular and doctrinal discourses invariably seek to legitimate politics and policy on religious grounds, and preferably out of biblical texts. This language—of revolutionary Christianity—is also frequently spoken by FSLN leaders themselves (who freely refer to the Kingdom of God, speak of Christian praxis, and are fond of drawing on Biblical parables and analogies).

The Popular Church in Nicaragua is simultaneously a *cause* and *effect* of the Sandinista Revolution. In the events leading up to the 1979 revolution, a reinterpretation of Christianity was underway on a more or less popular basis: spontaneously, and in the Christian base communities, the radical impulses of the traditional religion were being refined, systematized, and rationalized into a new variant of Christian practice.[5] New masses were being written, and in working class barrios and rural communities, study groups evolved distinctly proletarian interpretations of the Bible as a message of hope and liberation for the poor. (See E. Cardenal 1982.) In many areas, revolutionary Christians took up a "vanguard" role in the events leading up to the revolution. But this much also remains clear: the consciousness of the *bulk* of the population lacked such refinements as could be achieved by an even minimally systematic or studied basis, and remained at that time a mix of militant populism, nationalism, and a general religious sensibility based on the traditional popular religion.

It was a result of the success of the revolution that the Popular Church absorbed and displaced large areas of the antecedent popular religion, in much the same manner that the FSLN absorbed and displaced large areas of the antecedent populism and nationalism. Growing and consolidating as the revolution grew and consolidated, offering a systematic ethos in place of magical manipulations, and offering a rationalized ideology that organized the diffuse militant impulses of the poor, the theology of hope, in effect, collected the pieces of the old religion into a new constellation and articulated them into a new structure. It thereby became, after the fact, the dominant ideology of the revolutionary culture.

It is also true that the revolutionary Popular Church still coexists with a popular religion of tradition—and perhaps it will, if not forever, then surely for a long, long time. Paradoxically, in sparking a greater overall interest in things religious, liberation theology may actually be promoting the traditional popular religion as well as itself. By providing a strong moral center for religious practice in place of the decaying influence of the official church hierarchy, the Popular Church, in the very act of assembling itself, also resuscitates the traditional religion in the margins of the ideological system. As long as the social basis for magical manipulations continues to exist, the popular religion will continue to exist, and these show no signs of disappearing. To the extent that the revolution consolidates *religion* as its dominant ideology, it also creates the space for magic in the margins of that system; moreover, to the extent that the revolution blocks the path of progressive capitalist development through increasing rationalization of the productive apparatus along cost-benefit lines, it also leaves room in life daily-lived for enchantment.

And the revolution *has* "re-enchanted" things. It is true that the revolution brings aspects of society under rationalized, even bureaucratic control, and that it has moreover streamlined, simplified and rationalized the core of religious belief. Yet the magical and the miraculous, if banished from some procedures, reappear at the very heart of revolutionary ideology itself. The slogan "Sandino lives"— a clear parallelism to the religious slogan "Christ lives"—both elevates Sandino to the level of sainthood and proclaims his resurrection in and through the new state. This image of a sacred spirit animating the masses may in effect "rationalize" and "instrumentalize" the sacred, but it also simultaneously re-enchants life and clings irrevocably to the content of politics thus shaped. Here, the miraculous meets the commonplace, or, as one militant priest put it: "We are living the miracle of Christ's resurrection through the Sandinista Revolution."

At this level, the experience of revolution participates in religion in two ways: first, it generates a new faith or mythology that binds society together, and second, it interprets every act of revolution as a form of worship. It is not only that revolutionary practice follows certain historical rules, then. Rather, revolutionary practice simultaneously enacts God's will on earth and magically manipulates *things* as though through prayer and worship. This is the magic that clings most irrevocably to the core of even the most ethical religion. The magic of revolutionary transformation, then, is not unlike the magic of transubstantiation or transfiguration. "It is this way now, but it will be otherwise tomorrow." Matter itself is no obstacle to the revolutionary, for by closely following a revolutionary practice, or by working for nothing but the effectuation of God's will, matter itself will be transformed. Personal transformation through faith proves this magic to the body of believers (see Hobsbawm 1959:62–63). "The revolution has changed us. We are a new people."

It is here, on the borderline between the distinctly "magical" (or miraculous) and the "ethical" that revolution really multiplies the possibilities for enchantment and mysticism. Many of the houses whose members adhere most directly to the traditional religion have images of saints above their beds: Christ, Mary, Santo Domingo. In the houses of people who adhere most directly to the new Popular Church, one sees a phenomenon so similar that at first the observer fails to notice the depiction very closely and is likely to think that he is viewing a representation of Christ. But on a second inspection, beyond the cursory glance, it is clear: the image of the "saint" hanging on the wall is that of Che Guevara, the magical spirit that is identified with revolution in Latin America. Or, less commonly than Che, one finds Carlos Fonseca or A. C. Sandino occupying this place of the saints on the wall. The attitude cultivated toward the new saints is not so different from that cultivated toward the old ones; new figures fill the voids left, in some houses, by old ones.

What is evident is that religious belief and practice have found a new moral center, a new "exemplary center" (C. Geertz 1980). In their coexistence and symbiosis, the Popular Church provides the raison d'être for faith, while the popular religion carries this out at the margins of the system, enmeshed in magic and preoccupied with practicalities. The theology of hope thus provides the rationale and the rational basis for religious belief, and the popular religion takes refuge in the practice of the irrational.

In one sense, the traditional practice is "in contradiction" to the rational and systematic basis for the new religion; in another sense, the new faith is only the fulfillment or extension of the logic of the popular religion. This latter sense is sometimes quite explicit: in Nicaragua's liberation theology, the logic whereby this or that patron saint is locally known as "the Saint of the Poor" is extended *up* the sacred authority structure, so that the Godhead itself becomes the clarifier of the poor to themselves—that is, "the God of the Poor," or "Christ of the Poor." This motion is of course appropriate only when there is in development a sense of class consciousness that both encompasses and transcends local interests, local problems: when there is in play a national (or even trans-national) sense of class consciousness. Writ another way, then, the "contradiction" between the Popular Church and the popular religion is the same as that between units of a structure: the units can never be homologous, nor can the specific and local ever be identical with the general and total.

The nature of the contradiction between the Popular Church and the official hierarchy is another matter. That contradiction is neither benign, nor is it the dialectical play of pieces that all lie readily within a given gestalt. It is a conflict over which vision of God and the Church will provide the moral center for Christian practice. It is, then, the conflict between two radically opposed interpretations of the Bible, with implications for the continent of Latin America potentially as significant as were the implications of the rift between Catholicism and Protestantism for European history. This contradiction is also, at bottom, a class conflict. Between the traditional religion and liberation theology, then, lies a series of *grades*, and each is, in its way, a religion of the poor. Between the church of the religious hierarchy and the church of liberation theology, however, lies not a series of grades, but a radical disjuncture: the one a religion of elites, the other a religion of masses. This conflict could be nowhere more evident than in the discourses generated from the *base* of the popular Christian movement.

What follows is an interview with—actually, the testimony of[6]— Norma López. She has been a Christian base community lay worker in Managua's poor barrios for more than twenty years. Her testimony bears examination: in themes and temperament it is typical of Christian lay activism, but it also resonates quite closely with typical non-activist concerns and sentiments. Norma López is not a nationally famous or even locally prominent woman, but a relatively anonymous lay activist. Not atypical of such lay activists, she lacks formal education beyond the elementary grades, yet has achieved a remarkable verbal facility and a deep reading of the Bible. What is unique is the duration of her experience and the depth of her involvement from its very origins in the movement that was to become the Popular Church in Nicaragua.

TESTIMONY OF A LAY WORKER

My name is Norma López. I am a widow and grandmother. I am going to tell the story of our involvement in the Christian base community movement over the last twenty years.

The state of the Nicaraguan youth in the 1960s, when we began base community work, was poor, desperate, and oppressed. I was a mother of four children at the time, living in Rigoberto, and how I feared for the moral state of the children! Many of Managua's youth had given up all hope. Gangs were becoming commonplace. Prostitution was rampant. The children were falling into despair. Many had fallen into drug addiction. That is the way the life of the poor was in the time of Somoza. The corruption of the regime and the corruption of the capitalist system had produced in the poor neither hope nor anger, but despair.

For us, the first question was, how to recuperate the youth from this terrible slumber? This was the concern that propelled us Christian lay workers when we organized the base project in 1966. Our efforts were part of the broad lay movement that established Christian base communities throughout Latin America, under the directive of the Vatican II, "Go to the Poor."

At first our efforts were met with miserable results. We tried to talk to the youth. We tried to tell them that their problems were *social* problems. And they responded that they did not believe in God any more.

Our task was born, then: to display a *new* face of Christ to the poor and oppressed. We, the lay workers, began holding regular meetings to reexamine the Bible ourselves, and see what its message was for the Nicaraguan poor. We realized that the old church was failing to carry out the true mission of Christianity. And we discovered then that the priests must use their robes to keep the community off its knees. We decided that mass should be given in Spanish, not Latin, so that it could be understood by all the people. And we knew that we had to continue working with youth.

With the youth of the barrio, we reread and rethought the Bible, from start to finish. Exodus was a *choice* to move forward, out of slavery and oppression.[7] The major and minor prophets embodied a radical stance against the sin of exploitation. The mission of Christ and the message of the Bible is that of God stooping down to help the poor, of God drawing the poor closer to him, of God intervening in history to save the poor from sin.

And then we realized that politics did not lie outside of religion. We realized that we were victims of Somoza and of exploitation; that the poor are victims of the radical sin of social injustice.

How can I tell you of the excitement that propelled our project? Daily, weekly, monthly, yearly, we could see our headway, and feel it in our hearts. We had found the fire of Christianity that the hierarchy had hidden from us, and it was beginning to illuminate the eastern barrios like the rising of the sun or the coming of Christ. The youth were coming around, more and more, drawn by this message of the Christ of the Poor.

We didn't tell the bishops right away what we were doing. Truthfully, we went about our work in an almost clandestine way, like the early church of the New Testament.

The youth developed for us a popular mass: with guitars, drums, and new songs. When we performed it at last in front of the bishop, to show him what we were doing, he said, "This is not good. It is prohibited."

And then the people responded, "To shit with this bishop! The people have accepted their historic project. We will not turn back. We will continue moving forward, just as the children of God moved forward and out of bondage in the book of Exodus."

Marriage became a problem. Under the old dictums of the church, divorce was prohibited, and many women were living with their second *compañero* (companion), to whom they were not married. And when they saw the good work of the base community with their children, they wanted to move closer to the church. But the rules of the old church demanded that they not be permitted to take communion. We broke with that official practice: it was the work of Christ to draw the poor closer to him. These archaic dictums of the old church were designed to put distance between the poor and Christ. They had to be abolished, if the church would be a church of the poor, and if it would worship the true Christ.

We developed new songs, protest songs, and eventually, forms of passive resistance against the regime. These brought down massacres upon the community. For the one who died in a hunger strike, a dozen more were killed by the Guardía Nacional. We then realized that passive tactics were not enough, and that we had to join or support the armed struggle. Many went away to the mountains;[8] others stayed in the community and did clandestine work. And our understanding of the Bible was developed enough now that we knew that there was no contradiction between being Christians and participating in the struggle for freedom. We were learning that we could *only* be good Christians by participating in the struggle for freedom.

The church hierarchy behaved in a reactionary manner. It showed its true face by siding with the interests of the rich. From its offices and pulpits it admonished us not to struggle against the regime, and told us to wait and not act, and told us that we must love and tolerate the rich, and that there was justice in the unjust system. We had learned, however, and we knew from our experience as workers and Christians, that capitalism is the enemy of the people because it engenders hatreds, and that the exploitation of man by man is the most radical sin of all because it denies the divine light that exists in every man, and persecutes the body of Christ itself. And we knew that some must die in martyrdom so that other could live in happiness.

And now the base community has become a parallel church, entertaining relations with another church. We can no longer consider ourselves subject to the authority of a hierarchy that actively pushes the poor away from Christ. Moreover, the base community is a *geographic* area, embracing *all* the people therein, Catholic or not. We count not only Catholics, but also Episcopals, Baptists, Pentecostals, and Jews in our base community. We have thereby broken with many of the tenets of the old church in pursuing the authentic message of Christianity. God is in the people. The true face of Christ is in each one who is suffering. You can't look for Christ in the Vatican or in the church hierarchy. This is what our experience has taught us. Our directive, then, is to incorporate ourselves *in the people*; that is the gospel, that is the message of the true Christ, that is the work of the church of the poor.

Therefore we are loyal to the gospel, which is to say, to the people, rather than to the church as such. We lack any equivalent of the centralized hierarchy of the official church. The Popular Church can only exist in the body of Christian believers, which is to say, the body of Christ. The base community then, is a series of small cells, whose purpose is to illuminate the whole community. We do not say as Paul said that "I have the way," but rather that everyone has the answer . . . and that many times the children of darkness are more enlightened than the children of light.

Now, some have wondered about the appropriate role of women in this Christian movement. Especially, some have asked whether it is right to have women out fighting in the military, or in the militia. Some were not only lay workers, but also clandestine activists during the insurrection, and many have daughters who have served in the military. This sort of thing has given some people cause to stumble. But we read our Bible, we Christian mothers and daughters, and it is from the scriptures—and no other source—that we take our inspiration. God called up women as prophetesses and warriors to lead God's children against the oppressors when there were not enough men to do the fighting. Deborah was a prophetess, and Jael took a nail and drove it through the head of the oppressor.[9] And we Christian women of Nicaragua are willing to heed God's call and take up the rifle against the oppressor. If our revolution needs it, our faith requires it.

More and more, we are also doing battle with the hierarchy of the church. The bishop that once said, "This is not good, it is prohibited," now serves as cardinal of all of Central America, and he is still saying that the authentic message of Christianity is not good, that it is prohibited.

Under Pope John, the Vatican was at least a little more sensitive to the needs of the poor of the world. Even so, I am sure that the hierarchy had no idea what it was doing when it encouraged the base community movement and issued the directive, "Go to the Poor." Now that the Vatican understands the implications of this message it is desparately trying to stop what has been set in motion. This intention was made quite clear on John Paul's visit to Nicaragua, when he told the mothers of children who had been massacred by the contra to shut up and stop clammering. Or take Obando. He has made trips to Honduras and Miami to give special masses for the Guardía Nacional in exile there, and he says it is because they are Nicaraguans, and that he cannot withhold the mass from any Nicaraguan. Yet not once has this man who was the godfather of Somoza's son ever found the time to take even one trip to the border areas and comfort the mothers and families of the victims of the contra; not once has he ever offered a mass for the sons who died fighting these Somocistas.

So now, little by little, more and more, the church hierarchy in Nicaragua openly sides with the counterrevolution against the people's government. There is talk of excommunication, of open schism in the church. But we are not afraid of the Pharisees and Sagisees, because we recognize only the authority of God. We are loyal to the gospel of Jesus Christ, the word of God, the body of believers that is the true church. Let them excommunicate us. God has already excommunicated them.

Will we give up? Will the Church of the Poor, the body of Christ, surrender? No. Neither to the hierarchy nor to Yankee imperialism. And we always remember that some will have to give themselves to martyrdom so that others can live in happiness.

THE SPIRITUAL AND THE MATERIAL

The themes in Norma López's testimony are perhaps clearer and more articulate than usual, but they are not at all atypical of popular political/religious discourse in Nicaragua. Moreover, one encounters a similar facility with historical expression and interpretation in a surprisingly large number of people. Of course, not everyone can tell a tale that spans twenty years and integrates local and national history with an interpretation of the Bible, but a large number of people are surprisingly articulate about such things. When I remarked upon this to one of my informants, he observed, "The revolution has given us a voice."

What appears to be a non sequitur occurs early on and signals our interest in the subject matter: "We tried to tell (the youth) that their problems were *social* problems. And they responded that they did not believe in God any more." As long as this statement is seen as a non sequitur, the experience of the poor in Nicaragua remains unintelligible. The basic dilemma here echoes that of the Psalmist, who despairs at the oppression perpetrated by the rich against the poor, and finds faith only in the promise of liberation by a God plainly identified with the poor and oppressed. Not a non sequitur at all, the connection between social problems and God's existence is actually crucial to the message of revolutionary Christianity, and this connection is evident at all levels of the faith, ranging from most popular to most doctrinal. Liberation theologians have since worked out the specific mechanisms for this premise (see, for instance, Miranda 1982:65–67), but the insight was intuitively reached in the base communities early in the movement, and is continually regenerated at that level in lay practice. The position may be summarized as follows: *the classical distinction between the spiritual and the material, the religious and the political, is contrary to authentic Christianity.*

It is significant that this perspective is always situated within the framework of *authentic Christianity.* Like the Protestant Reformation before it, the Popular Church does not generally present itself as "new" except in the sense that early Christianity was "new"— and it likewise presented itself ambiguously as being both completely "new" *and* as the continuation and fulfillment of Judaic law. Liberation theology, as it understands itself, only tells the "good news" of the original message of Christ, a message that was driven underground by hostile conditions or lost in the subsequent Christianity of the church hierarchy. Its struggles with that hierarchy,[10] then, are all the more crucial, for "escapist religion" undermines authentic Christianity, while liberation theology is its reclamation. This approach again parallels the self-understanding of the Protestant Reformation as the reclamation of original Christianity from the constraints of an errant theology. It likewise signals a real church schism in that it revokes the exclusive proprietorship and interpretation of the sacred scriptures by trained church specialists, and puts those texts in the hands of popular masses. The key difference in the approach of the Protestant Reformation and the Popular Church movement lies in the nature of the interpretation of those sacred texts: if in Protestantism every man is theoretically his own interpreter of the scripture, the caretaker of his own soul, the charge of liberation is from the beginning collectivist. Interpretation and caretaking is theoretically a *class project,* a *community project,* and not an individual one.

The equation of the social and the spiritual is also the original demarcation between the new Popular Church and the traditional popular religion, for it allows the Popular Church to set in motion a series of interpretive streamlinings that "demystify" traditional practice. It entails that religious beliefs may not only be representationally radical through various indirections, symbols, metaphors and subverted languages, but that those metaphors and symbols become consciously bound to revolutionary and class aims. Thus, like Protestant revolutionaries before them, the activists of the base communities in Nicaragua sometimes express contempt for the formal trappings of traditional practices (see Randall 1983:53–55), and similarly deemphasize the saints and the practico-magical. ("On our knees in front of mute statues," was how one lay activist described pre-base community practice.) The "ends" of the new religion thus become more remote; not miraculous cures, badly needed rain, or good fortune, but the salvation of humanity becomes its major active concern. In other words, springing out of a traditional popular religion, the Popular Church ultimately embodies itself as a genuinely "ethical religion," in Weber's terminology.

Yet the connection between the new Popular Church and the traditional popular religion is perhaps greater than what would be immediately apparent, even on this discerning terrain, and that connection is certainly greater than the relationship between the Popular Church and the clerical religion of the hierarchy. Like the new religion, the key concern of the traditional popular practice is emphatically with divine intervention in human and earthly affairs: an intervention mediated by saints and directed at individual concerns, perhaps, but an intervention nonetheless. The traditional popular religion may separate the spiritual from the material, then, but it can never draw that distinction as sharply as will the clerical religion, because its concerns are inherently practical. Like the traditional popular religion, the new Popular Church is also primarily concerned with practicalities, but with practicalities more remote than those of the antecedent practice: practicalities that are rationalized, and given a clear class perspective. The new Popular Church thus shares with its antecedent a strong notion of divine intervention in human affairs, even insofar as establishing the criteria whereby one may *bend God's will to human needs*, although the backdrop of that intervention is the panoply of class history, and the subject of God's intervention collective rather than personal. Thence, the conclusion drawn, after a decade of community practice, was that "we could *only* be good Christians by participating in the struggle for freedom"—for what better proof than the fact of class struggle that God exists in the world and brings his assistance on behalf of the poor and oppressed?

This equation of the social and the spiritual is crucial. When the youth in Norma López's tale respond that they could not accept the message of *social* liberation because they no longer believed in God, the distinction drawn is not between the *social* and the *spiritual*, but between the *social* and the *individual*. Allied with and superimposed upon the category "the social" is the spiritual, the divine, the religious; *social vision* is thereby identical to *faith*. (Thus, the real church of Christ can only be synonymous with the solidarized community of the poor.) Allied with and superimposed upon "the individual," then, is sin and acquiescence to sin, alienation, and despair; to lack the faith of social vision is to be lost in the self, estranged·from God (and "all sin ultimately springs from egoism, which is to say, greed").

Therefore there can be no contradiction between "retrieving the souls of the lost"—the project of Christianity—and "engaging in radical social action on behalf of the poor"—the project of Marxism. On the contrary, the contradiction would lie in their separation or hypostasis, for the minimal conclusion of liberation theology is that the two are complementary activities; its maximal conclusion is that they are identical tasks.

According to this interpretation, the Bible is simultaneously a social and spiritual document. What does the Old Testament recount? The real history of the Jews. Who were the Jews? They were unambiguously identified as the poor, the enslaved, the oppressed, and as God's chosen people. And what is the subject of their history? It is their spiritual relationship with a God who is unambiguously identified as Yaweh of the poor. The history of the biblical Jews is also simultaneously a social history of their emancipation from slavery in Egypt, and of their long path to freedom, interrupted by captivities and oppressions by the great empire states of the ancient world. The children of God are the marginated, the poor, and the oppressed. The messianic promise of God to his people is the promise of emancipation and justice.

The New Testament continues these themes. Through Christ, God fulfills his messianic promise. Through Christ, God "breaks into history" to offer redemption and liberation to the poor of the first century, living under the exploitation of the Roman empire. If this emancipation is seen as "purely spiritual," it is meaningless, for even as Yaweh appears in the Old Testament, arms aloft to strike down the oppressor, Christ appears in the New: sword raised and eyes afire, accompanied by his army of saints, to overthrow the world order: to elevate the poor, oppressed, and suffereing, and cast down the rich, the oppressors, the wanton.

The poor of the Third World today occupy exactly the same social position as the poor of the first century: simultaneously exploited by local elites and oppressed by a world empire. And the message of the authentic Christ to the poor of the world today, simultaneously spiritual and social, is the same as his message in the first century: the destruction of an evil world order and the salvation of the poor. And the logical extension of this is embodied in the Popular Church's slogan *"Entre Cristianismo y Revolución No Hay Contradición"* (Between Christianity and Revolution There Is No Contradiction).

ATHEISM, DRUG ADDICTION, AND PROSTITUTION: THE LANGUAGES OF DESPAIR

In Norma López's testimony and in Nicaraguan culture more generally, the revolution is presented as a diminution of despair, lawlessness, and godlessness. The Somoza regime is characterized as corrupt and anarchic; the revolutionary government as a transcendence of those conditions. More concretely, this is typically expressed through two sets of idioms: on the one hand, atheism; on the other, prostitution and drug addiction.

Either of these two sets may be used to frame the origin and ongoing work of the Popular Church in Nicaragua, and in practice both are used. "They did not beleive in God anymore" defines the extent of the existential despair of Managua's youth before the revolution, because atheism signifies an individual *lost in the self* and unable to establish communion with either God or the community. The atheist is the quintessential individualist, because he lacks faith in spiritual or religious categories superordinate to the individual. And the threat of atheism continues to define the work of the Popular Church, most notably in its struggle against the official hierarchy. Explaining the role of the Popular Church, another lay worker develops the following example:

> I talked to a youth the other day. He had been fighting in the mountains, and he came to me and said, "The contra propaganda is all 'Viva el Papa' and 'Viva el Cardenal.' The contra invokes the name of the church in all its propaganda and leaflets, while slaughtering women and children. Yet the Pope says nothing to disassociate himself from this, and the cardinal says nothing to refute the use of his name by these antisocials, criminals, and murderers. Well, if this is the church, I do not believe in it any more, nor in its God!"

> We see the despair in youth like this one, caused by the treachery of the hierarchy and those who invoke the name but not the message of Christ. The work of liberation theology is to

try and save them by showing the true face of Christ, and telling the authentic message of Christianity.

Every Christian lay worker with whom I spoke has referred to the threat of atheism as a stimulus for his or her own activism. This theme occurs among lay workers with a consistency far beyond the actual occurrence of that phenomenon that most non-Nicaraguan observers would call "atheism." (At no time in all my fieldwork did anyone describe himself as "atheist.") Indeed, from its persistent use it is clear that atheism is employed as a metaphor for despair, especially extreme despair: before the revolution the youth of Managua had fallen into a despair so bleak that they had, in effect, ceased believing in God.

Moreover, delinquency in general, and prostitution and drug addiction in particular, occupy privileged and, as we shall see, pivotal, positions in liberation theology's discourse on sin, as carried out at the most popular levels. As in Norma López's testimony, these are most typically linked to the category of youth (*los jóvenes*). *Despair* is defined as the acquiescence to sin, and therefore liberation theology is frequently referred to as "the theology of hope." Recurrently and consistently, even as despair is *metaphorically* represented as atheism, it is *metonymically* represented and concretized through the examples of prostitution and drug addiction. Thus, in the end, it is not so much atheism or drug-addiction or prostitution proper that frame the told histories of the Popular Church in the revolution; rather, it is the underlying theme of *despair* and the threat of despair—as Nicaragua's poor understand these.

"Before the revolution there was rampant prostitution, and the youth were falling into drug addiction." If the revolution was a triumph of Christian principles over godlessness, it was more specifically characterized by the reduction of *urban vice*. In this context, we can understand the testimony of a reformed prostitute: "The revolution has taught me that it was capitalism that marginated us women, from the community and from God." Or consider that a common pejorative leveled against the contra (and anti-Sandinistas more generally) is *"marijuaneros"* (marijuana smokers). A prominent graffito in one of the working-class barrios proclaims: "The CDS[11] in Action: Against Delinquency and Drug Addiction."

Why this recurrent theme, "Before there was much atheism, drug addiction and prostitution, but afterwards, no"? The moral depiction is distinctly "conservative," even "authoritarian"—especially in the sense of literal or figurative parental concern for endangered youth—and diametrically opposed to libertarian or individualist social-political thought. In the popular thought, prostitution and drug addiction represent most pointedly the larger categories of urban vice and social disorganization. Each is seen as corrupting the poor with bourgeois values—and Nicaragua remains a place where "bourgeois" (*burguesa*) is used to denote simultaneously "urban," "elite," and "corrupt." Both represent sin, but the origin of that sin is social and systemic. Exploitation overwhelms the poor and disorients them; estranged from God, they acquiesce to despair. But these themes of drug addiction and prostitution do not just represent "moral" categories of boundaries and transgression. They link the moral conservatism of the urban peasants to their radical stance against capitalism and exploitation.

Drug addiction and prostitution each symbolically represent the most socially disruptive extremes of commodity circulation on "free markets," as seen from the perspective of a "conservative" or "traditional" peasant society. In the case of drug abuse, physically and socially disruptive substances are commodified, marketed, and circulated in a process that embodies the more subtle destructiveness of commodity circulation generally. And in the case of prostitution, the human being itself is appropriated in the marketplace, transformed into a commodity, and bought and sold to other people's satisfaction, in a process that grotesquely parodies the commodification of labor in the market. Each category, then, represents capitalism at its most extreme: simultaneously on the map of the human flesh and on the larger terrain of social relations. And each is indeed an expression of the functioning of the capitalist economy and its tendency to appropriate the entirety of human existence— against God's and man's laws—into the marketplace of commodity circulation. Each pointedly represents the dissolution of community norms under the assult of marketplace rationality.

We will understand neither the radicalism of the popular religion nor the politics of the Popular Church, then, unless we see that the image of prostitution and drug addiction deployed therein is *both* "conservative" (in the sense of pursuing a stable and normative community) *and* "revolutionary" (in the sense of identifying the capitalist market as the main obstacle to that stable and normative community). This image is simultaneously moral, spiritual, social, political, and economic. The words of the reformed prostitute, now a witness for the messages of revolutionary Christianity and the new

Sandinista state, are telling: "capitalism marginated us from the community and from God."

SIN AND ALIENATION

Liberation theology revitalizes Christianity by breaking open and re-constructing the biblical notion of *sin*. Its theory of sin underlies and contextualizes the entire discourse on the aforementioned cat-egories of despair, atheism, prostitution, and drug addiction, and likewise generates the particulars of its dialectical opposite, *re-demption*. By speaking this language of sin and redemption, base community activists simultaneously mobilize both the tradition-alism and the radicalism implicit in newly urbanized popular classes. This theory of sin remains traditional in its framing, conservative or normative in spirit, while being consciously revolutionary in its content. Base community activists like Norma López point to the origins of the new theory of sin: in the very salient features of urban social life in recent Nicaraguan history. To understand sociologi-cally the meaning of that concept of sin, and hence the origins of the Popular Church, it is necessary to keep in mind the conditions that gave rise to these interpretations.

Land concentration and the dislocation of rural populations is nothing new to Nicaragua or Central America. Consecutive waves of large-scale capitalist agricultural expansion have continuously transformed the countryside since the coffee boom of the 1880s. Yet, as recently as 1950, Nicaragua was still an overwhelmingly rural country: 65 percent rural as opposed to 35 percent urban, with Man-agua's population at 110,000. The pace of rural dislocation quickened in the 1950s, '60s and '70s. Some of that dislocation was directly related to the acquisition of large tracts of land by Somoza and his close associates, and especially the growth of the land-intensive, la-bor-scarce cattle industry. These trends all accelerated after the 1972 earthquake, which destroyed much of Managua and unleashed a wave of unusually corrupt government and business practices by the So-moza family.[12] At the time of the earthquake, Managua's population stood at 400,000. By 1979 it had grown to 600,000. Owing to war, continued dislocation, and the world recession in agricultural prices, urbanization has continued apace after the revolution. In 1986 the population of Managua stood at nearly one million. In this same time period, the rural-urban ratio had dramatically realigned: it now stands at approximately 58 percent urban and 42 percent rural, with nearly one third of the country's population concentrated in Managua.[13]

This period of Nicaraguan history provides a textbook case of what has been called a "lumpen-development" (Frank 1972), for in the midst of all this dislocation and relocation—growth without development—Nicaragua's economy remained agricultural export-oriented, and virtually no industrial development took place. A nominally better urban condition drew uprooted peasants to the city. Managua had grown rapidly and sometimes anarchically before the 1972 earthquake, and this pace continued and accelerated after the earthquake, against a background of growing corruption and political violence. The city grew rapidly without adequate facilities and without adequate employment of a productive sort. It has been estimated that, at the time of the revolution, fully two-thirds of Managua's residences lacked some combination of electrical lights, potable water, and secure roofs. The national quality of life figures for prerevolutionary Nicaragua are staggering: "some 71 percent of all housing units had no potable water, 55 percent had no garbage disposal facilities, 62 percent had no sewage system, 77 percent had no electricity, and 83 percent of Nicaragua's children had suffered from malnutrition at some point in their lives" (Rudolph 1982:81).

The conditions of life thus generated are clear enough: reductions in the rural labor sector without concomitant expansion in the urban labor sector; massive rural dislocation and urban migration; increasing levels of corruption and violence in the Somoza regime, whose credibility was rapidly unravelling.

What has been called a "culture of poverty" (Lewis 1966)—and what my informants would call a "culture of despair"—was clearly growing up in Managua's poor barrios. Migrants from the countryside found in Managua a world of poverty, predation, and insecurity.

There was much prostitution and drug addiction. The national guard would come around and prey off the people. They would demand money, just because they could, and you had to give it to them. Gangs of delinquent youths roamed the whole city, robbing and stealing.

The holy days, like Santo Domingo and Holy Week, had become perverted and corrupt. They were little more than bacchanalia of public drunkenness, open prostitution, and delinquency. The prostitutes used to set up little portable houses along the side of the road, and the celebrants would stop in and visit them along the route. Gangs roamed the crowd snatching off people's jewelry. Sometimes they would demand a watch with the phrase, "The watch or the wrist?" If the victim resisted, they would cut off his hand.

Here it is useful to recall Oscar Lewis' observations on the culture of poverty and revitalization movements:

> It would seem that any movement—be it religious, pacifist or revolutionary—that organizes and gives hope to the poor and effectively promotes a sense of solidarity with larger groups must effectively destroy the psychological and social core of the culture of poverty. (1966:8)

The "culture of poverty" thesis has been vigorously criticized (Leacock 1971; Valentine 1968) as a "blame the victim" strategy. Lewis' analysis, it is maintained, lays too much emphasis on the idea that it is the culture of poor people (and not the economic structures they inhabit) which reinforces poverty and makes it self-perpetuating. And surely, this aspect of the theory has been much-abused, as in Moynihan's recommendations that the Nixon administration pursue a policy of "benign neglect" toward black poverty in the United States (see Moynihan 1965, 1967; Glazer and Moynihan 1963).

But no such "blame" was ever the intention of Lewis' own work (and indeed, he minimized the self-perpetuation aspects of the theory), which depicts the culture of poverty as an adaptation to social and economic conditions beyond the control of the affected poor: such is the nature of their rendezvouz with Fate, which ultimately awaits every one of the Sánchez children (Lewis 1961). It would seem a far less tenable position to contend that multigenerational poverty in an urban setting produces no cultural and psychological effects in its victims. Like victims of acute poverty the world over, Nicaraguans speak of the perniciousness and disorientation of despair.

This is how the politicized poor in Nicaragua reconstruct their own past and tell their own history: lay activists, adherents of the Popular Church, Sandinista activists, neighborhood militants, and government supporters *all* tell their story as *the decision to resist despair.* But it is liberation theology that tells this story most convincingly, because it establishes not only its connections to the present-day poor, but to their received traditions of popular Christianity, and more generally to the transhistoric poor, as revealed in the Bible and in Christian myth. By reinventing the concept of *sin,* the Popular Church simultaneously establishes the "community of the poor" as a *sacred body* and establishes the *normative rules* that link that community to its past and—messianically, prophetically— to its future. It establishes in the nature of the enemy the origin of sin itself. Liberation theology, then, *mythologizes* its subject matter and audience—the poor—more effectively (in this case) than similar coexisting ideologies, and thereby is able to absorb those ideologies and articulate them into its powerful discourse on sin and redemption. And it is here that the very *conservatism* of Christianity propels its radical message and reconstructs religious faith as a conscious bulwark against the radical dislocation and anomie of the capitalist marketplace.

Sin is defined as that which estranges man from God. The original state of humanity, in the Book of Genesis, was sinless perfection and perfect communion with God. Sin is, then, the alienation of the human from the divine; ambiguously, it is both the *cause* of that alienation and the process of that alienation as well. To say that "Man lives in sin" is to say that he is estranged from God.

This is no doubt inherent in Christianity generally, but the point is underlined in liberation theology and developed in a particular fashion, for liberation theology collapses the distinction between the social and the spiritual. One may ask, then, "How do we measure this estrangement? How do we know that we live in sin, which is to say, in a state of alienation from God?" And liberation theology answers: "We can only know sin in the nature of our dealings with our fellow man." That is, the measure of our estrangement from God is ever our estrangement from the community of man.

Any number of scriptures may be cited to this effect. The story of the Good Samaritan provides a central parable in the mythos of liberation theology. This parable provides a clearly material and social measure for God's presence and proximity. The caretakers of official religion—a priest and a Levite—both turned aside and ignored the traveler who had been attacked by thieves and lay wounded by the side of the road. Yet a Samaritan—a non-Jew and heathen, by the measures of the official religion—stopped and aided the stranger. Christ upholds this material and social action as the path to salvation, and instructs: "Go, and do thou likewise." (See Luke 10:25–37.)

Likewise the message in which Christ reveals the content of Judgment Day: the basis for its perfect justice is how one has expressed his love of God, which is to say, how one has treated his fellow man. "I was hungry, and you gave me food; I was thirsty and you gave me drink; I was a stranger and you took me in; naked, and you clothed me; sick, and you visited me; I was in prison and you came to me." The righteous, duly confused, answer by saying, "But Lord, when did we see you hungry, or thirsty, or sick?" And God responds, "Inasmuch as ye have done it unto one of the least of my bretheren, ye have done it unto me." At the same time, God condemns into everlasting fire those who have turned away when he was hungry, thirsty, homeless, naked, sick, or in prison—which is to say, who turned their backs on the sufferings of the poor. (See Matthew 25:31–46.)

We may rest on the surface of things and cite the specifics that visibly separate man from the community, and hence from God: hatred, envy, spite, selfishness, gossip, deceit, and treachery are cited often enough, and their opposites are also apparent as the measure of proximity to the community and to God: love, straightforwardness, selflessness, honesty, loyalty, and the like. And again, these are all inherent notions in the traditional religion's understanding of sin as well as its measures of one's godliness or ungodliness. But liberation theology presses further, beneath these "surfaces," to identify *that which most radically divides man from man and estranges humanity from God: exploitation.* The attention of the poor is ever drawn to those passages of the Bible that condemn wealth and exploitation. Miranda has shown how *differentiating wealth* enjoys a special status in the ontology of sin in the Old Testament (1982:21–56). Base community activists emphasized this immediately in their studies: Exodus is liberation from slavery and servitude; the major and minor prophets embody a radical stance against the sin of exploitation; Yaweh is the avenger of the poor, Christ the liberator of the oppressed.

It is thus *exploitation* (and/or oppression) that stands as the metalanguage of sin, and engenders its specific variations (hatred, envy, gossip, deceit). Repeatedly, the Bible establishes this thought, identifying evil with wealth and denouncing the persecution of the poor. This is the long theme that runs through the Bible, from Exodus to Revelation: that it is the radical sin of exploitation that spiritually estranges humanity from God, and that socially estranges man from man, the individual from the community.

The poor are always the primary victims of this alienation of the community from itself and from God, which is to say, then, that the poor are victims of the radical sin of exploitation. This is important in what follows, for the origin of sin lies *outside* the category of the poor proper; they are its victims, subject to a force beyond their control. The same may not be said of the rich. The rich, in pursuing their wealth through exploitation, set in motion the engines of sin, and their continued existence *as the rich*—quite beyond individual intention or volition—depends on the perpetuation of sin. Sin must thus be said to originate, if not from the deliberate actions of particular persons (the rich), then certainly in the process of their accumulation of wealth. *Sin divides the community from God precisely by the measure that exploitation stratifies the community internally.*

If sin originates outside the poor, then the poor—as victims of sin, exploitation and injustice—are indeed "God's chosen people." But exactly like the Hebrews of the Old Testament, who would on occasion lapse into polytheism, pursue false gods, or evince a lack of faith, the poor are likewise prey to a special and pernicious category of sin beyond their simple victimization by exploitation. *Despair* is this *internalization of sin;* it signifies the loss of faith in God (and humanity). Despairing of faith, the poor prey on each other even as the rich prey on the poor; despairing to believe, the youth turn away from God; despairing to uphold community norms, the poor turn to crime, alcoholism, drug addition and prostitution; despairing to believe in the goodness of ourselves or our fellow man, we are disloyal to our friends, faithless to our spouses, unkind to our families.

THE COMMUNITY OF THE POOR, THE BODY OF CHRIST

Weber long ago noted the striking correspondence of "religions of salvation" with "urban proletariats." The need for radical redemption is born alongside and within these proletariats and are as natural a concomitant of certain socioeconomic conditions as are those proletariats themselves. The message of Christianity in liberation theology is *redemption of the poor from sin,* which is to say, externally from exploitation, and internally from despair. The very concept, *redemption from sin,* central to the message of Christ in the first century, stood isomorphically linked to the socioeconomic process, "redemption from slavery": a process whereby slaves could buy themselves out of, or be bought out of, their servitude (see Weber 1963:99–100; also Burridge 1969:4–8).

In liberation theology, God redeems the poor through a process that is indissolubly linked to *social vision* and *social action.* The process of reconstructing the community of believers—of building the kingdom of God—is the process of diminishing the reign of despair. Revolution thus redeems the poor by sweeping aside despair, godlessness, drug addiction; it moves the community closer to God by diminishing the realm of exploitation that constitutes sin and estrangement. It rolls back the culture of despair *and* the "theology of death" (Borge, n.d.).

If the atmosphere of socialist revolution is most intensely an atmosphere of religious revivalism, it is because the Nicaraguan revolution has delivered socialism out of the womb of Christianity. In the New Christology, the new ideology, soteriology meets eschatology in an old/new synthesis: the path to salvation through Christ is fused with the prophetic vision of a new state, a new order, and the reign of justice. The agent of human salvation and of these transformations is of course Christ himself; at the same time, the body of Christ, really and ever-present on earth, is the community of the poor. There is no contradiction, then, in saying that "Christ saves the poor" and that "the poor save themselves," for both of these propositions are dialectically intertwined aspects of the New Christology.

A recurrent image of Christ found in the Popular Church is that of *Cristo Campesino* (Christ the peasant). It is usually a very straightforward depiction: a simple peasant, obviously poor and usually barefoot, bearing a large cross. A variation of this image depicts *Cristo Obrero* (Christ the worker), and sometimes even *Cristo Guerrillero*: a Nicaraguan Christ in guerrilla fatigues, bearing a cross, supported on either side by the community of the poor, and struggling to liberate humanity.

It is through such arresting images that the most political and studied segment of the Popular Church presents an image of the poor to themselves: the project of the poor to liberate themselves is a sacred undertaking; Christian faith *is* the solidarity of the lower classes against sin and oppression. The liberation mass celebrated in many services in Nicaragua is not incidentally called *la Misa Campesina Nicaragüense* (Nicaraguan peasants' mass). Its opening hymn, "El Dios de los Pobres" is a simple and straightforward embodiment of this message and holds up a series of striking images of the God of the poor:

> *(Chorus)*
> *You are[14] the God of the poor,*
> *the God humane and simple,*
> *the God that sweats in the street,*
> *the God with a weather-beaten face.*

> *That is why I talk to you*
> *just like I talk to my own people,*
> *because you are the God of the working people,*
> *Christ, you're a working man too.*

> *You give my people a hand,*
> *you struggle in the country and in the city;*
> *you fall in line there in the camp*
> *where they pay you your day's wages.*
> *You eat sweet ices seated there in the park*
> *with Eusebio, Pancho, and Juan José*
> *and even protest for the syrup*
> *when they don't give you much honey.*

> *(Chorus)*

> *I have seen you in a pulpería*
> *installed behind the counter,*
> *I have seen you selling the lottery*
> *without feeling ashamed of that piece of paper.*
> *I have seen you in the gas stations*
> *checking the tires of a truck,*
> *and even working the highway,*
> *with work gloves and overalls.*

> *(Chorus)*

The service's second hymn, "Kyrie," is both an invocation to worship and an invocation to class struggle:

> *Christ, Christ Jesus*
> *identify yourself with us*
> *Lord, Lord God*
> *identify yourself with us*
> *Christ, Christ Jesus*
> *solidarize yourself*
> *not with the oppressor class*
> *that wrings out and devours*
> *the community*
> *but rather with the oppressed*
> *with my people*
> *thirsting for peace.*

Likewise, the song "Gloria"—sung to a popular bullfight tune—establishes a parallelism: we sing to the glory of a natively Nicaraguan God in natively Nicaraguan places, and we simultaneously sing to the glory of the poor who struggle against injustice.

> *Glory to God in Siuna, Jalapa and Cosigüina,*
> *in Solentiname, Diriomo and Ticuantepe*
> *Glory to God in Tisma, Waslala and Yalagüina,*
> *in Totogalpa, Moyogalpa and Santa Cruz.*

> *Glory to those that follow the light of the gospel*
> *Glory to those who denounce injustice without fear*
> *Glory to those who suffer prison and exile*
> *and give their lives fighting the oppressor.*[15]

In the dialectical synthesis of sin and redemption, the poor are both subject and object of history. Liberation theology sacralizes the community of the poor, which is to say, the body of Christ, and deploys it as both the agent and subject of salvation/revolution in the world. In the image of *Cristo Campesino*, the poor see themselves as the victims of sin and exploitation; in *Cristo Obrero*, they see themselves clarified and sacralized; in *Cristo Guerrillero*, they view the military aspects of the millennium and see themselves as its active agent. Liberation theology thereby establishes the nature of the movement, solidarizes it around a key symbology, and lays down the new rules of conduct and struggle.

Liberation mass itself takes the form of a dialectical tacking back and forth between the traditional sacraments and the new interpretations of those sacraments. A traditional passage is read; a new interpretation is offered. The traditional lines are recited over the host. Then, the new commentary is added:

> Bread is the food of the poor. It is what we give our family, our friends, our loved ones to show that we love them. God has given us bread. Bread is also our work, the product of our own labor.

Any number of variations may be found in local practices: sometimes the host is *given* in the traditional fashion; other times it is most emphatically *taken*; i.e., the officiating priest may place the bread and wine where worshippers can get it themselves, in a service with minimal mediation by the priest between God and humanity. At least one priest makes a point of donning his priestly robes over dungarees *in front* of the congregation, so all may see that he is, after all, an ordinary man officiating the service.

It is inherent in the nature of religious services that they provide exhortations to the community, and a clear aspect of liberation mass

is "political exhortation." Like other exhortations, these are sometimes scolding. But the term "political exhortation" does not capture all the nuances involved. The meshing of new messages with
old ones, modified forms with received ones, and the general her-
meneutics of liberation mass, combined with religious music in a
sacred setting, often surrounded by murals that depict politico-religious themes, can produce powerful emotional responses in the
congregation. Political exhortations from the pulpit are suffused with
religious authority, even when they are distinctly programmatic (i.e.,
vote, do communal work, join the coffee-harvesting brigades)—and
liberation mass contains both general exhortations and programmatic ones, the latter always developed from the former. The following was taken from a service whose general topic was the sin of
individualismo or *egoísmo.*

> We know that egoism is the sin of greed, and that greed is the
> root of all evil. We know that individualism separates and divides
> the community, and that individualism is counter to Christianity.
> We go to church on Sunday, and denounce individualism, and nod
> our heads at the service . . .
>
> And yet the sin of individualism is rampant in Managua. We are
> being individualistic when we know fully well that there is a water
> shortage, and yet we leave the water running the whole time while
> we brush our teeth. It is such a little thing, such a simple thing, to
> turn the water off! And yet a whole city of individualists, running
> the water, each thinking, "this is such a *little* bit of water, surely
> it will do no harm."
>
> It is this same evil of individualism that causes us to waste toilet
> paper, and then to run out and buy more on the black market,
> knowing fully well that this hurts the national economy and all the
> people. These are little things, and everyone is thinking, "these are
> such little things," but multiplied a dozen times a week, amplified
> a million times for the entire population of Managua, they are not
> such little things at all, and we begin to see the full weight of this
> problem of individualism . . .
>
> And yes, mothers, it is individualism when some mothers hide
> their sons from the draft, saying, "not my children, let somebody
> else's children go off to the mountains and make the sacrifices."

Having ranged from the general explanation down to the specific
exhortations, this priest's sermon ended again on a general exhortation:

The Sandinista Revolution, this people's revolution, our *evangelical* work in Latin America, has all the forces of evil in the world aligned against it: all the might of the United States military, all the riches of that giant nation . . . And we are a tiny country, a poor country. But Christ has shown the way for us, he has set the example. If we are selfless and dedicated, we will persevere. But this revolution, this evangelical work, will not survive unless Christians renounce the evils of individualism and make the necessary sacrifices to defend our country, our people, and our faith.

CHAPTER THREE

Liberation Theology and the Spirit of Socialism in Nicaragua

For the oppression of the poor, for the sighing of the needy, now will I arise, saith the Lord; I will set him in safety from him that would ensnare him.
—Psalm 12:5

It is worth repeating that liberation theology provides a "normative," even "conservative" vision of social good. The ideal state of the community envisioned therein is normative in a sense that recalls the stability of the closed corporate community of traditional peasant society. Its stance toward "the individual" as a differentiated entity is hostile and may almost be summarized as "that which deviates from the community norm."

The popular language bears the mark of this social conservatism in a number of ways. A common pejorative is the term *vago*, which may be used as either an adjective or a noun, and which literally denotes "vagrant," "tramp," or "tramplike." More generally, it connotes something that is deviant, or out of its proper place. Hence, children who wander, adolescents who stay out too late, even household cats, dogs, or birds are scolded with the charge, *"Muy vago!"* which says simultaneously: you are vagrant, idle, deviant, and out of place. Indeed, the conception that things belong in their proper place is so compelling that it frequently enters into the political discourse. For instance, I have heard the opposition newspaper derided in the following matter: *"La Prensa es muy vago."* Which is to say, in colloquial English, *"La Prensa is way out of line."* While similar to its English equivalent, "bum," the image of *vagancia* is somewhat richer, more nuanced, and is capable of being put to a wider range of meanings: it conjures the image of public idleness, social nuisance, potential destructiveness. The moral force of such a term is undeniably conservative: people and things always belong in their proper place, well-centered, and appropriately occupied.

In the place of the traditional category *pinche* (stinginess), liberation theology elaborates the newer, more powerful, parallel categories *egoísmo* and *individualismo*. Strong prohibitions against individualism and egoism strengthen the normative power of the community to regulate itself in much the same manner that the derogative *pinche* served (and serves) to level distinctions in the more traditional setting. In a word, revolution augurs the reestablishment of the traditional image of social order—real or mythical—lost when sin divided the community and capitalism stratified the society.

It is also worth reiterating the indigenous origin and development of the Popular Church, as well as its genuinely popular following. It has become a routine procedure in some circles to impugn the authenticity of the Popular Church in Nicaragua by suggesting that it does not represent a variation of Christian faith at all, but rather a jerry-rigged system imported and imposed on the poor by Sandinista bureaucrats.[1] On the contrary, lay workers and base community activists are typically not "outside agitators," nor is the Popular Church in any sense a foreign "imposition." One can readily trace its emergence out of the traditional popular religion and show how its theology was arrived at through local reflection and meditation.

A similar criticism, often mounted by the church hierarchy, has been that liberation theology provides an unsystematic mixture of Marxist materialism with Christian theology (see Cardinal Ratzinger's *Instructions*, 1984). I have found no real basis to substantiate this claim, and it seems to me that liberation theology may well be quite wholly derived in all its major principles from the Christian tradition and from biblical sources in a manner far more systematic and consistent than many of the dogmas of the official church hierarchy. A textile millworker and base community activist from Barrio Peru succinctly comments on this point:

> They say we are Marxists, or that we are mixing Marxism and Christianity. Really, we do not know anything about this Marxism. We have never read Marx in my barrio, or in the base community. All we know is what we read in the Bible. That is the source of our Christianity and our politics.

RELIGIOUS PLURALISM AND REVOLUTIONARY HEGEMONY

A substantial majority of the population in Managua's popular barrios affiliates with, identifies with, or supports the activities of the Popular Church to one degree or another. Of course, degrees vary, and the milieu may be characterized as a "pluralism of religions." There are many exceptions, but as a general rule, younger Nicaraguans, growing up in a revolutionary milieu, more readily tend to identify their religious loyalties with the Popular Church. Older people may remain attached to a more traditional religion, and some retain respect for the symbols and offices of the church hierarchy. Many people accept some of the messages of the Popular Church, question others, and even reject some. I have heard one Nicaraguan mother argue vigorously against the notion that Nicaraguans "live the resurrection of Christ through the Sandinista revolution," only to argue later with much greater vigor that Christ is, indeed, the Christ of the Poor. ("And not of the rich?" I ask. "The rich have Caesar—and all the modern caesars.") Another praises the Popular Church on all points—except that it has diminished the role of the *santos* and their incarnation in particular statues, so important in the traditional religion.

> When I go to mass, I like to see the saints in their places. It seems to me that the saints are losing their place in Nicaragua. The Popular Church displays only the cross, the Sacred Heart of Christ, and the Virgin Mary, and nothing more. I don't understand this. It seems to me a church ought to have some saints in it, like the churches in Masaya and Granada. I understand the right of people not to believe in them, but I like the saints. I like to look at them. They comfort me, and I miss them when they aren't in the church.

Many people, like the above informant, are in fact inclined toward both the political theology of the Popular Church *and* the magical practicality of the traditional popular religion. For others, of course— and this attitude defines the rationalizing trend in the Popular Church—the magical practicality of the saints has given way to a *popular rationality*. This tendency is far more common among the adherents of the Popular Church. The following opinion was expressed by a grandmother living in the very poor barrio Sergio Altamirano:

All the saints were invented, except the ones in the Bible: Saint Christ, Saint Mary, Saint Peter, Saint Paul, and the like . . . As for the rest of them, they were invented by the clergy in order to get money out of the poor people. So it won't do you any good to pray to them! You should only pray to Christ, or Mary, or the biblical saints.

Skepticism of the hierarchy; an insistence that the clergy are corrupted by money; a simplification and streamlining of the religion: the above statement simply and eloquently distills many of the concepts key to the development of a current of popular rationalization in Nicaragua, and illuminates its relation to both the official hierarchy and the traditional popular religion.

In theory, numerous relations could attain between the traditional popular religion, the new Popular Church, and the official religious hierarchy. In practice, all of these do occur, although some relations occur with greater frequency than others, and provide the culture with its dominant structure and social trends. Part of the complexity here is the fact that substantial numbers of people, in practice, adhere to more than one set of religious beliefs. For instance, one informant believed the essential message of Christ of the Poor, retained some respect for the offices of the official church, participated in the *fiestas patronales,* and prayed to Santo Domingo when there was illness in the family; if that illness was protracted, she would sometimes consult spiritualists. Thus, depending on context and occasion, she made use of the full range of options in Nicaragua's religious pluralism. Like the majority of Nicaraguans, she attended no service regularly, although she prayed nightly and said her rosary, and no one could describe her as an irreligious woman.

Another family was internally divided. The conservative father identified with the official church, while the militant mother supported the Popular Church. Some of their children were Sandinista Youth activists, and all of them identified with the values of the revolution. Yet some of the children were regularly sent to popular mass, and others to official mass, without any apparent basis for assignment. The eldest daughter, a neighborhood militant, along with her mother, a former Sandinista Police officer, were key actors in planning and executing an elaborate *Purísima,* in keeping with the traditional practice.

Despite such complexities, the general trend is quite unambiguous: the Popular Church continues to grow in strength and credibility, and the official hierarchy continues to decline in strength and credibility. Oddly, this is true especially among people who do not go to church regularly and therefore do not *appear* to be especially devout. The traditional popular religion, after all, was not a religion of regular church attendance, but rather, one of belief and only occasional practice (for instance, in the *fiestas populares*). "Rich people go to church to show off their new clothes," was one worker's comment on church attendance. "The message of Christ of the Poor cannot be confined within the walls of a church. The Popular Church grows because it attracts the loyalty of the poor, who do not have new clothes and are not in the habit of going to mass every Sunday." "Some people worship God in the church on Sunday; we choose to give glory to God in how we live our daily lives."

This is a crucial point. What has replaced reliance on the religious hierarchy in many working-class areas of Managua is not so much a new liturgical religion as a *faith* or an ideological religion. Various observers, well-acquainted with bureaucratic structures in Managua but only superficially acquainted with belief in the popular barrios, have commented on the "weak social base" of the Popular Church, especially in comparison with the very active social base of the Protestant evangelicals. But in fact the strength of the Popular Church now lies less in its activism at the base community level and more in its relative hegemony over popular religious ideology. Much of what would ordinarily constitute the base community of the Popular Church has in fact been incorporated into the community base of the FSLN, the CDS, and other mass political organizations. That is, much of the popular base of the FSLN is simultaneously Sandinista and revolutionary Christian.

A POLITICAL RELIGION, A RELIGIOUS POLITICS

Some may find the actively political orientation of the Popular Church a distinctly nonreligious trait. I hope I have recreated the theology and ideology of the Popular Church well enough that its political activism is seen to flow naturally from its status as a religion of the poor. At any rate, the function of the Popular Church in Nicaragua is only rarely programmatic propaganda. More typically, its function is, like that of other religions, to provide general exhortations and to enunciate the general principles of theology and ideology around which the society may be said to be solidarized or unified. What distinguishes liberation theology from religion more generally speaking is the same thing that distinguishes the revolutionary state from other types of states: both are consciously reforging the society and its ideology by "the logic of the poor." In the case of the Popular Church, the community that it seeks to solidarize and sacralize is the community of the poor. And liberation theology's relation to the Nicaraguan state is special: both the revolutionary state and the revolutionary church originated under the same conditions, developed along parallel and mutually reinforcing routes, and apparently share a fate.

Sometimes North Americans ask me about the relationship between the Sandinista state and the Popular Church in a manner that reveals an implicit bias: "Is there a danger that the political aspects of liberation theology will eventually crowd out the mystical aspects"—in effect leaving the Popular Church an empty shell, and something of a fraud? We after all—or rather, those of us in the Anglo-Protestant tradition—do have a bias for religions that emphasize the personalistic, the individualistic, and the mystical, and we tend to define religion in these terms from the outset. But clearly an anthropological understanding of religion, cognizant of the enormous historical and cultural variation in religious practice through history and across cultures, cannot afford an ethnocentric equation of this sort. And the clear bias of liberation theology is from the beginning *against* what we would understand as mystical, individualistic, or personalistic religion: whatever segregates the spiritual/religious from the material/social, and whatever isolates the individual in the self, is inherently counter to real Christian faith with its communal values. Indeed, "escapist religion" progressively approximates *sin* according to liberation theology, because it turns the poor away from God and away from meaningful social solidarity.

Another common question about the special relationship between the Popular Church and the Sandinista state goes more to the heart of the question: "Is the Popular Church a state religion?" Again, North American culture entails a strong bias against state religion, and the notion runs counter to our history as a nation. Nicaraguans do not necessarily share this bias. Many workers look forward to the day when the Popular Church will altogether displace the official church hierarchy and become in effect, if not the state religion proper, then the religion of clear consensus. A relatively homogeneous society with a strongly *normative* ethic (as opposed to an individualistic, libertarian, or marketplace ethic) could naturally be expected to evolve something like a "state religion."

It may justly be said that the Popular Church is progressively ap-

proximating the status of a state religion, in the sense that it originated with the present state, and its fate is tied to that of the
Sandinista state. It is unlikely, however, that any formalized, officially sanctioned relationship of this sort will ever materialize. One
of the long-range strategies of the revolutionary government in un-
dermining the authority of the official church hierarchy has been to
promote meaningful denominational freedom, a move which has led
to massive Protestant conversions in some areas. More importantly,
the foundations of the Sandinista state itself are secular (Borge et al
1982:110). Its *language* is often the language of the religious movement; its ideology, especially at the community level, is often quite
unambiguously religious. But the official self-conception of the
Sandinista state is modern and secular, and will probably preclude
the emergence of a genuine church-state or state-church.

REVITALIZATION, RENEWAL, AND
CHARISMA

In its origins and development, liberation theology in Managua's poor
and working-class barrios represents a *religious revitalization movement* (Wallace 1956) in classical anthropological terms. The community was facing a protracted social crisis brought about by the
disorganization and anomie of the capitalist marketplace; indeed,
it had faced a serious natural disaster (the 1972 earthquake) that
seemed to serve as a metaphor for the protracted social disaster of
colonialism (see Barkun 1974). Likewise, the traditional religion was
deeply immersed in a crisis of credibility, unable to account for the
present situation, impotent to solidarize a fractured community, and
unwilling to confront the real conditions of life in a constructive
manner.

The new religion was thus innovated: out of the stuff of the old
religion, and in response to the historical predicament of the community. It achieved a prophetic stance with regard to Nicaraguan
history, and forged its chiliastic mission. Unlike many such revitalizations in the anthropological literature, however, liberation theology supports no single *living* charismatic prophet or savior who
has galvanized the movement. It draws the charisma of its prophetic
vision from the example of Christ, who, in original martyrdom, "paid
the price" for the redemption of humankind. (As Leonardo Boff has
put it, "The price of liberation is the cross.") Likewise, its house of
"saints" is in fact a house of martyrs: Antonio de Valdivieso, Che

Guevara, Augusto César Sandino, Carlos Fonseca Amador—men who, following the example of Christ, have likewise "born the cross" of martyrdom on behalf of the poor and oppressed.

Charisma in the Popular Church, then, is derived not from a living prophet, but from dead ones—or perhaps we should say, resurrected ones—who were martyred for their prophetic faith. From one angle, then, this is a *decentralized* charisma: it centers on no one living individual. As a corollary, this model of charisma insures that whatever charisma accrues to living individuals will be a function of their willingness to make sacrifices and forego individual gratification for the good of the community. This built-in leveling mechanism deflates the material utility of charisma from the outset. Its incentive must always be altruistic.

From another angle, however, this model of charisma strongly *centralizes* the authority structure of the Popular Church. By making Christ its central referent, liberation theology undermines the decentralized and diffuse charisma of the popular religion with its burgeoning house of magical saints. Where once a variety of diffuse procedures might confer charisma on the basis of general magical principles—healing, magical cures, miracles—the new charisma is simplified. Effectively, only one procedure confers it: the example of Christian sacrifice. Or perhaps it could be said another way: in the traditional religion, it is the magical healing of individuals that confers charismatic authority; in the new religion, charismatic authority is conferred by the social healing of the community. Thus, while diminishing the real or potential authority of any one individual, this charisma simultaneously maximizes the authority of the collective church community.

But if the Popular Church has its martyrs, it conceives of itself not as a church of martyrdom, but of resurrection: the ultimate triumph of life over death. Christianity is always the shedding of innocent blood to atone for sin—that is, it is sacrifice. It is also redemption and a new life.[2] The mystical core of liberation theology thus draws on the deepest blood-redemption symbology of Christianity in the following manner: the death of the individual brings new life to the community. This is both a real and a figurative relationship: concretely, the revolution requires its martyrs, and death in the defense of the revolution is seen as bringing new, revitalized life to the whole community; figuratively, the death of the individual—in the sense of the death of individualism—signifies the rebirth of the collectivity and the origin of the collectivist "New Man." The price of liberation, then, is the cross; struggle is a cross to bear, but revolution is its ultimate triumph. And echoing the biblical texts, revolution resurrects the dead, for it proves the prophetic vision of the martyrs; in effect, it is also proof of the resurrection, for the body of Christ that was once dead is now resurrected. Thus, as popular slogans have it, "Sandino Lives," and "Carlos Fonseca is more alive than all the living."

This link between martyrdom and resurrection, which is the essence of Christianity, is also the essence of revolution. In tellingly religious language, one young man recounts an experience as an insurrectionist in the battle for Rigoberto:

> All around me in the dark, there were boys crying out in pain. One *compañero*'s leg had been completely blown off by a mortar shell. Another was missing his arm.
>
> And then I saw a girl, a friend of mine, who had been wounded in the fighting. Her leg had been cut off by the explosion, but unlike the others, she was not shouting out in pain. We began carrying our hurt friends away to the hospital to be treated, and this *compañera* looked at me and said, "Listen, my pain will animate you in the struggle against Somoza."
>
> When sunrise finally came, the sky was all red. We wondered, what could it mean? Someone said it was the color of blood. But no, it was the color of our freedom.

THE RATIONAL IRRATIONAL

Weber's major work, especially *The Protestant Ethic and the Spirit of Capitalism*, aims to describe the transition from economic traditionalism (with its aversion to work beyond the necessary minimum (1958:36, 59ff)—and, we might add, with its ceremonial fund, leveling, and aversion to accumulation) to the modern capitalist economy (with its rational accumulation, open-ended reinvestment, and profit-seeking imperative). Much has been written, for and against Max Weber's interpretation of Calvinism as the early "motivational system" in the development of capitalism.[3] While any number of nuances and revisions may be added to Weber's original thesis, it remains a powerful paradigm in terms of both its method and content.

First, regarding the method: Weber's is an attempt at integrating economy, culture, and ideology into a dynamic and historic model that might still be called "Marxist" if we recall Engels' polemic against the vulgar and reductionistic (Marx and Engels 1968:688–690) distortions of Marxism:

> According to the materialist conception of history, the *ultimately* determining element in history is the production and reproduction of real life. More than this neither Marx nor I have ever asserted. Hence, if somebody twists this into saying that the economic element is the *only* determining one, he transforms that proposition into a meaningless, abstract, senseless phrase. The economic situation is the base, but the various elements of the superstructure— political forms of the class struggle and its results, to wit: constitutions . . ., juridical forms, and even the reflexes of all these actual struggles in the brains of the participants, political, juristic, philosophical theories, religious views, and their further development into systems of dogmas—also exercise their influences upon the course of the historical struggles and in many cases preponderate in determining their *form* (692).

Contrary to a common misrepresentation of Marxist thought as economic reductionism, that ideology and motivation can and do sometimes take a "lead role" in historical developments is a premise recognized by both Marx and Engels (701) and by all subsequent Marxisms.[4] Weber's analysis is quite compatible with this dynamic perspective; it, too, begins with a description of the "material base" or economic preconditions that were necessary before Calvinism could act as an engine of history (e.g., free labor, non-household production, substantial cities) (1958:21–27); and indeed, Weber emphatically envisions a dialectical relationship between economy and religion (1958:27, 183) of which *The Protestant Ethic* only traces "only one side of the causal chain."

Second, regarding Weber's findings proper: by instilling into its adherents a "this-worldly asceticism," the idea of a calling, and hence a high degree of individual self-restraint and work-discipline, the Protestant Revolution indeed prepared the way for subsequent social, political, and economic revolutions leading to liberal capitalism. Some have taken up this latter revision of Weber with a twist: in the Protestant revolutionaries are also prototypes of the modern revolutionary man: self-restrained, disciplined, engaged in an all-consuming movement (Walzer 1965; Cohn 1961).

As we have seen in the case of liberation theology, Weber's thesis, appropriately modified, remains vital and productive—albeit in a sense Weber might not have forseen. Like the Calvinist revolutionaries before them, Nicaraguans found themselves estranged from God and encountered the world in a state of wicked disorder; they undertook a spiritual and social revolution to set things right. But how are we to understand the nature of that spiritual and social revolution? the role of liberation theology in the revolutionary society? in the transition to socialism? And what is the nature of the streamlinings and revisions it undertakes on the traditional popular religion?

A new system of charismatic authority, liberation theology also represents a *rationalization* of the popular religion. But it is not an unambiguous rationalization, in which the mystical and the traditional disappear. Rather, the specific rationalization of religion produced by liberation theology retains at its core an image of stability, the normative, and the timeless that defines "tradition." If "modern" society always entails the notion of progress-through-maximalization as its image of social good, then the revolutionary Christianity takes a distinctly anti-modern, *traditional* image of social good. Its ideology is a specific mix of the rational and the "irrational." Like the revolution proper, it employs modern or rational techniques to the traditional end of social conservation and stability.

We may distinguish, then, between means and ends: the means employed by liberation theology are essentially modern, rational, and calculated (the strike, the demonstration, civil disobedience, syndicalism, class struggle, guerrilla warfare). Its *ends*, however, are "traditional" in the sense that they are normative, and the means and the ends are legitimated by an often "irrational" appeal to divine intervention and a collective mythology quite above the utilitarian plane.

The rational/irrational mix may be traced along any number of routes. Weber distinguished between "formal" and "substantive" rationality, with each roughly corresponding to the more commonplace concepts, form and content. *Formal* rationality/irrationality refers to the degree whereby decision making and action are controlled by rigid or received procedures as opposed to intellectual calculation; the more calculation enters into the process, the more rational it is. *Substantive* rationality/irrationality refers to the extent to which general rules, regular laws or consistent principles are employed; the general, the regular, and the consistent—as in ethical religion or regular law—is "rational." Formal rationality may naturally breed substantive irrationality, and vice versa. One could say, then, that *formally*, liberation theology lingers in the shades and shadows of the irrational, with its rituals of mass, prayer, and hosts, but that *substantively*, it streamlines, clarifies, and rationalizes the general symbology of Christian faith in such a way that removes much of the lingering ambiguity of popular practice and makes its general rules of the faith sharper, clearer, and more universal.

This formal-substantive dimension may be analyzed even further, if one distinguishes social practice from ritual practice. Liberation theology entails a formally rational, empirical, and calculated social practice; it conceives of social reality as subject to conscious intervention and manipulation. At the same time, this positivism is balanced and supported by formally irrational ritual practice: prayer (appeal to spirits or the divine), baptism (sanctification by divine forces), the rosary (mechanical and magical invocation), etc. Along the substantive grid, a parallel situation manifests itself: liberation theology's claims and aims—its deep theory—are legitimated by substantively irrational and sometimes magical concepts that would seem to undercut the possibility of empirical social science (God, Christ, church; ultimately, the belief in a real intervention in the world by a divine force irreducible to natural observed phenomena). At the same time, it is substantively rational and empirical on the nature of its aims (redistribution of wealth, egalitarianism) and its generally prescribed social methods for achieving them (class struggle, revolution).

One could no doubt pursue this basic configuration through many more degrees of complexity, for the revitalization of religion in Nicaragua simultaneously pushes forward rational, ethical, modernizing, and calculating trends, *and* at the same time preserves a space for and multiplies the facets of the irrational, the magical, the traditional and the received. This peculiar mix of the traditional and the modern, the magical and the rational, the conservative and the revolutionary, may well define predominately peasant societies in revolutionary periods more generally. Such a mix, in broad strokes, constitutes the emergent states and cultures of Third World socialism. The revolutionary ideal, the revitalization ideal, as we are reminded by Wallace (1970:377–378), may appeal to apparently opposite themes: the salvaging of tradition, the coming of the future utopia. In practice, revolutions and revitalizations appeal to each simultaneously. Even the image of the future utopia is conceived as the stuff of tradition, for tradition is not a dead hand, but a living social force. At the same time, even those who undertake to "preserve the tradition" are already firmly in the grip of a type of rationalism, for they must now and ever after go about appropriating and measuring reality in a conscious and empirical fashion—that is, employing rational means—with their end of stability in mind.

THE LIBERATION REFORMATION

There is a religious "Reformation" going on in Nicaragua and throughout Latin America, but it is not like Weber's Protestant Reformation. At first glance it appears to offer a quality strikingly similar to the asceticism of the Protestant Reformation. But no ethic of real sensual asceticism pervades the Popular Church. Its theoretical conception of sin has curiously little to say about such things as sex, moderate drinking, and the standard sensual gratifications. What it addresses is the issue of *wealth*—"socially differentiating wealth" (Miranda 1982:21–30)—and what it condemns is not sensual pleasure, but individual self-enrichment at the cost of the community. Anti-individual, yes, but it is not at core anti-*sensual*.

Like the Protestant Reformation, the present one projects the biblical texts "out of the monastic cells and into daily life" (Weber 1958:181). But what it interprets in those texts is not "progress" through increment, saving and stewardship, but *justice* through equitable distribution and social order. Where the Protestant ethic emphasized work, the Liberation ethic emphasizes *struggle* as the key to the Kingdom of God. Certainly, the Popular Church promotes the idea of work, too, especially in the new society. But where Protestantism centered on the individual as the subject of the Bible, the interpreter of its texts, and author of work, liberation theology centers on the community as the Bible's subject and interpreter, and as the author of struggle and work.

The present Reformation, then, is surely not the Protestant Reformation, nor need it lead, ultimately, past the "charismatic stage" (1963:229–235) to the terrible "iron cage" (1958:181–183) of rationalization foretold by Weber. In liberation theology rationalization is powerfully present but also powerfully restrained by the presence of the traditional; instrumental reason (Horkheimer 1974) is chained to magic in a manner that precludes its colonization of every sphere of human existence. The spirit of the rational cohabits there with an equally powerful spirit of the irrational.

The oft-invoked "logic of the poor" *is* popular rationalism, and the revolution deploys this form of rationalization in any number of directions, along any number of paths. We have surveyed that trend toward rationalization in the field of religion. But popular rationality is not the same thing as the rationality of the capitalist marketplace, for it takes fixed, even rigid ends. Those ends are ever "traditional" or "conservative," and this fusion of popular rationalism with traditionalism is legitimated by a religious ethic that combines the rational and the magical in a particular mix. Barring its destruction, the ideology of the revolutionary society could not lead to the alienation and anomie of capitalism because it preserves the spirit of tradition; because it erects "the irrational" as a high bulwark against capitalist rationality.

Of course, whether one sees traditional or corporatist society as its own "iron cage" will all depend on one's point of view. The traits characteristic of such social formations are seen, from the wholly exterior point of view of capitalist rationality, as so many fetters on productive rationalization, and as so many restraints on the individual. But from the point of view of the "traditional rationality" ever-present in traditional masses, these traits represent safeguards against exploitation, disruption, and anomie.

The desire to reassemble these shattered customs and resurrect the traditional corporatist image of society—to vanquish the dislocations of *vagancia, ateísmo, delincuencia*—is the form that class consciousness spontaneously takes everywhere the marketplace impinges on traditional society. This "rational irrational" consciousness—always tinged with mysticism, millenarianism, and corporatism—has typically been quite inaccessible to the Western Marxist academics who purport to study such phenomena. Cosmopolitan Marxism fantasizes the image of a "pure class consciousness," calculated and legitimated in the manner of a utilitarian rationality quite out of place among real revolutionary masses. Real class consciousness among real revolutionary masses operates differently.

A rational irrational, modern traditional consciousness defines and *is* class consciousness in real, revolutionary milieus. This consciousness defines and legitimates the emergent revolutionary state. Therefore, as a corollary, the perennial inaccessibility of the revolutionary state to Western Marxists flows not from any "perversion" or "distortion" of revolutionary praxis by elites in the new state, or by conditions of underdevelopment, or as a result of colonialism's persistent attacks—as theory often holds—but from the very inception of the revolutionary movement itself in popular masses. Cosmopolitan Marxism and rationalist capitalism thus share a common aversion to revolutionary movements and states as they are really articulated: an aversion to the irrational, religious and corporatist aspects of traditionally minded people activated in revolutionary movements.

The attitude with which the West more generally surveys these revolutionary movements might best be called a "schizoid gaze."

On the one hand, the Western intellect sees these traditional, even "conservative" aspects of revolutionary mobilization and consolidation as barbaric, backward, even psychopathic phenomena. Surveying the landscape of a restless and rebellious world class of laborers, economic development theory converges with the bureaucracies of psychotherapeutic practice to show how the insoluble dilemmas of the modern situation produce native resistance, and how native resistance always comes under the rule of social pathology. Where dwells there a Western commentator who has not shaken his head over the religious fervor of the Shiite fanatic? who has not carped over peasant excesses during periods of revolt? This discerning gaze finds in revolutionary masses only a grotesque parody of their nonrational aspects.

On the other hand, a coexisting and complementary current of Western thought characterizes revolutionary mobilization wholly in terms of its *rationalizing* consequences. In this equally enduring scenario, the revolutionary state is typified as the ultimate triumph of modernity: atheistic, rational, demystified and impersonal. The gaze embodied therein sees in revolutionary society a Kafkaesque mirror-world of the modern industrial factory.

Weber clearly believed that socialism (of either the reform or revolutionary variety) would ultimately push foward rationalization in the particular form of bureaucratization. In this paradigm, socialist revolution is modernization and rationalization, in a particularly rigid and repressive form: to the extent that it is like Western capitalism, it brings various compartments of society under the rule of rationalization, and modernizes the productive apparatus; to the extent that it is unlike capitalism, the rationalization it brings is not that of "blind" market forces, but rather those of an impersonal bureaucratism far more efficient at regulating and controlling society than at maximizing the economy proper. This model has not only become standard in academia and among Western Marxists, but has long since passed into the sphere of common knowledge and may be encountered in various simulated forms in any metropolitan newspaper.

I would suggest that the trends involved in revolutionary mobilization are far more complex. Paradoxically, revolutions are great social upheavals made in the pursuit of the traditional, the timeless, the stable society. Nicaraguan masses are, simultaneously and without contradiction, both "conservative" and "revolutionary." The legitimation of such revolutionary regimes flows not from their incremental or rapid assertion of social control through bureaucratization, but rather, from a type of religious-political consciousness endemic in popular masses in revolutionary periods. The emergent revolutionary state retains the allegiance of popular masses to the extent that it fulfills its obligation to recast society in the image of tradition.

Revolutionary society is, in its way, the last respite of tradition in the modern world.

CHAPTER FOUR

The Theology of Creative Despair: Evangelical Protestantism

*Therefore, if any man be in Christ, he is a new crea-
ture: old things are passed away; behold, all things
are become new.*
　　　　　　　　　　　—II Corinthians 5:17

---

*That ye put off concerning the former conversation
the old man, which is corrupt according to the de-
ceitful lusts; And be renewed in the spirit of your
mind; And that ye put on the new man, which after
God is created in righteousness and true holiness.*
　　　　　　　　　　　—Ephesians 4:22–24

Nicaragua's Protestant evangelicals occupy an ambiguous, sometimes contradictory, and quite often volatile position in the emerging political-religious configuration. North American new right TV
evangelists have been key organizers of private aid for the contras,
and these same right-wing networks have attempted to manipulate
Nicaraguan evangelicals against the Sandinista government. A number of local evangelical clergymen have gladly obliged their U.S.
counterparts in this respect (see Stoll 1986).

Within the general framework of confessional freedom, the approach of the Sandinistas to the evangelical movement has varied
greatly. Troublesome foreign missionaries have indeed been expelled or prevented entry into the country; on one occasion the
properties of several denominations were seized; and most recently,
a crackdown on the conservative Catholic and evangelical clergy drove
several figures into exile. At the same time, practicing evangelicals
are sometimes held up as exemplary role models for the nation at

large, and the FSLN has made increasingly vigorous efforts to include evangelicals in the revolutionary process.

This chapter considers evangelical practice as a popular phenomenon, and is based on extensive interviews and participant observation in the heavily evangelical barrios of Sergio Altamirano and Catalonia. As with the Catholic clergy, it may safely be said that only a substantial minority of perhaps one third of the evangelical clergy is "with the revolutionary process" in a consistent or profound way. But as is the case of the Catholic Church, if we distinguish clergy from congregation, a different picture of evangelical practice emerges.

RELIGION AND CLASS STRATA: THE CONTEXT

In Managua's very poorest barrios, the religion that competes with liberation theology for the status "religion of the poor" is neither the traditional popular religion nor the clerical religion of the official hierarchy, but rather, evangelical Protestantism, most typically of a pentecostal variety. This may seem surprising in a revolutionary state whose "overarching ideology" is liberation theology, but evangelical Protestantism has grown rapidly since the late 1970s, and especially since the 1979 revolution: from approximately 5 percent of the population in 1979 to more than 15 percent of the population in 1985.[1] It seems altogether plausible that a fifth of the population will be evangelical by the close of the decade.

The association of Protestantism with dire urban poverty is noted by native observers, and confirmed by my research in distinct barrio types. Protestantism is not really much at issue in middle-class and professional neighborhoods *(las residencias)*, which remain predominately Catholic and predominately devoted to the clerical religion of the official hierarchy. It is here, among urban (and rural) elites that Cardinal Obando y Bravo and the conservative clergy find the bedrock of their social support, more or less openly opposed to the Sandinista government.

Below the middle-class *residencias* and at the level of the middle working-class *colonias* like Erasmus Jiménez, one finds a split between the popular and clerical churches. That division generally operates to the substantive advantage of liberation theology. But liberation theology in Erasmus Jiménez coexists alongside strong remnants of the traditional popular religion, and this traditionalism occasionally acts to the clerical church's *formal* advantage. For instance, I have seen the children of Sandinista militants baptized in the church of a conservative priest. Why? It would seem that the parents wanted the additional measure of assurance that a traditional—and "official"—baptism confers.

A variety of religious issues resist firm resolution here in middle working-class barrios like Erasmus Jiménez. Many residents are torn in conflicting directions between their respect for the priestly offices (which sometimes pulls them in the direction of the hierarchy), and the conditions demanded for that respect (humility and sacrifice, which generally pulls them in the direction of the Popular Church). A third tendency also operates here, roughly analogous to a rural situation: insofar as middle peasants are the primary carriers of tradition in the countryside (Wolf 1969:292), the middle working class takes up an equivalent position in the cities and acts as a *culturally conservative* force there. In other words, the urban middle working class tends to retain a strong current of the traditional popular religion. The traditional leveling mechanisms are prominently practiced here. Various residents engage in economic activities that generate an economic "surplus," but a traditional mentality strongly militates against "rational" savings, investment, and accumulation. The expense levied by Purísima is especially apparent here. Such neighborhoods, popular but comfortable, are not, then, the primary sources of popular rationalization in the religion; despite their educational aspirations, they remain more entrenched in tradition than poorer barrios, who actively reshape tradition in the light of popular interests.

It would not be inaccurate, then, to see such middle working-class neighborhoods as roughly evenly divided between two or three religious tendencies, depending on one's configuration: clerical vs. popular, or clerical, popular, and traditional. Erasmus Jiménez is less than 5 percent Protestant—well below the national average, and this seems to be true of similar neighborhoods throughout the city.

In the lower working-class barrios Rigoberto and Peru, only a fragment of the conservative clerical religion remains. There, the Popular Church's numerical advantage is striking, supported by active congregations, base communities and Bible study groups. While the traditional popular practice persists, it persists in the framework of a more radical mix with liberation theology. Here, in these barrios, the base community has been active since the mid-sixties, and increasingly powerful since the early seventies. Residents cite the intransigence and reaction of the clerical church in dealing with the plight of the poor as the chief reason for their widespread defection from official authority, and it is here that the message of *Cristo de los Pobres* is most enthusiastically embraced. But it is also here that Protestantism begins to put in its first notable appearance: about 15 percent of the residents are evangelical, according to informed speculation by residents.[2]

In the poorest and newest barrios of Managua—the economically marginal shantytowns, marked by widespread reliance on the "informal economy"—the conservative clerical religion all but disappears. Barrios Sergio Altamirano and Catalonia are suffused with a smoldering anticlericalism. It is difficult to find anyone here who will defend the Pope or the Cardinal; strong denunciations of the clergy are the general rule. Moreover, belief in the traditional popular religion has also eroded. Some people believe in the saints, but many do not. There is little surplus in these barrios to level, in keeping with the traditional popular religion, and little benefit accrues to the residents from traditional leveling practices. It is here, under conditions of direst necessity, that the rationalizing impulses of the popular classes is most visibly unleashed in the field of religion, but that impulse follows two distinct paths: roughly half these two *repartos* adheres to the teachings of liberation theology, the other half to evangelical Protestantism, and especially to a variety of doctrinally similar charismatic sects.[3]

Sergio Altamirano, in particular, is a striking example: it is one of Managua's largest and most densely populated barrios. While other marginal and semi-marginal barrios have not been as vigorously or successfully proselytized as Sergio Altamirano, they too appear much more Protestant than the national average. The Protestant percentage in the poorest barrios of Managua, then, is generally double the national average, and, by extension, these barrios comprise the bulk of the Protestant movement in Nicaragua.

Moreover, a lower-income bias also shapes the Protestant phenomenon in the entire range of popular neighborhoods. In marginal, lower working- and middle working-class barrios, the Protestant families tended to exhibit one or more of a variety of characteristics that indicate a fragile social position. As a general rule, the Protestants are among the very poorest people in their given barrio, whatever that type be. Female-headed households, or households with other special economic disadvantages (recent or persistent illness, for example) are overrepresented. Finally, tolerance of the evangelicals is also correlated to special social and economic disabilities. I have observed at length the reaction of many families in various neighborhoods to Protestant proselytizing. Most people in the lower working- and middle working-class neighborhoods refuse to discuss religion with the evangelicals when they come around testifying, door to door. The families that will sit and talk with evangelical proselytizers—in essence, to *consider* conversion—are largely marked by the same characteristics as presently practicing evangelicals: especial poverty, absence of a male household head, recent or persistent illness.

The roster of evangelical churches operating in Nicaragua reads like a telephone-book directory of churches in the rural South of the United States: Baptists, Pentecostals, Church of God, Assembly of God, Jehovah's Witnesses. Introduced by North American missionaries, largely from the southern United States, these denominations are taking on a native life of their own, and are now largely self-sustaining and self-reproducing entities, with their own special relation to social class and the Nicaraguan revolution. In some respects, evangelical Protestantism has been as vigorous a movement among the poor as liberation theology: its numbers may be smaller, but its religious activism is often far greater. Each sect, every formal or informal congregation, *each cell*, is consciously envisioned and organized as an *actively proselytizing* body that is always seeking new converts. And as the figures show, the evangelicals have registered remarkable success at initiating widespread conversion among the urban poor.

PROSELYTISM AND CONVERSION

It is clear that the special traumas and dangers associated with dire poverty provide the major stimulus for Protestant conversion, in both pre- and post- revolutionary Nicaragua. The stimuli that trigger conversion to Protestantism are not dissimilar to those that also generate liberation theology. Similar problems and preoccupations are continuously cited by adherents to each faith: drugs, delinquency, and crime; despairing poverty and social disorganization.

Liberation theology and evangelical Protestantism are both quintessentially "evangelical" discourses. Both renounce the formalism of clerical practice on behalf of active scriptual study, both emphasize the importance of God's word over liturgy, and both entail a strong conception of Christian praxis in daily life. And both represent, in Walzer's (1965) phrase, a "revolution of the saints." While the traditional popular religion demands that ordinary people recognize and endorse the ideals of Christian comportment (as embodied in the saints), both liberation theology and evangelical Protestantism participate in the same reformation process in that each demands of the ordinary people ideal Christian comportment, which is to say, *saintliness*. The key difference would seem to be that the especially marginal milieu of the *repartos* generates a more radical need for personal salvation than the relatively more socially integrated barrios of the lower working class.

One might, for shorthand, call the conversion techniques of the Popular Church "soft" and those of the Protestant evangelicals "hard." The liberation Catholics, after all, are only calling upon fellow-Catholics to renounce the conservative clergy's leadership and to interpret the scriptures and the mass in a new light. Affiliates remain Catholics, and the message of the new gospel spreads by a process of community consensus on the communal nature of religious interpretation. Liberation theology's iconography and hagiology, while simplified, remain identifiably Catholic.

Protestantism, in contrast, offers a "harder" break with tradition. The evangelicals vigorously renounce Catholicism, its mass, the saints, and all varieties of "formalism" and "idolatry," opting for a new religion. Like liberation Catholicism, evangelical Protestantism presents itself as "authentic Christianity" in opposition to "debased religion"; like liberation Catholicism, it displaces responsibility for scriptural interpretation away from the bureaucratic offices of the Church; but unlike liberation theology, which retains and resynthesizes some traditional liturgical forms, evangelical Protestantism's ritual is wholly anti-traditional. And it spreads its message less by a process of community consensus, and more by a tumultuous process that breaks down the resistance of whatever lies in its path. Indeed, enormous community resistance initially stands in the way of Protestant conversion, and the evangelical movement, as an aggressive and antagonistic religion of despair about the present world, feeds on this resistance to its spread.

Like the "soft" conversion techniques of the Popular Church, the "hard" conversion techniques of the evangelicals generate a standard form of argumentation, a standardized testimony, and a standardized "text" of conversion. Assembly of God member, Carlos Ocón Gonzáles explains his conversion in a manner designed to solicit other conversions. No less sincere for being routine, his presentation indicates the activist and proselytizing orientation of the evangelicals. As we spoke, he turned through pages in his Bible, citing scriptural justification for each assertion. Well-read in the Bible, he in fact attained literacy primarily through Bible study. Our interview, ostensibly designed to discuss Protestantism, was in fact quickly subverted into an attempt to convert *me*; Carlos ran through his litany as though I were a potential Catholic whom he might convert to Protestantism.

The Catholic Church teaches that God is dead. The priests make images of him, idols of wood and stone. They cause the people to worship a dead god. The Bible prohibits this, in Exodus 20: "Thou shalt have no other gods before me. Thou shalt not make unto me any graven image, or any likeness of any thing that is in heaven above, or that is in the earth beneath, or that is in the water under the earth. Thou shalt not bow down thyself to them, nor serve them: for I the Lord thy God am a jealous God . . ."

Because of their idolatry, the Catholics live in sin. Because they worship a dead god who can neither see nor hear, they can drink and rob and still be good Catholics. But the evangelicals know that God is alive, and that he lives in heaven and on earth.

Catholicism, like Judaism, is religion, but it is not salvation. This is what Christ told the Pharisee in John 3. The Bible says you must be born again, you must be made a new man, to enter the kingdom of God. So you see, we Christians do not practice religion at all. We have *salvation*.

The law of Moses isn't enough. Nor is it enough to baptize your children and confirm them into the church. It is just this sort of religious idolatry that stands in the way of true salvation. The Catholic clergy are exactly like the Sagisees and Pharisees who tempted Jesus, and whom Jesus admonished. You must be made into a new man.

Now, how do we know that we are saved? How do we recognize it? First, it is necessary to remember that we are saved by God's grace and not by human works. But when we are saved, we are made into new beings, we live a new life, and all our works are changed. We give a testimony to God—a testimony not of how we talk, but of how we live. If I am saved by grace, you will see that my works are good, that I don't drink, that I don't rob the people, that I don't fight with or beat my wife, that I live in peace with my neighbors, and that I rear my children the same way, by God's word.

Another informant continues this same theme. More analytic and less categorical but taking up the same idea, he explains the appeal of Protestant conversion.

The people are very confused, and the official church has helped disseminate that confusion. Many Catholics, for instance, don't ever read their Bibles at all, so they have no idea what the scriptures say. Most of them end their spiritual life with baptism or confirmation, and go on to sin, drink, steal, and exploit the people with impunity.

The evangelicals set a higher example. They read their Bibles, and they exalt God in their daily lives. They do not sin with impunity, and this example is noted by many Catholics, who choose to convert.

Of course, there are good Christians who are Catholics. And there is only one church that God recognizes: the Church of Believers. But it does seem to be more difficult to be such a believer in the Catholic Church.

The conscious preoccupations that lie behind Protestant conversion are not so different from those of Popular Church activism. Each religion emphasizes as its nemesis the characteristic social traits associated with urban poverty and lumpen-development; each cites the threat and the reality of social disorganization. If prostitution and drug addiction are the master metaphors of liberation theology in the barrios, the themes that preoccupy the evangelicals are perhaps only slightly more familial, in keeping with the more personalized approach of Protestantism: drinking, wife-beating, stealing . . . If distinct at all, these preoccupations are continuous with liberation theology's, and more frequently entirely interchangeable. In essence, each movement tries to reclaim and reestablish the conservative or normative social milieu lost with urbanization and lumpen-development.

The spiritual career of Carlos Ocón Gonzáles and his family is not atypical. The family originated in a rural mountainous department. Eventually landless, the family largely depended on Carlos' agricultural and manual day labor, supplemented by his wife's food-vending on foot in the local market town. While still in the country, his wife developed severe ulcer infections in her lower legs that have lasted several years now and have seriously curbed her ability to work. The family subsequently moved to Managua, in search of better employment opportunities for Carlos, which were available in the form of day labor: cutting vegetable growth by hand with his machete, construction work, lifting and loading, and sometimes hauling. The family's major setback came when Carlos' neck was broken in a work-related accident. As a result, he lost several months' work, and is even now prevented from performing strenuous manual labor.

It was after his broken neck that Carlos and his whole family converted to Protestantism. This case exemplifies something of the nature of Protestant conversion: special trauma followed by the conversion of the entire family seems to be the general rule. Carlos now makes a meager living through a nonproductive routine that exemplifies the large, decentralized informal economy of his marginal barrio: he waits in line all night twice a week outside the *panadería* (bread factory), where he purchases a bulk amount of bread, which he takes by foot from *pulpería* (neighborhood store), to *pulpería*, selling to small merchants at a very slight commission for himself. He goes the entire route by foot (about five miles total) to avoid the unnecessary expense of the bus, or three córdobas.[4]

Carlos would prefer to work with his hands, he explains, but mishaps have forced him into this means of making a living, which is both unproductive and less lucrative than manual labor. "But you will see that I, as a Christian saved by grace, do not try to rob or cheat the people in my dealings like other vendors," he explains. Although he would never describe it in such terms, it is clear that Carlos' conversion to Protestantism was shaped by his experience of the social and economic traumas that have been especially acute in Nicaragua for more than twenty years.

The social practice of evangelical Protestantism in these barrios is not so difficult to deduce. According to another informant, a mother, textile mill worker, and Jehovah's Witness:

> Crime is very bad in this barrio. There is a lot of delinquency, and it can be very dangerous here. Our neighbors in front over there have been robbed three times in the last six months: an iron, some clothes, and a sewing machine . . . We have a CDS, and it keeps fair vigilance, but that is at night. So now the thieves come in the daytime, while people are out at work . . . We are already poor, and this makes things worse.
>
> A good Christian does not act that way. He reads the Bible and does what it says. A good Christian acts . . . *good*, and godly. He doesn't rob. He lives in peace with his neighbors, and all people. He works hard for his living, and is not a thief or a parasite.

Even according to most *Catholic* informants in Sergio Altamirano, Protestant conversion produces an exemplary effect on the individual's comportment. Said one Catholic mother who is surrounded on three sides by Protestant neighbors:

It is very simple, why so many people are converting. The evangelicals set a good example, they lead a godly life. They don't drink, they work hard, they believe in education for their children. I am very impressed by the evangelicals. . . . Whenever they have a *junto* (meeting, especially open-air gathering) over there, I go to it. I like the service a lot. It is very beautiful, simple, and informal, and you don't have to dress up or have money to go to it.

This sort of commentary is not at all unusual in Managua's *repartos*, especially Sergio Altamirano, where many of the remaining Catholics are potential Protestant converts. Indeed, the power of Protestantism to shape religious perception here is so impressive that one informant, when queried about his religious identification, responded: "No, I am not a Christian. I am still a Catholic."

Not all Catholics, of course, are so generous in their assessments. The impression of Protestantism in the poorest barrios is almost unanimously, even monotonously, positive. But increasingly, as one moves outside the marginal barrios and into lower and middle working-class neighborhoods, one encounters an often-intense hostility toward the evangelicals. "They come around door to door, annoying[5] people and twisting the Bible." "It's disgraceful the way they broadcast their religion in the market, like vendors." Liberation Catholics sometimes insist that the evangelicals are counterrevolutionary, and are plotting the overthrow of the Sandinista state: the type of conspiratorial stereotype to which minority sects are often subjected.

Sometimes, Catholic workers who are not economically marginated—even those who are oriented toward the message of liberation theology—are irritated by the evangelical assault on Catholicism and express this through counter-insults that, intentionally or not, highlight the status differentiation between themselves and the marginated poor. One informant (from Barrio Peru) who was usually restrained and analytic commented on Protestantism with the following protracted insult:

The evangelicals, as you have seen, stand out in the marketplace proselytizing, and go from door to door visiting people. And when they go from door to door all day, after reading the Bible and insulting your faith, after denouncing the Virgin Mary, what do they do? They ask you for money. The majority of people just close the door in their faces and won't talk to them.

Now, what do you call someone who doesn't work, but who goes from house to house all day, talking and asking for money? I call them *vagos* (vagrants), and I call *evangelismo* a religion of *vagancia* (vagrancy).

RATIONALIZATION AND THE INDIVIDUAL IN PROTESTANTISM

Unlike the Protestantism of the Reformation, Protestantism in Nicaragua has been most emphatically a religion not only of the poor generally but more specifically of the most marginated poor, especially those living in urban slums. While it does seem equally plausible that peasants in the process of becoming farmers might opt for a Protestant religion that stresses savings, stewardship and rational investment,[6] this is clearly not the logic of developments in Nicaragua. Landed farmers have not taken up the cause with any great enthusiasm, and poor though relatively comfortable urban workers have singularly resisted the conversion attempts of the evangelicals. Lower working-class barrios embrace the more moderate sects at figures that hover near the national average. Where the evangelical faith is taken up in large numbers and in the more extreme form of charismatic sects is in the *repartos* (urban slums) and among landless peasants (Escorcia 1985). Massive conversions there have apparently produced a permanent demographic shift in religious practice in Nicaragua, for the children of evangelicals are reared in the faith of their parents, and go on to reproduce that faith themselves.

The propitious circumstances which have led to these wholesale Protestant conversions are similar to the circumstances that likewise gave birth to liberation theology two decades ago. A foremost factor has been the intransigence of the clerical religion when confronted by the political, economic, and spiritual needs of the poor. This factor has been amplified by the remoteness of the clergy from the daily life of the poor. For instance, only two parishes served the entirety of Managua as late as 1961, when that city's population was 200,000. Under such circumstances, the clerical church was very much a church of the rich: its offices staffed by elites, its congregations filled with elites. The only time it came into contact with the masses at all was at the end of the giant *fiestas patronales*, like an afterthought, to baptize the popular religious practice with the authority of the official church. For the vast bulk of Nicaragua's poor population, even minimal clerical care was virtually unheard of until the Vatican II reforms that gave birth to the base community movement. The determinate factor that finally wrenched the masses of poor Nicaraguans away from the sway of the clerical authority was the anomie and disorganization implicit in proletarianization and urban life, especially for the most recent immigrants from the countryside.

Thus, beginning before the revolution, and accelerated by that revolution, a new religious constellation has crystallized in Nicaragua. Evangelical Protestantism plays a key, if underreported, role in that new constellation. Like liberation theology, it "rationalizes" the popular Christianity of traditional practice. Strangely, this doctrine diverges from liberation theology on most every fundamental point, but nonetheless runs a parallel course to liberation theology and produces many of the same sociological effects.

Where liberation theology's key referrence point is "the community," evangelical Protestantism's is *the individual*. It is the individual who stands responsible for his interpretation of the Bible, his own sins, his own spiritual well-being. But this is not to say that Protestantism thereby represents a "religion of individualism," especially in the sense of individual accomplishment, competition, or greed. It does not. Its emphasis on the individual is not to exalt his social role but to apply more rigorous criteria of individual responsibility and accountability: *the individual is more effectively circumscribed if his accountability for sin is effectively maximized.*[7]

In liberation theology, the individual is pitted against the community as well as the divine, and the doctrine pronounces the superiority of the communal and spiritual over the individual or egotistical. In the case of the evangelical or Pentecostal sects, however, this sort of dichotomy never fully emerges. Rather, it is the pursuit of the physical, the tactile, the sensual that distracts the person from his all-important relationship with God. The dichotomy here, then, is most explicitly between the physical and the spiritual, a dichotomy which may be played out in its entirety on the terrain of the individual person without ever resulting in "individualism" as recognized by the radical Popular Church. The spiritual task of the individual, in the Protestant sects, is to be drawn closer to God by means of self-renunciation, especially renunciation of things physical.

Through radical, ascetic conversion, evangelical Protestantism in Managua's marginated *repartos* rearticulates the anomic and sinful individual into a new community of believers whose demeanor is, theoretically, exemplary, and whose actions are rationalized and calibrated by the read or revealed word of God. In this sense, then,

Protestantism does indeed re-create a normative community. And it is clear that the *example of evangelical deeds* (i.e., good works) is the key witness to the power of Protestant conversion. But it is also crucial to Protestant ideology that "deeds" are the *consequences* and not the cause of personal salvation. Thus, while the real practicality of this religious experience lies in the realm of deeds, the *magic* of conversion lies in the ineffable concept of *grace.*

Through this mystery of "grace" and "deeds," the evangelical conversion experience is saved from the shallowness of mechanical emulation. One's deeds are only the evidence, the epiphenomena, of the Holy Spirit effecting its true work of personal salvation: a process of divine grace that reaches its most intense expression in the spectacular forms of "speaking in tongues," hysterical weeping, "shouting," and faith healing. This myth of grace is the overarching myth of Pentecostal salvation: one does not simply *behave* differently, one is in fact transformed into a new creature. Grace is that irreducible and indescribable quality of God stooping down, by means of the Holy Spirit, to lift man out of sin and worldliness.

In spite of Protestantism's strong rationalizing tendencies, prayer, like the concept of grace, for many evangelicals progressively approximates the status of *magical manipulation.* This aspect of Protestantism represents a retreat away from the purely ethical aspects of a streamlined religion, and recreates the practico-magical orientation so at home in the traditional popular religion. We might expect this in Managua's marginated *repartos,* where persistent and cyclical sickness is a major fact of life, and where uncertainty has a meaning absent in the economically integrated working-class barrios. Few there retain the traditional faith in the patron saints, but the idea of a religion without magical cures and personal intervention by God would be too harsh to bear.

The words of one new convert underscored this point. A bout of dengue had detained me for nearly a week from either visiting his house or, more importantly, from accompanying him to the nightly services of a local *primitivista* cult. When he finally saw me coming down the road, and having heard of my illness by word of mouth, he immediately began chiding me for my lack of faith.

> God wants only good things for us, not bad things. It is the devil who is the author of bad things, bad works. That is why Jesus died for us. He died not only for our sins, but also for our sicknesses, our poverty, our sufferings. He took all these evils upon himself, so that we would not have to bear such burdens.

You did not have faith in the Lord, or you would have come to the service anyway, and He would have healed you. The Holy Spirit is a wonderful thing. If we have faith, and if we go to God in prayer and earnestness, he will give us what we ask. God is good, He is our father, and he does not want any of us to suffer.

In contrast to the Appollonian daily life of the convert, the nightly services of these Pentecostal cults give full vent to Dionysian excess. Replete with ecstatic music, shouting, weeping, and speaking in tongues, the service's general form duplicates similar practices found in poor North American congregations of the same denominations. And nightly, the pastor acts as dispensary of divine cures and blessings.

In sum, the process of religious rationalization is clearly unleashed in evangelical Protestantism. This process is particularly pronounced in the evangelical concept of individual accountability, in precise, practical measuring rods of salvation, as well as in the radical simplification of belief that renounces the saints and their efficacy. Echoing developments along the same lines in the radical Popular Church, evangelical Protestantism *simplifies* the core of belief, *centralizes* spiritual authority around the Godhead, and *decentralizes* the church's political authority and bureaucratic organization—in this case into a confusing array of sects, each of which lacks national as well as interdenominational coordination. But, as in liberation theology, these trends toward rationalization are kept in close check by the powerful presence of "the irrational," the magical, the mystical: that which is irreducible and unanalyzable—in short, that which *resists* rationalization. Unlike liberation theology, in the case of evangelical Protestantism, this "mystical" aspect of religious practice is ever bent toward the practico-magical ends of divine cures and personal blessings.

Sociologically, as well as logically, evangelical Protestantism runs a strangely parallel course to liberation theology. A doctrine of renunciation and mysticism, avowedly apolitical, it is nonetheless a religion of the poor in a revolutionary milieu. As such, it produces radical social phenomena, but *indirectly*, rather than through the directness of the radical Popular Church.

As in liberation theology, evangelical Protestantism posits an indissoluble link between sin and wealth—a relationship arrived at by different mechanisms, to be sure, but a nonetheless indissoluble connection. If in liberation theology differentiating wealth is that which separates man from the community and both from God, for the evangelicals wealth, especially of a mercantile sort, is that which most profoundly and most powerfully distracts men from their true spiritual pursuits. The Pentecostals are fond of citing the encounter between Christ and the rich young man and the parable of Lazarus. They often cite biblical aphorisms that highlight the connection between sin and the pursuit of money: "Lay not up your treasures upon earth . . ., for where your treasure is, there will your heart be also." "You cannot serve two masters, God and money" (Matthew 6:19–21, 24).

In the evangelical sects, then, wealth and the aspiration to wealth are seen as master metaphors for all that is worldly (sensual, tactile, material), and hence *sinful*. Because it is easier for a camel to pass through the eye of a needle than for a rich man to enter the kingdom of God (Matthew 19:23–24), it also follows that the poor are closer to God—and are demonstrably more inclined to convert—precisely because they have less invested in the worldly, the sinful, the mesmerizing pursuits of the flesh.

Now evangelical Protestantism clearly does not espouse an active, politically revolutionary message in keeping with *Cristo de los Pobres y Oprimidos*. But in this religion of asceticism, one encounters a powerful hatred of capitalism, exploitation and markets, intertwined with an austere renunciation of the flesh.

> Listen, it is because the rich are always enriching themselves that we have so much sin and vice in this city. The merchants of pornography and the merchants of *guaro* (liquor), they are responsible. I don't go to the movies any more, praise God. It is just a wicked distraction. They lead people astray, these movies about "breakdance" and "flashdance." Why do you think we have so much delinquency in the barrio now? Because the youth went to see movies where they learned the corrupt habits of North American youth. This filth is of the devil, straight from the devil, and it is criminal that it should be marketed without regard for the spiritual state of the people.

As such sentiments demonstrate, Pentecostal sects in Nicaragua, albeit through radically different logic and substantially different sociological mechanisms, ultimately share with liberation theology an orientation toward *social order* that is somewhat class conscious, anti-capitalist, morally "conservative," and (at least implicitly) economically "radical." As a religion of the poor—in fact, of the marginated poor—evangelical Protestantism's relation to the revolution is indirect, rather than direct: it creates order out of disorder, without overtly "political" intentions, through the notion of individual responsibility and accountability. It thereby indirectly and unself-consciously exemplifies certain revolutionary values. One could put this particular relationship another way: whereas liberation theology's relationship to the revolution is primarily ideological, evangelical Protestantism's relationship to the revolution is primarily sociological.

Through its powerful motivators in the concepts of personal sin and salvation, evangelical Protestantism radically reorders and regulates the lives of the very poor. Despair about this veil of tears and fear of punishment in the afterlife prevent practicioners from falling into the ever deeper states of anomie that threaten to engulf the community of the marginated. Thus, in a real sense, the religion of renunciation and despair opens up a space of order in the midst of disorder, morality in an immoral world, and a deferred hope in a prevailing social terrain of hopelessness. It ultimately combats the culture of despair by causing the poor to lead more exemplary lives. In opening up this space among the poor, the sects of radical personal salvation—despite their renunciation of things worldly—thereby open up the possibility of revolutionary participation, rather than lumpenproletarian delinquency, in the very poorest barrios.

EVANGELICALS AND THE STATE

Some of the evangelical ministers, especially foreign missionaries, have attempted to rally antirevolutionary sentiments in Nicaragua, although the social stratum of evangelical strength has not proved amenable to counterrevolutionary politics. And according to their own fund-raising material in the United States, any number of foreign mission projects directed at Central America take anticommunist principles as their chief raison d'être. With good reason, various foreign missionaries in fact have been expelled for using their offices to disseminate antigovernment political propaganda. Some Nicaraguan evangelicals have resisted the military draft on religious grounds.

But on balance, the evangelical sects have accelerated, not impeded, the revolutionary process. Just as there are many ways to skin a cat, there may be many routes to consolidating a revolution. Liberation theology is direct, ideological. Evangelical Protestantism is indirect, sociological.

For instance, there is no evidence that evangelicals evade the draft in greater proportion than Catholics, and my own observations over a period of some months indicate that they may evade it *less* often— although this probably correlates more directly to the relevant social strata in which religious faith is embedded, rather than to the nature of faith itself. As the natural transition presently underway continues, and as the evangelical sects become nationally and locally self-perpetuating and self-reproducing, with ministers converted out of the *repartos*, and as the involvement of foreign missionaries recedes, antirevolutionary and antigovernment tendencies likewise tend to minimize themselves. Indeed, many practicing evangelicals praise the revolution precisely because the prevailing climate of religious freedom, which they say is greater than under Somoza, promotes and facilitates conversion. "Before, people were afraid to convert— Oh, we were afraid of everything, and conversion was just one more thing. The hierarchy of the Catholic Church and the Somoza government were very close. We were intimidated. It is not like that now, and people feel free to worship God as they choose."

It is also clear that, despite suspicions about the evangelicals' otherworldly orientation, the revolutionary government is a substantial if indirect beneficiary of the evangelicals' activities. First, the evangelical movement erodes the moral and spiritual authority of the conservative Catholic clergy, which now serves as the chief facilitator of internal political opposition. Moreover, the fragmentation of effective spiritual authority into an acephalous and uncoordinated variety of small churches and sects likewise benefits the government indirectly: this trend obviates the possibility of organizing sources of power and authority alternative to the revolutionary government's. Protestantism thereby dissembles the religious bureaucracy that could really or potentially rally non- or anti-Sandinista sentiments. At the same time, Protestantism effectively *privatizes* those religious practices that are not expressly pro-Sandinista, accelerating a development which is highly desirable to the consolidation of the revolutionary state. Practically, this means that the ideologically revolutionary religion of liberation theology is carried out as a public discourse; evangelical Protestantism, on the other hand, as an individual-oriented religion, neither pro- nor anti-state, is relegated to the sphere of private belief, personal conviction.

Equally importantly, Protestant evangelism operates in potentially problematic barrios to lower crime and delinquency rates. It encourages greater social and work discipline, and concomitantly, higher labor productivity. Many evangelicals actively participate in the revolutionary process—in the mass organizations, and a few in the FSLN itself: some because they have innovated variations of Baptist or Pentecostal doctrine that are continuous with the theology of liberation. Some evangelical congregations affiliate with the informal Popular Church, or are members of the *Centro Valdivieso,* which coordinates relations between the Catholic base communities and Protestant congregations aligned with liberation theology. And when Miguel D'Escoto undertook his 1985 "fast for peace" as part of an "evangelical insurrection" against the counterrevolutionary positions of the church hierarchy, he was supported in rallies, vigils, and prayer services by several of Managua's evangelical churches. Indeed, some evangelicals speak of the emergence of an eventually consolidated, new Popular Church in Nicaragua, based on a fusion of liberation Catholicism with a variety of receptive evangelical churches and sects. But outside of a few barrios, this sort of relationship is still rare, and it is difficult to imagine such an overt alliance spanning the significant doctrinal gap between liberation Catholicism and evangelical Protestantism.

Largely, the relationship between evangelical Protestantism and revolutionary participation is indirect, not direct, for Protestant doctrine contains few principles that would appear to prescribe revolutionary political praxis. His radical salvation prevents the convert from pursuing the paths of delinquency and criminality that always run through these marginated *repartos,* and, in so doing, makes the person more morally, hence socially, responsible. It is only, then, in the last analysis that this doctrine of personal salvation increases the possibility of the convert's active participation in the civic aspects of the revolutionary process.

It is also worth pointing out that such participation generally comes later on rather than early in the moral career of a convert. The novice to evangelical Christianity is likely to put special stress on the other-worldly and mystical orientation of his faith, with a radical renunciation of things worldly, including politics. When pressed on political subjects, he is likely to exhibit classical no-nothingism, responding to each query, "I don't know," "I don't know," then pressing his own missionizing agenda. Few converts retain this especially zealous state of renunciation beyond a period of several months, however, and after a few years the convert may begin to emphasize the ethical aspects of his faith over the mystical ones. It is at this later stage that evangelicals seem more likely to make common cause with liberation theology.

Carlos Ocón Gonzáles' particularly cogent discussion of the concept "the New Man" is indicative of the important if indirect relationship between evangelical morality and revolutionary participation.

Well, we should be clear that the New Man of the revolution and the New Man of salvation are two different things: one is political, the other is spiritual. It would be wrong to confuse them. However, the political New Man, what does he do? He works hard, he studies, and he tries to develop new ways of living with other people, free of theft, corruption, and vice, and based on justice, equality, sharing. . . . This is good, it is very good. We are, in this family, spiritually New Men and Women, saved by grace. But we like the political New Man, too.

And we need a political New Man, because there has been a change in the ways of doing things. The old system was very corrupt, and the rich used it to exploit the poor people. The humble people can now achieve some dignity in this life, and that is new. Before, for instance, only people with money could buy food, and we would often go hungry. Now, everyone gets a card, and the government keeps basic food prices low, so the poor people can eat. This is just. It is right. This is a better way of doing things, and I would even say that it is a more Christian way of doing things than through the rule of money and force.

Despite the fact that evangelical Protestantism does not conceive itself as a revolutionary religion in the political sense, its personal revolution of the soul generates real political consequences, and in the milieu of Nicaraguan society, these act to effectively bolster the revolutionary process. It is a religion of the poor, and it provides the doctrinal material by means of which the poor organize themselves in the face of exploitation and margination.

The Sandinista government has not interfered with the explosive growth of the evangelical sects, which it would almost certainly do if it felt the sects to be a threat to either the revolutionary process or Sandinista authority in that process. Moreover, the government is making increasingly visible attempts to include the evangelicals in various consultation processes; for instance, in 1986 evangelicals participated in several open hearings on the subject of the new Nicaraguan constitution. The traditional interest blocs of the revolutionary process were all consulted in these months of televised hearings, nationally and regionally: women, youth, labor, the CDS, the Christian base communities. The symbolic importance of the evangelicals' inclusion should not be understated. In effect, their inclusion in these consultations signal the recognition of evangelicals as a legitimate—read non-counterrevolutionary—interest group or bloc in the revolutionary process and in the emerging conception of "popular democracy."

On occasion, members of the government have gone beyond tolerance and coexistence and have even spoken quite warmly of the evangelical presence in Nicaragua. Tomás Borge, Comandante of the Revolution and Minister of the Interior, has included Protestant evangelicals in his conception of the Popular Church or church of the poor in Nicaragua. Indeed, he pointedly alludes to a Protestant example as something of a model in constructing a new church of revolutionary believers (n.d.:21).

While the evangelical sects clearly proved less significant during the revolution proper than did the radicalized Catholic Church, it has become increasingly significant in the postrevolutionary society. Of course the exigencies of postrevolutionary consolidation and reconstruction—work and discipline—are substantially different from those of revolutionary insurrection. And it is on precisely those grounds that the evangelical sects figure so prominently in the new religious crystallization.

What is the future of Protestantism in Nicaragua? That would be difficult to say. I suspect that the evangelicals are approaching, although they have clearly not yet reached, their theoretical growth limits. As an antagonistic faith, Protestantism in Nicaragua would seem to require a strong Catholic presence, if for no other reason than to rail against it and despair about the evil state of the world. At any rate, it seems unlikely that the evangelicals will convert all of Nicaragua's economically marginated population, and their prospects in more socially integrated segments would seem dim at best. A substantial upturn in that country's economic fortunes could actually reverse Protestantism's advance, although we are unlikely to see wholesale de-conversion. Of course, under the right conditions, the theoretical limits of Protestantism's growth could be revised upward—and recent Nicaraguan history is marked by radical transformations and upheavals. The nature and outcome of Nicaragua's ongoing spiritual revolution is clearly tied to the nature and outcome of its ongoing social revolution.

It seems obvious that, working within the broad framework of confessional freedom, the Sandinistas will continue to discourage Nicaraguan evangelical churches and ministers from receiving foreign sources of funding. Moreover, it can safely be predicted that the Nicaraguan government will act, brusquely on occasion, to sever their evangelicals' ties to right-wing religious networks in the United

States. Sects and congregations that resist these developments will naturally be subject to greater scrutiny and suspicion than those that do not. Finally, as is the norm of anti-imperialist governments, it seems improbable that Nicaragua will permit foreign missionary activity on a large scale (if at all) in the future. In short, the FSLN will guarantee religious freedom for the evangelicals, but will undoubtedly discourage coordinated clerical movements, international activities and organizational centralizations whose inclinations are perceived to lie *on the right*. Conversely, it will encourage those developments within the national evangelical movement whose orientation and consequences are perceived to lie *on the left*.

The ordinary evangelical citizens are quite impervious to these restrictions on their clergy and on foreign missionaries. During the 1985 state of emergency, several conservative evangelical clergymen were arrested and their national organization effectively abolished. I raised this topic with a number of Sergio Altamirano's Pentecostals. Most of them had not heard of these events, neither through their neighbors nor their churches. Some expressed skepticism about the wisdom of the government's actions, and a few expressed anger over the move. Others believed that the harassed clergymen must have been up to no good. Meanwhile, churches continued congregating, Bible study groups continued meeting, and proselytizers continued their usual rounds. Measured in terms of Mexico's laws, which prohibit religious proselytizing and propaganda, these measures seem minor indeed.

Given the spiritual and moral career typical of older converts, one may also speculate about a long-range cycle within the Protestant sects generally. The charismatic, mystical, and other-worldly phase may well give way to an increasingly ethical and even civic orientation. The gradual incorporation of the evangelicals into a formalized relationship with the revolutionary process, already well underway, would no doubt be accelerated by the development of a stronger ethical current in evangelical practice—especially if that ethical trend sought out those junctures between evangelical practice and liberation theology.

But even barring that sort of development, the process of coexistence and coevolution between the evangelicals and the revolution should continue. The possible relations between evangelical practice and revolutionary politics can be both subtle and multiplex. And here it is good to remember the example of Southern populism in the 1890s. On the social terrain of a region heavily dominated by pietistic and evangelical sects, substantially similar in theology to those found in Nicaragua, there developed and flourished a radical politics of class consciousness and class struggle. Unimpeded by such a religious base, Southern populism was actually spurred by the evangelical sensibility, its rhetorical forms often leaping quite spontaneously out of revivalist traditions. It would be inaccurate, then, to say that this remarkable history was accomplished "in spite of" the South's religious leanings. Neither was it effected through a grand theological revolution on a par with the Protestant Reformation or the emergence of liberation theology in Latin America. It was, quite simply, altogether possible for people to be religiously evangelical and politically radical at the same time. In this case, it was unnecessary to either reconcile or refute the one with the other: the two facts simply *were*, and they were welded together through the link of the cultural conservatism of the popular classes.

The affinity of evangelical Protestantism for political conservatism has been overstated. Like the example of the farmer-labor populism in the United States, the example of the urban poor in Nicaragua reminds us of this.

II

RELIGION
AND
POSTREVOLUTIONARY
RECONSTRUCTION

For, behold, I create new heavens and a new earth: and the former shall not be remembered, nor come to mind. . . .

And they shall build houses, and inhabit them; and they shall plant vineyards, and eat the fruit of them.

They shall not build, and another inhabit; they shall not plant, and another eat: for as the days of a tree are the days of my people, and mine elect shall long enjoy the work of their hands.

They shall not labor in vain.

—Isaiah 65:17, 21–23

And all that believed were together, and had all things common;
And sold their possessions and goods, and parted them to all
men, as every man had need.

—*Acts 2:44–45*

And the multitude of them that believed were of one heart and
of one soul: neither said any of them that ought of the things which
he possessed was his own; but they had all things in common.
And with great power gave the apostles witness of the resurrec-
tion of the Lord Jesus: and great grace was upon them all.
Neither was there any among them that lacked: for as many as
were possessors of lands or houses sold them, and brought the prices
of the things that were sold,
And laid them down at the apostles' feet: and distribution was
made unto every man according as he had need.

—*Acts 4:32–35*

In place of the old bourgeois society, with its classes and class antagonisms, we shall have an association, in which the free development of each is the condition for the free development of all.
—Marx and Engels, *The Communist Manifesto*

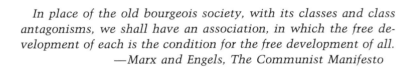

. . . Only then can the narrow horizon of bourgeois right be crossed in its entirety and society inscribe on its banners: From each according to his ability, to each according to his needs!
—Marx, *Critique of the Gotha Program*

CHAPTER FIVE

Priests, Saints, Martyrs, and Guerrilleros: Observations on the Structure of Authority in Sandinista Nicaragua

Those who give of their all, including their lives, have the right to demand sacrifices.

—*Carlos Fonseca*

ON THE NATURE OF POLITICAL OBSERVATION

George Orwell reports his strong impressions of socialist Catalonia during the Spanish Civil War: tophats had vanished, tipping was abolished, subservient and formal forms of address had disappeared, and churches had either been burned or commandeered by revolutionaries. For Orwell, Catalonia was the socialist and revolutionary spirit incarnate, tangible and unambiguously clear.

My first impressions of Nicaraguan society, in December 1984 and January 1985, were likewise bathed in the brilliant glow of socialism, equality, and fraternity. The almost boundless energy with which ordinary people threw themselves into their national project appeared to me remarkable. Self-interest and social solidarity had seemingly cojoined. Men, women, and children all stood vigil in their neighborhoods at night, and CDS activism remained high in the majority of Managua's working-class communities. A continuous human stream of volunteers, mostly high-school and college students, flowed through the gates of UCA (the University of Central America) and out again by bus for points north and east, where they would join the voluntary coffee harvesting brigades. And unlike the Spanish militants, who burned churches, the Nicaraguan poor were erecting a new image of Christ the Worker, whose mass was both revolutionary and devotional. What a contrast Nicaragua seemed to capitalist America! In socialist labor and community self-organization, the new man and woman—and the new society—were being born.

All this is a "true" picture—a powerful image—of revolutionary Nicaragua, but like all categorical and unqualified depictions, it is an incomplete one. The human condition is never so free from contradiction, conflict, and dissatisfaction, except in those utopian or messianic images deployed by the poor in moments of pitched battle with great adversaries. Which is not to say that messianism is therefore a "lie"—quite the contrary: it is a collective myth, expressing a social truth of a nonempirical nature. It can no more be a "lie" than can the concept of God, the sacred, or the collectivity itself.

From our own end of the world, we perhaps do more harm than good by viewing Third World revolutions as distant Rorschachs of our own idealism, desires, and dissatisfactions. It should indeed surprise us if our aims happened to correspond with *theirs;* and when such correspondences are asserted, we should always be willing to make inquiries concerning the production of illusion through the projection of ethnocentric assumptions.

In Western radical and intellectual circles, a distinct moral cycle has revolved around every Third World revolution: unrealistic, romantic, and Rousseauian images dominate the first stages of that cycle; antagonism, despair, and feelings of betrayal dominate the later ones. Fated not only to act as political Rorschachs for cosmopolitan intellectuals, then, Third World revolutions are also predestined to act out a classical tragic drama—or is it by now a comedy?—for Western observers: the promise of hope and liberation, inevitably and invariably followed by the reality of betrayal and new oppression. This script is fixed, for it is already written out in the first moments of the adoring gaze of cosmopolitan observers.

Hopeless before the structure of a political discourse that they themselves have generated, distinct generations of intellectuals have lived this tragicomic cycle with regard to China, Vietnam, Cuba, and now Nicaragua. Apparently incompatible with each other, the two ends of this cycle are in reality only graded moments in the continuous motion of a morality play, for within the Rousseauian imagery of the "pure" revolution, seen at a distance, is actually already immersed a *series of demands,* conditions for sympathy, so extraneous to indigenous politics and so rigorous that no society, least of all a revolutionary one, could possibly meet them.

What I have called these "Rorschach" images, seen from a distance, should not be confused with the messianic image proper. Both are indeed idealized impressions. But the one is an *indigenous* image, undefeatable and indefatigable by mere twists and turns of history because, as *myth*, it rests outside and above history. As dream, it distills the dreams of a people about their *own* history, about themselves. When this messianic vision encounters material difficulties, as it always does—whether those difficulties be in the matter of industry, economy, social organization, or in the matter of physical material itself—like religion proper it does not falter, but rather serves to motivate harder work, greater effort, more systematic application. The other image is a fleeting figment of the cosmopolitan intellect in repose. It embodies what Marx really meant by "idealism." It is not poised to action, and the slightest difficulties can leave it dispirited and despairing. One of many possible exercises in ethnocentrism, it is an alienated and ultimately alienating excrescence of colonialism, resting in well-intentioned but fickle elites.

We must always keep this in mind when surveying postrevolutionary societies, lest we lapse into comfortable babble about "revolutions betrayed" and dreams subverted.

"Authority" signifies legitimate power (Weber 1978:212–216; Bendix 1962:286–297); the concept draws our attention to the process of legitimation and delegitimation. This chapter is an inquiry into the concepts of formal and informal authority in Nicaraguan society. It traces the various and crisscrossing connections—indeed, the indistinguishability and synchronicity—of religion and politics, tradition and revolution. This interplay is most strikingly impressive precisely on the terrain of authority: How does a revolutionary regime legitimate itself? disseminate its ideals throughout the whole of society? adjust its own aims in the light of social facts? How does it go about establishing the new corporate community? Here, a variety of images, some "messianic," some "traditional," and some newly rationalized, converge. Previous chapters have already treated such questions in the specific areas of traditional popular religion, liberation theology, and evangelical Protestantism. This chapter considers the question of authority in a more generalized cultural context, and with a conception of social practice enlarged beyond religion and official ideology.

A substantial body of opinion and analysis exists on the delegitimation of old regimes: how authority breaks down in a revolutionary situation. We have less information on how new regimes legitimate and consolidate themselves. In many cases, these mechanisms are deliberately obscured by ideological constructs, especially the "totalitarian models" of revolutionary government that have long since passed from academic circles into the popular culture. Laboring under the rule of this paradigm, rightist, centrist (and even some liberal) political science can name a thousand subtle ways nonrevolutionary regimes reproduce themselves, but opinion is monotonously repetitive in assessing postrevolutionary regimes. It would seem that, once the romance is over, postrevolutionary regimes know one method only: force, either veiled or overt. This double set of intellectual books leads to a dubious form of intellectual praxis, as anyone can see by scanning a sample of major cosmopolitan newspapers or listening to a congressional speech in the United States: every whisper, every murmur of discontent uttered in Nicaragua is portrayed as a harbinger of counterrevolutionary insurrection. (For a particularly egregious example, see Leiken 1984.)

It quickly became apparent to me that, while murmurings and discontent are indeed widespread in Managua's working-class barrios, the revolutionary government continues to successfully consolidate its power and authority. Totalitarian models cannot convincingly explain *either* fact. What this chapter treats, then, is the political culture of Nicaraguan society and the process of legitimation in the new regime. Consequently, it also posits an alternative theory of postrevolutionary legitimation.

To do this, to rightly understand the process of consolidation and reconstruction, it is necessary to draw out some of the lines of fissure in the new political economy, and the *various* interplays of consciousness, representation and belief in the revolutionary process. This has been the most difficult chapter to write, and reflects an analytic maturity well beyond initial impressions. This sort of analysis is particularly difficult, for it calls for "bracketing off" any number of one's own political beliefs or desires, or at any rate, measuring them more carefully against the empirical evidence.

Seen from a prejudicial point of view, some of this material could be imagined an exposé—if one assumes Rousseauian or romantic standards, or if one proceeds with the purpose of "discrediting" a social-political type. If my preceding discussion is correct, though, the social scientist is not only justified but *required* to "maintain an adequate enough definition of reality" (Mills, 1959) that he falls into neither glowing adulation nor self-righteous condemnation. This definition maintained, the Nicaraguan poor may appear—at last—as actors in their own drama, rather than stock figures in a puppet show of someone else's devising.

The careful study of culture and revolution is a particularly perplexing and frustrating undertaking, and this chapter stems from my attempts at describing if not resolving these ambiguities. At times, in studying the juncture of revolution and culture in Nicaragua, it seemed to me that I was looking at nothing in particular at all: that the revolution was in fact all window dressing and public displays, nothing more than the new slogans annually splashed upon the walls of Managua in preparation for the anniversary of the Sandinista Triumph. Barrio life seemed to go on, much as it normally would in pre- or nonrevolutionary times: the routines of school and work, of eating and sleeping . . . Far from achieving a wholeness of society and culture, the revolution, in politicizing everything, seemed to spring loose a thousand *new* conflicts, many of them implicit in the shape of the emerging regime. "The same old shit," as an informant might say in a skeptical mood. What does the revolution really *mean?* What is "popular power"?

At other times, the theater of revolution expands, the monotonous routine is arrested, transformed, or imbued with greater significance, and the entirety of real life itself becomes the drama: when an entire street sits up all night, out on the sidewalk, observing the wake of a neighbor killed by the contra in a mountainous department; we drink coffee and rum, while revolutionary discourses freely comingle with simple conversations and mundane gossip, and the children play kick ball off to one side . . . Or, at a meeting of the CDS, where participants are attempting to revitalize that deflated organization; held in the open air under coconut trees and the tropical moon, this meeting is free of polemical grandstanding, and begins sketching out solutions to the real problems of the barrio: mosquitos, dengue, high food costs, a resurgent crime problem . . . Or an old woman defines the revolution, her revolutionary faith, in a widely used metaphor that is both unthinkably sad and resolutely optimistic:

Perhaps we will not succeed, and perhaps the Yankees will invade us again, like before, to impose their will on us again for another forty years. Only God can say. But we are only part of the Latin American revolution, which will go on. And we are all like ants crossing a stream, we people of Sandino: many of us may die before the others of us make it over to the other side, crossing over on the bodies of their fallen *compañeros*.

PUBLIC AUTHORITY:
SACRIFICE, CHARISMA,
AND THE MILLENARIAN VISION

Revolutions write and act out their own mythologies, which provide the new moral exemplars of postrevolutionary society. In Cuba, the so-called "Cult of Che" has filled this role. Through his example of self-sacrifice, in anticipation of the socialist new man and new society, the image of Che tinges even the most trivial political undertakings with an air of devotion and religiosity. This is not unlike the manner in which the Puritans transformed the world, imbuing their work and industry with the meaning of a devotional, even sacred calling. If the example of Che Guevara has proved useful in synthesizing a new moral/political order in Cuba, in Nicaragua the same iconography has proved even more pivotal. Drawing its powers from the preexisting hagiology of folk Christianity, the charisma of the guerrilla looms large in Nicaragua. This charisma may appear as any guerrilla; it may appear in the form of Sandino or Che; it may even appear as *Cristo Guerrillero*—and here the nature of the image, its peculiar syncretism of politics and religion, is most evident. In the same manner and with the same attitude that Christ hangs on the cross, suffering for and expiating the sins of mankind, the guerrilla endures his tribulation in the mountains—and to much the same end: each offers hope, liberation, and redemption.

Omar Cabezas has transcribed that mythology of the guerrilla: with the slogan "Be Like Che" the guerrilla ascends to his "Calvary" (1985:12, 53). Even as Christ was beaten on the path to Golgotha by Roman soldiers, the guerrilla endures the blows of his initial march up the hills (65). His sufferings, sexual deprivations, loneliness, hunger, and exhaustion: these gradually strip away the man's bourgeois impulses, his cosmopolitan vices and civilized artificialities (78–87). Like his surroundings, he becomes "more natural"—but neither less social, nor less intelligent (83–84). By undergoing his ordeal of struggle, the guerrilla is purified of sin; he is *sanctified*. "And little by little our faults faded out" (86); thus was born the new man.

Cabezas himself underwent a debilitating case of "mountain leprosy," and wears the stigmata of this mortification of the flesh, even as medieval lepers ambiguously exemplified Christian suffering to the whole community. Most of the figures in his account die as martyrs, and of the four brothers in his family who "go to the mountain," only the author himself comes back alive (73).

Even the profane language of Cabezas' narrative, in the mouth of a clandestine activist or guerrilla, takes on a sacred glow; its mission recalls that of the early dadaists: to assault the arbitrary and unjust rules of social and political discourse. The violence, committed against language and persons, is a *purifying* and even "tender" violence. Obscenity sometimes lies very close to the sacred, and Cabezas' profanity is on sound religious grounds: in elevating the profane over the sacred, he symbolically substitutes the popular for the elite (see Bakhtin 1984:145–195). Through the breaking of rules, higher orders of rules may be revealed. In a similar manner, Gnostic and Manichaean Christianities practiced sexual excesses in order to purify and ultimately free themselves of the lure of the sensual. But if violation of language implies excess, even sensuality, the austere example of the guerrilla's *form of life* is much the opposite. Like the priest, the saint, and the martyr, the guerrilla's life is one of deprivation and sacrifice. His passion is distinctly *spiritual*, not physical.

Revolutionary praxis, like Christianity, is also story, narrative (Roth 1985). Events follow in either a regular succession or form a repetitive cycle. God or the proletariat either intervenes or fails to intervene in history. As social action develops and events unfold, these become part of the collected repertory of acts and events; persons and events cease being distinct and come to represent transcendent principles. Once told, these tales are nothing; recited a thousand times, they become folklore, myth, collective representation; sung as ballads and told as tall tales—for how many centavos *did* Sandino sell the heads of Yankee Marines?—they ultimately pass into mnemonic devices of class consciousness, the guideposts and blueprints of future praxis.

In the case of the Sandinista revolution and radical Christianity, the story lines run parallel, more than occasionally converging, and their implicit convergences resonate strongly in the popular classes (see table 5.1). Indeed, if we see a continuous Judeo-Christian religion of *sanctification through sacrifice*, the new constellation appears as a reconstellation of the ancient messianism. Like the spiritual example of Christ the Redeemer and the moral authority of the priest, the social authority of the FSLN rests on its exemplary action through self-sacrifice. This authority of the FSLN may still be described as "charismatic," in Weber's sense of the term; it has

TABLE 5.1 Sacrifice and Charisma, Parallelisms

Narrative	The Story of Christ	The Authority of the Priest	The Charisma of the Guerrilla
Subject	Christ descends from heaven to earth.	Priest separates himself from ordinary humanity.	Guerrilla ascends from the city to the mountains.
Message	Christ brings the good news of salvation.	Priest perpetuates the message of Christ.	Guerrilla spreads the good news of revolution.
Exemplar	Christ eschews material comforts, victorious over the flesh.	Priest eschews material/sexual gratification, victorious over the flesh.	Guerrilla eschews material comforts and bad faith, endures pain and hardship, victorious over the flesh and capitalism.
Sacrifice	Christ is crucified, others carry on his message.	Through life and/or death, priest embodies the example of Christ; the Church as body of believers survives him to perpetuate the message.	Guerrilla dies in combat, others carry on the struggle.
Result	1. Christ is resurrected, insuring Christendom's victory, the "new man," and life after death.	1. Priest may live on, as martyr or saint, insuring the perpetuation of the gospel through his exemplary life/ death.	1. Guerrilla is symbolically resurrected in the revolution, insuring the victory of the poor, the socialist new man, and transcendence over the present conditions.
	2. Man ascends to heaven.	2. Saint intermediates between heaven and man.	2. Heaven descends to man.

not yet been quite routinized. In this sense we may speak of the new regime as *consolidating* rather than fully "consolidated."

Recalling Hubert and Mauss' definition, "Sacrifice is a religious act which, through the consecration of a victim, modifies the condition of the moral person who accomplishes it or that of certain objects with which he is concerned" (1964:13). Through the destruction of living physical matter, the sacrificial victim is "separated definitively from the profane world" (1964:35), and the *sacrificier*, on whose behalf the sacrifice is made, is likewise purified. For some purposes, the sacrifice, *sacrificier*, and the sacrificer may all be the same person; for others, they may be distinct persons. And, as Hubert and Mauss observed, the process may proceed in either direction, but there must be an ascent, an apex, and a descent. Thus, the divinity of Christ is actually profaned when he takes corporal form, and even more so when he is subjected to death, but the sanctity of his image is thereby insured at Golgotha; his saving powers stem from his sacred profanation. In reverse direction, the once-profane man is purified, and thereby separated from the world of the profane, through self-abnegation and sacrifice in the mountains. And even the image of the mountain no doubt resonates here with the site of Christ's crucifixion: an ambiguous place, in either case, halfway between heaven and earth; a no man's land; a bridge between the sacred and the profane, where a sacrifice may be appropriately offered. It is in just such a religious sense that Nicaraguans speak of "going to the mountains."

Beatific and violent, the sacrificial ritual of both Christ and the guerrilla acts first upon the victims themselves, sanctifying them. The one is a precedent for the other. Christ the divine may have been perfect, but he could not be truly *sacred* until he had put off the old human form to be transfigured into his divine form—the model procedure for both the Christian and socialist new man. The guerrilla's actions, likewise, at first only sanctify *himself.* In both cases, the *sacrifice* and the *sacrificier* are originally one and the same. It is only then that the sacrificial example acts, long-distance upon ordinary humanity, to save and redeem them as well. In the second sense, the sacrifice is offered on behalf of a much wider community of *sacrificiers.* Indeed, sacrifice is a meaningless act, a notion sealed in upon itself, unless the sacrifice and the *sacrificier* come to be distinct. The halo bestowed by the act of sacrifice on the sacrosanct, then, ultimately illuminates the entire community of believers who, in a less extreme manner, duplicate that practice, and illuminate the whole world. The new man is first born in the sacrifice of Christ, or the martyrdom of the guerrilla, and then in the collective body of believers, or in the community of the poor.

If sacrifice implies redemption, and each is implicit in the millenarian impulse, then we must ask, "What is redemption?" It would not be enough to posit redemption, monosemically, as simple liberation from economic oppression, although that may indeed be seen as its central metaphor. But no messianic movement, religious or secular, has ever envisioned redemption in purely economic terms, by the calculus of surplus value. "Redemption" is largely the state that accrues *after* and as a result of the elimination of exploitation. The promised redemption is thus always an idealized state, and the ecstatic antics of the charismatic cults offer a mere foretaste of the promised joy of final redemption. It is not enough that we will experience a sort of "negative freedom"—the removal of restraint—but that *our whole being is redeemed,* and that the nature of social life is totally, unimaginably transformed: thence, the new man of the Bible, and the new man of socialism; the kingdom of heaven, which is not of this world, and the new society, which bears no resemblance to the old one. All of creation strives for such joy.

Burridge, following Weber, sees redemption appropriately in the context of *debt;* and redemption is indeed the cancellation of economic, social or spiritual debt. But Burridge's resulting conclusion is that redemption therefore signifies a state of "unobligedness" (1969:6)—a conception that would surely be labeled antisocial and anti-Christian in Nicaragua. Certainly, the concept of a cancellation of debt is appropriate here: from slavery, from peonage, even from the usurious loans of the IMF that reduce entire nations to debt peonage. But redemption, in wiping out an old debt, does not destroy obligation, but rather, *restructures* it. In place of a free state of unobligedness, the economics of millenarianism universally promise a state of *perfect obligation,* that is, of balanced reciprocity, instead of the negative reciprocity of exploitation. True reciprocity, in restructuring social obligation, thus perpetuates reciprocity and multiplies one's equal interdependences. The conception of freedom here—and this is the conception of freedom in either the Kingdom of God or in socialism—is neither a wholly negative one (freedom from restraint), typified by the absence of oppression and exploitation, nor is it the conception of a social vacuum, in which obligation is removed or diminished; it imagines instead a dense social space, characterized by an aggressive equality, which actively perpetuates interdependence and reciprocity.

It is the nature of the millenarian vision that this ultimate redemption always lies in the future. For no matter how many advances are achieved in leveling the old invidious distinctions of social stratification, new inequalities and conflicts perpetually reassert themselves. And no matter how many laudable achievements a revolutionary government makes in the fields of health care, literacy, agrarian reform, etc., the new society produces its own fissures and imbalances—less destructive ones, it is hoped, than those of the old society, or no transcendence at all has been affected.

If no earthly project can ever live up to the millennial dream of perfect wholeness—then what? Does the dream die? Rarely, even given the cruelest buffetings. Belief in the ideal is not an empirical sort of thing. The Jehovah's Witnesses have in the past set two different dates for the end of the present world and the beginning of the Kingdom of God; the world ended on neither of them, but the cult continues to exist and grow. The believers, like Jehovah's Witnesses, may well conclude that the signs were misread; that the time was not yet right. Politically, one may conclude that the formula for successful actuation of the ideal has not been followed closely enough, and then dedicate oneself even more fervently to the politico-religious task at hand. Or, the religion may opt for a more "pragmatic" approach, keeping the messianic impulse in check by reserving its display for special occasions, meanwhile emphasizing the more ethical and civic aspects of belief. All of these paths have been followed, many of them simultaneously, in a variety of millenarian contexts, both Christian and Marxist.

What ultimately cements this messianic vision together and gives it credibility—whatever its real achievements may be—is the example of the perfect, i.e., altruistic sacrifice. Sacrifice is thus the bridge to redemption in two ways: first, the martyr establishes his quasi-magical authority—his charisma—from the power of his practice, because his example, in a sense, redeems us all. It is an article of faith that Christ's death redeems mankind; likewise, the sacrifices of the guerrillas did in fact lead to the overthrow of Somoza. But moreover, the altruism implicit in his act—the destruction of the individual, the mortification of the flesh—is exemplary of the social values necessary if we are to achieve a conflict-free perfect state of man and society where individual and collective will merge. And how can the promise of this state of affairs *not* be true, when we have so many examples of mortals who have achieved this ideal state—Islamic martyrs, Christian martyrs, martyrs for socialism— *in advance* of the new society?

Sacrifice, then, is more than a mere event; it is more even than self-abnegation; it is a story, a narrative, an allegory of much wider significance, for it tells in a single image the entirety of the millennial vision. No doubt the appropriation of this allegory of self-sacrifice and self-abnegation would have horrified Marx, who took great pains to establish the unproblematic unity of individual and community wills in communist theory (1977:183, 189–191), and who eschewed those varieties of Christian socialism that draped themselves in hairshirt (238–239, 243–245). But in practice, while revolutionary situations and radical movements have clearly sought out the *pleasures* of socialism—a guaranteed minimum standard of living, full employment, subsidized necessities—it would run counter to a century of history to ignore the strong *antiliberalism* inherent in such moments of class struggle. Popular classes have also been at least as attracted to socialism's *denials* and *restraints*, especially as these apply to regulation of the individual, the maintenance or establishment of community norms, and the depiction of these through spectacular displays of sacrifice and martyrdom. What more effective strategy, then, than to seek out precisely those *religious* aspects of socialism that Marx sought to evade, even suppress?

Out of such charisma is Sandinista authority constructed, and it is on the basis of their example of self-sacrifice that the Sandinistas ultimately rest their claim to being the "vanguard organization" of the Nicaraguan people. The price has been high, and the example set extreme. Of the original three founders of the FSLN in 1961, only one survived the struggle against Somoza: Tomás Borge, who was himself tortured and imprisoned, and whose wife was murdered by the Guardia Nacional. Like Christ's disciples, the early Sandinistas gave their lives in martyrdom—by the hundreds. The name "Sandinista" itself, and the organization's political-military formula, its conception of national liberation and class struggle, are largely derived from two martyrs, Sandino and Che, as interpreted by a third martyr, Carlos Fonseca. Nicaraguan history recounts itself as a succession of martyrdoms, and depicts itself as a series of martyrs. Those martyrs become the icons of class consciousness, emblems of religious hope.

The story of A. C. Sandino is most telling. The prototype guerrilla/martyr, Sandino demonstrated the efficacy of the guerrilla method in national liberation struggles. His example was noted as far away as China, and ultimately his techniques passed into a global repertoire of resistance methods. As the head of a band that never numbered more than a few thousand men, he engaged the U.S. Marines from 1927 to 1932 with varying degrees of success in the mountainous provinces of Nicaragua. Unable to defeat Sandino's band of peasants and workers, the Marines finally withdrew in 1933. Sandino then agreed to peace talks with Sacasa's government, and laid down his arms. Soon thereafter, and immediately following a dinner with figurehead-president Sacasa, Sandino and several of his generals were treacherously assassinated by Somoza's National Guard. It is not surprising that the Sandinista national program has always provided for "the veneration of the heroes and martyrs."

The position of the FSLN in Nicaraguan society, its role as "vanguard of the people," its practical examples: all these replicate, both consciously and unconsciously, the images of Christ the Liberator, of Christian martyrs, and in less depth, of priestly devotion. The issue here is distinct from, though also clearly related to, the question of authority in liberation theology. Sandinista praxis is a form of Christian praxis, not in the sense of being a subset of theology, but in the sense that it embodies a religious notion of the sacred and the profane, appropriated, perhaps consciously, perhaps unconsciously, from popular Christian culture. Clearly and emphatically secular, Sandinismo in no sense bases itself in theology, on the existence of God, or on divine inspiration. Yet its whole narrative is an allegory of Christian redemption. In a secular manner with these powerful religious resonances, Sandinista authority derives from the same fount as priestly or saintly authority. The popular attitude toward the Sandinista high command, and especially toward the revolutionary heroes and martyrs, often approaches reverential awe, for here the rules of political authority so closely resemble the rules of religious authority that the two very nearly merge.

THE STRUCTURE OF POLITICAL AUTHORITY: PUBLIC NARRATIVE, PRIVATE RUMOR

The narrative myth of *Sandinismo* so closely corresponds to both textual (biblical) and popular Christianity, that in Managua's non-propertied classes, only a tiny element actually opposes *Sandinismo* proper. This meshing of political and religious symbolism baptizes political undertakings with a religious charisma that few have any desire to confront directly. It may accurately be said that the Sandinista revolution is rapidly consolidating to the extent that (1) a substantial majority of the populace recognizes and validates the FSLN claim to leadership (its "vanguard" status), and (2) an even more substantial majority shares *Sandinismo*'s essential goals and symbolism. Those who reject both the validity of Sandinista leadership as well as the goals and iconography of the revolution are almost by definition marginated from normative political discourse, and this applies to activists both to the right and left of the FSLN.

As one could infer from the symbolism of sacrifice and millenarianism, the emerging culture of Sandinista Nicaragua is potentially quite "authoritarian" in the sense of an effective one-party monopoly on political power (whatever the actual electoral set-up, which is formally pluralistic), strongly legitimated by a quasi-religious symbolism and a shared meaning of authority. But before attaching too much significance to the label "authoritarian" or even "one-party," it is useful to remember that "authority," the root word of "authoritarian," is always a two-way street: since it is, at bottom, the *recognition* of authority, a populace in effect bestows it, and may thereby tinker with, modify, challenge, or even remake it. Strong authority, even "authoritarianism," is not at all incompatible with democracy, especially popular democracy. While this form of "authoritarianism" entails an *image* of stability, even impermutability, its *praxis* is in fact anything but static.

Especially for a fledgling regime like Nicaragua's, at war with a counterrevolution organized, trained, and financed by the United States, the question of authority is crucial. The FSLN calls upon the populace to make great sacrifices in the war against counterrevolution; it, in effect, asks that the populace at large duplicate the Sandinista example of self-abnegation and sacrifice. Thus, a country with no history of obligatory military service now has a universal military draft of two years for males between the ages of seventeen and twenty-four. In addition to military service, the people are called upon to endure sometimes acute shortages of basic necessities: meat, sugar, oil, beans, soap, toilet paper, and clothes are all in cyclically short supply, and sometimes altogether absent in the marketplaces. Moreover, Sandinista self-defense policy raises a huge popular militia and dispenses arms to large sections of the populace. The implications of this are obvious. If the Sandinistas failed at any moment to command a certain minimum of authority, then no amount of police or military force could sustain their government, for the very essence of the current arrangement requires popular participation, either directly in the military or militias, or indirectly, in the weathering of acute shortages and steep inflation.

The state of war, despite its dangers for the regime—and in fact, *because* of them—serves ultimately to reinforce *Sandinismo* in the general population. The counterrevolution continuously recapitulates the martyr/assassin dichotomy and images of national honor versus national shame, so powerful in engineering *Sandinismo's* triumph over *Somocismo* in the first place. Moreover, the war against counterrevolution allows the populace to experience the hardship and sacrifice that are seen as crucial to the emergence of the "new man." Acting the part of cosmic villain, the contras provide a reincarnation of the hated Guardia Nacional as the antithesis of the FSLN. And whatever the technical difficulties and legalistic qualifications in North American discourse about the composition and nature of the contras, they are seen by the bulk of the Nicaraguan populace as a literal and direct extension of the old Guardia Nacional. "Contra," "Somocista," "guardia," and various terms for drug peddler, are all used interchangeably, and, indeed, now constitute part of the lexicon of insult in popular neighborhoods. Finally, Sandinista officers take advantage of the recruits' period of military training and discipline to politicize the youth, and group study is a standard procedure in the army.

Repeating a long-established pattern with revolutionary regimes, then, the war against counterrevolution actually serves to consolidate the new regime on a number of fields: fueling the martyr/assassin dichotomy; equating national sovereignty with the leading Party; bringing discipline and organization to broad sections of the populace. Indeed, in the current configuration, the political-military threat of the contras is turned back upon itself, and not only legitimates the Sandinistas in a manner that their economic performance could not, but also marginates the internal opposition parties from the rules of normative discourse.

Forrest D. Colburn's study of agrarian policy and performance in Nicaragua asserts that "legitimacy for a revolution depends on political issues; legitimacy for a postrevolutionary regime depends on economic performance" (1986:22). It is the premise of this chapter that legitimation in Nicaragua rests substantially on bases other than economic performance. While no one would argue that economic performance is an insignificant or specious issue in the legitimation of governments, postrevolutionary or otherwise, a simple economic efficiency model overstates the case. Originally born of an economistic reading of Marx, this *Homo Economicus* theory has lately been taken to heart by even the most conservative circles of opinion, for it allows a single consumerist standard of "economic performance" in which quantitative standards of production and consumption appear as positive goods in their own right, severed from and independent of the qualitative issues of social power and class relations.

Historic evidence could just as easily be mobilized to show that populations tolerate not only lax standards of economic efficiency, but even gruelling levels of economic exploitation, as long as political legitimation and authority rest on noneconomic grounds, and provided that there exist nonrevolutionary means of expressing or reconciling social tensions. It would be a far less politically stable world indeed if political authority rested simply and directly on the base of "economic performance." Sebastian de Grazia, following Mosca, notes that the Polish peasants endured centuries of harsh, high-handed exploitation by their rulers, but became rebellious only when the aristocracy ceased upholding Polish norms to take up the alien language and manner of a French court nobility (1948:74–75).

Two recent revolutions do not readily affirm the "economic performance" model of political instability. In Iran, the Shah's rule corresponded to a rapidly rising standard of living and rising economic expectations. Neither recession nor inflation undermined the Shah's regime; it was secularization and Westernization that provoked a powerful revolutionary response in the people. Curiously, it was Iranian students, the beneficiaries of a generous public education system, that provided a popular base for the most militant anti-regime sentiments. In the case of Nicaragua, we may also note that the people endured dire poverty and grinding exploitation under the Somoza family, largely without revolting, but were moved en masse to revolution when the regime exhibited extraordinary levels of corruption timed to correspond with maximal levels of social dislocation.

Following Weber, Habermas (1975) distinguishes between "traditional" and "rational" legitimation. "Traditional" legitimation is *normative;* its model is religion. "Rational" legitimation is scientific and *empirical;* like the marketplace, its key measure is cost-benefit, efficiency, or performance. The former may be seen as a "conservative" system of authority, since it upholds continuity and replication ("norms") as key values; the latter may be seen as an inherently "radical" system of authority, with no genuinely independent values or variables, and an implicit, constant adjustment of means and ends in the light of ongoing experimentation. In the former case, society is seen as a space containing good and evil, experience is divided between the sacred and the profane, and government ideally acts much like religion, as a moral center, a moral exemplar, even a popular theater of normative rules. In the latter, society is seen as a vast apparatus of production and consumption, experience is likewise divided between work and life, and government is a cerebral, instrumentally oriented region concerned with the efficiency and smooth-functioning of the entire system. Every regime contains a mix of the two. Clearly elements of each may be found in Nicaragua's emerging moral economy, but the mix is trending rather more heavily in the direction of traditional, normative legitimation than what we find in Western capitalist democracies, which clearly lean toward rational legitimation.

Now, this is not to say that economic performance is entirely irrelevant in Nicaragua, nor that the resulting social structure is by any means free of conflict or tension. Quite the contrary: any political system entails pushes and pulls, thrusts and counterthrusts, in its system of authority. This is perhaps especially true for those political economies that make strong appeal to religious or normative means of legitimation. If the major cleavages emergent in any postrevolutionary society are loosely between "revolutionary elites" (Colburn, 1986; Sweezy, 1980) and "masses"—i.e., leaders and followers—then it is most precisely in the field of authority that we should expect to see the new society's conflicts manifested: i.e., in how the masses bestow, withhold, or modify authority. While popular masses in Nicaragua frequently complain about their deteriorating economic situation, it is important to note *how* they do so. Rarely are their complaints framed in terms of "rationalized" standards of measure. Instead, they are apt to be framed by normative ones that ultimately reinforce the moral economy of *Sandinismo* rather than undermine it. We shall see how this is so in the following examples.

"Somos gruñones" ("We are grumblers"), Nicaraguans say of themselves. Rocking in their chairs inside the house, or standing out on the street among their *compadres*, or speaking loudly in the marketplace, so as to be overheard by strangers, or even wagging a finger at an available policeman or soldier, they may indeed be heard grumbling.

There are dark spaces, hidden places, within any revolutionary process. This does not refer to secret police actions, state security measures, surveillance, or the like. These obscure areas are constituted within the populace in the process of revolutionary change and consolidation: rumors and counter-rumors, gossip, whisperings. This is how nonelites mobilize their power *as nonelites*. These discourses are always semi-private, no matter how loud the volume of their clatter, first because they are inconsistent with official (public) narratives, and second, because they draw their power precisely from their semi-covert status. They constitute a "conspiracy" of sorts among the popular classes: shared secret knowledge. Political elites rarely wish to raise these discourses from the private into the public arena, for such talk runs counter to the content of official talk. The popular classes likewise jealously guard the status of these discourses as whispered rumor, for it is only in this form that they can exercise the power of gossip. Once in the public domain, rumor may be denied, deflected, or even disproved with geometric logic, when we all already know that they embody a substantive truth. As whisper or murmur, rumor is infinitely more powerful than muckraking, or investigative journalism, or official criticism and self-criticism, precisely because it is *less knowable,* unanswerable, by elites.

Semi-covert language constitutes the thrust and counterthrust of popular sentiment within the new regime. Authority is essentially a *discursive* structure, and it is in the micro-discourses of rumor, gossip, and complaint that the people deploy their own symbols and countersymbols, tell allegories of heroism or betrayal, and mobilize their collective powers *as nonelites.* Thus it is that the populace organizes its own covert, informal, but nonetheless *real* powers in the new configuration of power. Because the power to give or withhold the normative authority of *Sandinismo* lies, as it were, in the mouths and on the tongues of the popular classes, it is here, in informal conversation, that we may ascertain both legitimation and delegitimation, endorsement and qualfication. The trajectory of a rumor circulating through the neighborhoods is in fact a *current of power* rippling through the populace. Whereas official, public display—macro-discourse—routinely affirms political norms, private discourse may affirm, deny, or qualify them.

The presence of these informal power mobilizations—in short, of "conflict"—is not necessarily a sign of systemic, structural instability in a regime. On the contrary, these vehicles allow the public a voice it may not choose to exercise in public, as macro-discourse. It may allow for complaint and conflict without ever confronting the government or without even negating that government's major claims to either power or authority. As such, then, these "murmurings" may serve to check government policy, to modify FSLN positions, and to gauge discontent or discomfort. In short, they may act as *stabilizing mechanisms* that *contain* the conflicts that might otherwise be expressed in more organized fashion.

We may go a step further. Gossip, rumor, and murmurings appear to be the implicit underside of the affirmative public displays which occur on official occasions (July 19, Carlos Fonseca's birthday, e.g.). Their function nationally, like their function in traditional neighborhoods (see chapter 1) is to *level wealth and power*. These microdiscourses, which *appear* from one angle to *dispute* the claims of the regime, may be seen from another angle: vital to the functioning of the Sandinista moral economy, they censure individuals and officeholders while leaving intact the *rules* of normative authority. That is, while they do not correspond to the language or messages of formal, official public displays, which unambiguously affirm the dominant structure of power, they do in fact constitute the necessary underside of authority, apparently in conflict with, but in reality vital to, the functionings of the authority structure. Thus, the micro-discourses of gossip, rumor and murmurings stand in relation to public display in the revolutionary state in exactly the same manner that they would function on a smaller scale in a traditional neighborhood setting typified by leveling and envy. They knock down and level differences in the interest of a status quo.

In the context of a shared symbolism of authority, how does one go about establishing claims and demands, and how does one check the power of one's leaders? One does so by holding them up to their own standards of morality.

PRIESTS, BLACK SUGAR, AND BUREAUCRATS

The natural parallel here is with the priesthood. People whose Christianity is never in doubt consistently denigrate the clergy, usually individually, sometimes collectively. The occasion of one young priest's visit to the barrio prompted a barrage of criticism from one resident of Erasmus Jiménez.

> That priest is a very *modern* priest. You see him over there now, drinking rum and dancing with his friend? Shortly, they will be going out womanizing (*mujeriando*) together, as they always do on these bacchanals.
>
> Most of the clergy are really not very pious. Oh, some of them

really are dedicated to a life of service, some of them live to help and comfort the poor. But others are just as materialistic as any businessmen.

Impressions like these dominate working-class depictions of the Nicaraguan clergy: "They live with their hand in the offering plate," or "They are in it for the money, so they can buy farmhouses and cars and other luxuries." A frequent vehicle for anticlericalism, this sort of gossip does *not* represent the transition to a more secular consciousness in the lower classes. It actually underscores and strengthens the religion (and perhaps even the *office* of the priest-hood)—as opposed to its *officeholders*. Thus, the populace bestows religious authority on those priests who serve the poor and lead a life of material self-abnegation, and takes a refractory stance toward priests who flout the ideals of abstinence, self-imposed poverty, and service to the poor. Not surprisingly, this has strengthened the po-sition of the radical Popular Church against the anti-Sandinista cler-ical hierarchy. And what this has facilitated is a popular reinterpre-tation of the church and its mission in Latin America. But the idea of "the church," the notion of clerical, exemplary authority, the es-sential symbology of Christianity: none of these are called into question by the sort of murmurings under consideration.

In the same vein, Managuans express concern over the material position of government and Party members with a frequency that would be considered quite unusual in the United States. The image of revolutionary sacrifice and self-abnegation is a difficult one to live up to, but it is an image that the populace jealously guards. This seems natural in a revolutionary milieu: to hold the revolutionary elites accountable, by their own standards of exemplary behavior, is to exercise a powerful check on the emergence of class and status stratification in the new regime. And given the history of how nu-merous bureaucratic elites in Latin America have used their lever-age to amass enormous personal wealth, this preoccupation repre-sents a very sensible collective wisdom.

Rumors of the sort in question frequently break out in connection with food shortages. No motive is too grubby, no scenario too out-landish, to prompt speculation of abuse and fraud. Many of these rumors revolve around sugar. Nicaragua is a sugar-producing coun-try, but various local conditions and international market forces sometimes result in an acute domestic shortage of white sugar. White sugar is a high prestige food favored by the entire population; often, only a grade of brown or black sugar is available for distribution at

the government-subsidized and CDS-rationed rate. The darker the
sugar, the darker the murmurings.

> Would you look at this? Black sugar (azúcar negro) again this week!
> The Sandinistas are hoarding all the white sugar for themselves.
> You can be sure the Sandinistas are eating white sugar today!
> We used to use the black sugar to feed the horses. That just goes
> to show you what the Sandinistas think of us!

Black sugar proves an especially productive subject for gossip and
rumor of this sort, in part because people insist it has dirt in it.
Nicaraguans express a variety of pollution fears primarily in terms
of the oral route, and I have heard this sort of sugar referred to as
azúcar sucio (dirty sugar). It does indeed leave a fine, black precipitant which resembles dirt in the bottom of one's glass of lemonade.

Around shortages of this sort, even in homes relatively close to
Sandinista policy, one is apt to encounter this basic framework of
explanation: the bureaucrats have commandeered the apparatus of
production and are using it to satisfy their own needs rather than
collective needs, and that is why we have shortages. This micro-
discourse, while truly conflictive in the sense of expressing envy and
hostility, is also continuous with the macro-discourse of official display. It only insists on "holding the leadership's feet to the fire,"
and that policy should benefit the people, not the powerful.

Another variant of rumor about black sugar maintains that all the
white sugar has been given away to X (the country varies). The complexities of the international market are thus reduced, in the popular
mind, to one simple transferal: a giveaway—which not too inac-
curately describes the nature of transactions between small, under-
developed countries and large, developed ones, in the capitalist marketplace. "Nicaraguan sugar should be for the Nicaraguans" is the
sentiment here expressed, both implicitly and explicitly. Rumors of
similar content break out, especially among housewives, whenever
the preferred vegetable or cottonseed oil is unavailable and the weekly
oil ration is replaced with pork fat.

Those most integrated into the revolution through political, educational, and health-care activism naturally are the least disposed
to rumor about the Sandinistas. And it is important to remember
that better than a third of Nicaragua has membership in one or more
of the mass organizations. Most of *their* murmurings are directed
against business elites, opposition parties, and the conservative clergy.
The content of these rumors is usually simple enough: a direct monetary interest is asserted as the basis for anti-Sandinista or counter-

revolutionary politics. For instance, "The Pope is on the CIA payroll" and "Obando receives a weekly secret salary for aiding and comforting the contra" are two of the most common rumors of this sort. One hears this sort of gossip repeated in a wide variety of neighborhoods, especially by activists, but also by large numbers of nonactivists.

Not all rumors involve equally large bases of discussants, nor play to equally large audiences, especially in Managua. Rumors to the detriment of anti-Sandinista forces are few, simple, and involve very large numbers of discussants. Rumors in which the Sandinistas come off badly are the opposite: numerous, and often quite complex, they involve comparatively smaller numbers of discussants in any given tale. Some are more disposed to rumor than others. By no means definitive, the profile of the most vigorous traffickers in rumor and gossip would seem to be female, older, less educated, and recently moved to Managua from a smaller town or rural area, especially a mountainous department.

The mysterious doings of government ministries, especially the ministry of health, provide ample grist for the rumor mill. A situation of ambiguity exists here, and this ambiguity toward medicine is an especially powerful generator of rumor. People naturally desire health and health care, but the esoteric knowledge of doctors, their mysterious equipment, and often-confounding language: these all make professional medical care simultaneously a mysterious and ambiguous affair. Despite various attempts to make medical practice "more popular" and to "demystify" it (Donahue 1986), reservations remain. For instance, I once heard that the hospital staff, especially its German doctors, were plotting to kill various categories of sick babies. The source of this rumor became clearer to me when one mother described an experience she had when she took a sick infant to the hospital. The child had a high fever. Short on medication, her German doctor suggested that they administer a cool water bath to lower the child's fever. Horrified, the mother took up her child and immediately left the hospital.

Understanding this incident requires some understanding of Nicaraguan popular beliefs and a pervasive folk theory of humoral pathology. Nicaraguan folk medicine largely revolves around the importance of "hot" and "cold" categories, and stresses the importance of maintaining a balanced temperature in the body. Especially dangerous to the individual are rapid or violent changes of temperature. Sudden exposure to cold water when one is sick, agitated, or fevered could harm or even kill the individual, especially those already vulnerable categories of persons, like infants. In cases like the one just recounted, then, a rather dark variety of rumor sometimes spreads in those families and neighborhoods where folk medical categories are particularly strong and unqualified by rationalized medical notions, and where distrust of foreigners and doctors is especially great.

A native Nicaraguan doctor at one of Managua's hospitals tells me that he has solved the problem: he routinely uses alcohol rather than water baths, despite the greater cost involved. Because of its "sting," alcohol is perceived as "hot," not "cold," and therefore could not shock or traumatize a hot child.

Wherever the activities of technicians, bureaucrats, or government officials appear to be wrapped in mystery—intentional or not— rumors will flow. After the announcement of an anti-rabies campaign by the ministry of health, various households in Erasmus Jiménez connected this campaign to the theft of several dogs over the previous two years: it was concluded that the ministry of health was exterminating household pets across the city.

Sometimes language can be tricky. Upon my routine visit to one family, a distraught mother wept to me, "They've grabbed my little boy! They've taken him into the military! It happened while he was at work, and I didn't even know about it, but he managed to send me word that everything would be all right." I imagined the worst sort of scene. There had been rumors of the military staging surprise visits to forcibly take some seventeen- and eighteen-year-old boys, so as to preclude the possibility of their evading the draft. This son's impending draft had been a source of much conflict and tension in his family, and after the fact of her son's conscription, the mother took to bed with severe headaches, stomachaches and symptoms of acute grief for three days, telling all visitors that her son had been "grabbed."

As it turned out when I visited him several weeks later, he had not been "seized" by the authorities at all. He had merely kept his appointed date for the medical exam and induction. He had not told his mother in advance of the date, "so as not to worry her"—but more likely, so she would not worry him. He had in fact notified his *madrina* (godmother) in advance, and sent a brief message to his mother by way of one of his co-workers.

A very scarce but ominous variety of rumor involves speculations about the state security apparatus. Again, these are quite rare, and it is remarkable to note the lack of fear that ordinary Nicaraguans feel toward their police and military officers. It is not unusual to hear an irate citizen vigorously scolding a police or military officer in very strong terms. In one case, however, a young man who had been a guard for imprisoned members of the Guardia Nacional was found dead in the prison where he worked. His bereaved mother spread the rumor that her son had been killed by his fellow guards, the Sandinistas, rather than by the prisoners, "because he wouldn't torture the prisoners." This powerful charge was not given much credence in the neighborhood, except by the handful of anti-Sandinistas living there. The same rumor is vigorously denied by the mother's other son, who is a career enlisted man in the military. (He characterizes his mother's tale as "ridiculous," insists that the prisoners killed him, and adds, "There is no torture in our prisons.")

Penny Lernoux writes about the difficulty of ascertaining "the truth" in such rumors: "It's like a *Rashomon* story in which it ultimately becomes impossible to establish the truth" (1986:27). I would conclude that there is indeed no "bottom" to such rumors: they are typically truths only of themselves. They do express apprehension and sometimes angst, but to take a purely empirical approach to the nature of such rumors is to misapprehend the nature of those rumors. Rumor constitutes a discourse on power; it is itself an embodiment of power, deployed in and by the popular classes. Its real subject is not this event or that event, but the position of the popular classes—and especially that of the discussants—in the revolutionary process.

The more esoteric or extreme rumors, such as those involving the state security apparatus, are quite rare. The most common rumors, after those with a clearly leftist and unambiguously pro-state content (i.e., clerical conspiracies on the right, business treachery, theft in the marketplace) are simpler, and express relative consumption differences between political elites and masses. The existence of a *Diplo-tienda* (diplomatic store) in Managua provides a particularly magnetic lightning rod for hostile gossip and envy. Formerly operated by the U.S. embassy, the *Diplo-tienda* has since been turned over to the Nicaraguan government. Its continued presence is considered offensive by many. A large emporium of imported luxury items and packaged foods unheard of in Nicaragua, the *Diplo-tienda* sells everything from smoked cheeses, fine chocolates, and caviar to summer sportswear, movie cameras, color televisions, and home video equipment. All sales are conducted in U.S. dollars. Theoretically, the store serves only international diplomats, embassy staffs, and foreign journalists. Actually, it is also frequented by Sandinista officials and local businessman with access to dollars. In practice, anyone who dresses the part stands a good chance of being waved in through the entrance checkpoint.

Some of the members of the FSLN directorate subject themselves to criticism by inhabiting what are considered to be "mansions" by Nicaraguan standards. It is generally agreed that the President of the Republic requires the special protection of a guardable presidential home. Other members of the directorate, however, may be subjected to praise or gossip, depending on the relative scale of their houses. And some in fact inhabit very ordinary houses in very ordinary neighborhoods; their residences are distinguishable only by the presence of a pair of armed guards in front of the house.

These rumors, while expressing conflict and reservation, do not necessarily act to destabilize the political system. They may serve to reorient factions within the system, to apply brakes to unpopular policies, or to diffuse discontent. Their key role is to maintain a vigorous leveling mechanism; in this case, one that operates against political elites vis-à-vis popular classes.

IN DETAIL: THE CASE OF THE CDS

Over the period of my fieldwork in Managua, the CDS in Barrio Erasmus Jiménez underwent a distinct transition in its functioning, a transition mirrored in other working-class barrios nearby and in the system of neighborhood vigilance and communal labor on the whole. I use this as a case study because it illuminates the various actions of macro- and micro-discourse in a system of authority and political praxis typical if not exemplary of the concept "popular democracy."

Formed during the neighborhood insurrections, the CDS (Comités de Defensa Sandinista) represents the largest and most important of the Sandinista mass organizations. It is charged with community vigilance against counterrevolutionary activities and crime. It also organizes and mobilizes communal labor tasks, such as cleaning the streets, playgrounds, and playing-fields, planting communal gardens on vacant lots, or mobilizing dispensable labor into the volunteer coffee-harvesting brigades. Theoretically, it administers the vaccination, health-care and mosquito-control campaigns. It is also in charge of the food-rationing system, whereby the CDS *tiendas populares* (popular stores) sell fixed quantities of basic staple foods to families at government-subsidized prices. During the 1984 elections, the CDS served to mobilize the Sandinista vote, and it routinely works to mobilize large turnouts to public events and large revolutionary displays. In short, the CDS is a crucial link between the vanguard FSLN and the popular masses. Charged with a variety of community responsibilities, it embodies more fully than any other organization the concept of "popular democracy," and the nature of its communications are two-way: from the FSLN down to the populace, but also from the populace back up to the FSLN.

Politically, the CDS is independently organized from barrio to barrio. Its smallest unit is the *andén*, or walk, along which a distinct neighborhood of people live. The *andén* is indeed a significant social unit: united by long-term friendships, marriages, kin ties, and systems of fictive kin, it is natural that each *andén* be responsible for its own oversight and vigilance. It is here, in the mass of *andenes* to which every CDS member ultimately belongs and which is ultimately the most meaningful level of organization, that community norms and political control most strikingly fuse. Some have portrayed this clearly corporatist form of political organization as "totalitarian." But it is evident that the power involved here is anything but "total," and that most of the members of the *andén* never experience the CDS as any more constrictive than is the envious and often gossiping gaze of one's neighbors. Indeed, the CDS has only a limited concern—public security—whereas one's neighbors, apart from their role in the CDS, might have a much more total concern (in the person's marital and familial relations, extramarital affairs, and personal idiosyncracies). That is, the "gaze" of the CDS is only a special case of the gaze of one's neighbors. The checks against political abuse at this level are powerful, for one's neighbors are also apt to be one's kin, *compadres*, etc.

The next highest level of organization is the barrio CDS itself, which is presided over by a *dirigente del barrio* (barrio director) and administered by a *comité del barrio* (barrio committee), whose members are individually responsible for overseeing specific project areas (construction, communal labor, health, etc.). Charged with administering CDS policy on a day-to-day basis, the office of *dirigente* proves the most powerful in the barrio CDS.

The uppermost and maximal levels of organization are the city and national CDS. Generally representing the barrio organizations to the national organization are the *dirigentes* and *comités*. Municipal and national CDS policy is set at this maximal administrative level, in consultation with lower levels. Again, the lower levels exert powerful checks on the upper levels; should the municipal or national organization set a policy that fails to arouse enthusiasm in the *andenes*, nonparticipation and noncompliance are likely, even certain, outcomes.

The FSLN is integrated into the CDS at all levels and clearly exercises a great deal of influence over that organization's policies and activities. The vast majority of CDS activists, however, are not members of the FSLN, and the CDS provides an important bridge between the political leadership and popular masses. Originally, membership in the Frente was a prerequisite for membership in the barrio committee or for the post of barrio director. However, as a result of the reforms detailed below, one need not be a member of the FSLN to be either a CDS activist or officer, and, indeed, now many of the *dirigentes* themselves are not FSLN members.

The major visible function of the CDS, other than its oversight of the food rationing and distributing system, is its coordination of community vigilance. During my December 1984–January 1985 stay in Erasmus Jiménez, community vigilance was still in effect. A stroll through the barrio at any hour of the night was revelatory: posted on every *andén* (walk), a CDS activist kept vigilance, and would shout "hello!" or "God go with you!" at passersby. If strangers, either singly or in groups, responded suspiciously to such greetings, the vigilante was charged with loudly rousing the whole neighborhood, who would then turn out of their beds to investigate the trouble. Persons caught committing crimes would be turned over by the CDS to the Sandinista Police and questioned or arraigned for trial. Obviously, either crime or counterrevolutionary activity would be difficult to execute under such circumstances, and the efficacy of CDS vigilance was reflected in low crime rates and the striking security of popular barrios on their interiors.

In the period of June–December 1985, CDS vigilance all but disappeared not only in Erasmus Jiménez but in most other popular barrios as well. The reasons for this decline in participation are multiplex. Upon first questioning, CDS members complained of fatigue: "I'm too tired at night to do vigilance," or "I need my sleep." More concretely, economic dislocation was beginning to take its toll on the population. The war consumed up to half of all government spending in 1985, and the economic embargo declared by the United States—which had been Nicaragua's major trading partner until that time—was beginning to be felt. Inflation ran in the double, then triple, digits; material expectations were revised downward, and many people began working extra hours and taking on extra jobs. Moreover, the economic effects of the military draft on poor households were multiplied in this period: obligatory military service signified not only the possibility that one's son might die fighting the contra, but the *certainty* that an important source of income for the family would be deactivated for two years during a period of inflation, shortages, and economic duress.

Thus, after working extra hours and, in many cases, attending day or night school as well, people felt they had less time left over for vigilance. With daily material sacrifices being made, CDS members felt overtaxed by the additional once a week sacrifice of vigilance. *Fatigue* proved an appropriate means of summarizing their harassed situations; CDS participation became demobilized in proportion to the real or perceived exertion of energies in the daily routine of work. While this decline in CDS participation did in fact correspond to an increase in crime, the increase was not uniformly, immediately, or dramatically felt in all the neighborhoods, so that the effects of the relaxation of vigilance provided no ready check on this process of demobilization.

In addition to the fatigue motif, it was also at this point that another, more significant complaint appeared in Erasmus Jiménez. Sometimes directed against the entire *comité del barrio*, it was usually directed solely against the acting *dirigente*, an FSLN member who had been in charge of the barrio CDS for several years. Charges of corruption, featherbedding, and exploitation gradually became commonplace in private discussion, and even several members of the *comité del barrio* itself echoed the charges. Similar accusations were duplicated in barrio CDS's throughout the city.

The FSLN leadership responded logically to this widespread rise in dissatisfaction and nonparticipation by encouraging new elections for *dirigente* and *comité del barrio*. Well-publicized special elections in two popular barrios set the precedent: *comités* and *dirigentes* were turned out of office and the leadership structures within the two barrios were renewed. Plans were then put into effect for widespread CDS elections covering most of Managua, in an obvious attempt to discipline or remove current leaderships and renew the flagging organizations on a citywide basis.

Andén meetings were called in Erasmus Jiménez and across the city in November 1985 to select candidates for *dirigente*; voting was scheduled for the second week of December. The vigor of the murmurings involved may be gauged from the following complaints aired at an *andén* meeting of the Erasmus Jiménez CDS.

This organization has fallen because Ortiz (the *dirigente*) is a thief and a criminal. What is the use of participating, if all the people don't share the results of our collective work?

He has stolen hundreds, perhaps thousands, of dollars donated to this barrio by visiting *internacionalistas*. What has he done with all that money, given in good faith to the people of this barrio, by our *compañeros* from other countries?

He always comes around visiting, and he always asks, "give me a soda," or "give me a cigarette"! I say, to shit with this worthless *vago* (vagrant, bum).

And when you go to his house to get his signature, he says, "not now, I'm drinking this *'fre'co* (*refresco*, refreshment)." Can you imagine such a thing? It takes two seconds to sign a form, and he can't do it unless you give him a gift!

He always was a big Somocista in the time of Somoza, and now he goes around a great big Sandinista. Where is the sacrifice for him? Enough of this shit!

Do you realize that he has four sons, and that somehow not one of them has ever been drafted? He is using his connections to keep his sons out of the military, so that they can all bring in income for his family.

He's always exhorting us to do communal labor, to work for the revolution, and making his long speeches. And when you go there to work, there he is, standing around giving orders, or making speeches, or saying, "give me a *gaseosa*." Who here among us has ever seen him work?

Two particular tales of malfeasance proved especially damning, in each case corresponding to the barrio's special advantage as a host-barrio for international visitors to Managua. Various programs locate visiting *internacionalistas* in spare rooms with a dozen or so of Erasmus Jiménez's families. Friendships are often sealed by the exchange of small gifts, but it is an ideal of the CDS that significant gifts and donations should be given not to individual families but to the barrio as a whole and distributed by the CDS. In the aforementioned case, following the will of the barrio CDS, the *dirigente del barrio* had collected contributions, largely in dollars, for the eventual construction of a *casa comunal*, or community center, which would serve a variety of local functions for the entire barrio: a site for collective baby-sitting; a public meeting house; a place for social functions and dances; a game room. Months, then years passed, and while a number of much poorer barrios nearby had long ago completed the building of their community centers, Erasmus Jiménez lagged behind. The *dirigente* continued collecting more and more money over a period of years, with no visible progress on the project. Even more suspiciously, the *dirigente* never opened a bank account for these contributions, but rather kept the money in his house. Public opinion widely held that Ortiz was simply spending the money raised on himself and his family, and when the *dirigente* undertook the project of enlarging his house, his action did nothing to quell such suspicion.

Another case involved the misdirection of clothing donations given to the barrio by similar groups of visiting *internacionalistas*. Visitors had been leaving small gifts of clothes as *recuerdos* (mementos) to individual members of the CDS in whose homes they had visited. In Nicaragua's economy of chronic shortage and acute envy, even small gifts of clothes can be significant, and this uneven enjoyment of privilege created envy and conflict in the neighborhoods. It was democratically decided that such gifts should be collected by the CDS and then distributed evenly throughout the barrio. Ortiz put himself in charge of that project and collected several large donations of clothes from the international visitors, who could then make contributions to the neighborhood, secure in the knowledge that their goods would be distributed by an egalitarian and communitarian scheme. According to my informants, however, no clothes were ever distributed; instead, the *dirigente* and his family expanded their wardrobes, sporting a luxurious collection of blue jeans, T-shirts, tennis shoes, and backpacks.

These ample suggestions of corruption and malfeasance, widely recited by CDS and barrio members, demonstrated the CDS leader's lack of credibility and the need for new elections. But organizing these elections nonetheless proved difficult. Every *andén* produced its own candidate for *dirigente:* more than fifteen in all. Ortiz was among the candidates. Public forums held in advance of the elections failed either to promote widespread participation or to coalesce support around one of the opposing candidates. CDS elections entail no runoff mechanism, so it would have been altogether possible that in a crowded field of candidates, the well-organized incumbent's faction could win reelection with less than 10 percent of the total vote. Worse yet, a major mobilization of volunteers for the coffee harvesting brigades further undermined participation for CDS elections, and in Erasmus Jiménez several major candidates were in the mountains picking coffee beans for the entire month of December. (Ortiz was not among them.) Amid growing signs of lethargy and disorganization, and with fear that incumbents would be reelected by default, CDS elections were postponed, not only in Erasmus Jiménez but in other barrios as well.

The elections were finally held in February 1986, after more preparation had insured greater participation, and a manageable list of candidates had allowed the consolidation of opinion behind major contenders. The incumbent lost his office as *dirigente del barrio*, and, following a pattern established in other barrios, a housewife was elected to replace him. In other barrios, women have moved into these positions: sometimes housewives, sometimes former beauty queens at the *fiestas patronales*. The nature of their special qualifications inheres in their status as women. It is felt that they will be less aggressive, less posturing, and less greedy; that they will make fewer public demands and exude less revolutionary rhetoric, while actually doing more of the work themselves.

Most of the barrio was happy with the results of this election. "Now we have a *dirigente* and *comité* that can get on with the hard work of the revolution, in the fields of health care, construction, and vigilance." Some felt it unfortunate that Ortiz was retained on the *comité del barrio*, but expressed relief that he had not been put in charge of anything involving money.

But even with the widely unpopular *dirigente* thrown out of office, attempts at reviving all the functions of the CDS have proved less than successful. While the organization clearly enjoyed greater prestige and had resumed most of its health-care functions in May–June 1986, vigilance was still being kept on only one of Erasmus Jiménez's *andenes*. The situation was much the same throughout Managua's popular barrios.

At the same time, the need for reviving vigilance was growing greater than ever. For the first time since the revolution, serious crime was becoming a weighty fact of urban life again. More than two dozen street gangs roamed the streets of Managua at night, especially on weekends, holding up whole buses, mugging pedestrians, and occasionally beating or stabbing to death their victims.

This atmosphere of criminal terror also tends to diminish some of the marked gains women have made in the revolution. Women, especially, fall prey to victimization by delinquent gangs, and almost all of my women informants in this period reported curbing their movements outside their own *andén* at night and even in the afternoon. And women's fears of victimization have also reinforced the special difficulties in raising community vigilance. Said one woman,

> Nobody on this *andén* keeps vigilance anymore because of the *pandillas* (gangs). It's mostly women who keep vigilance, you know, and the *pandillas* roam around with knives and small arms. There were several rapes, not here, but in other parts of the city by these gangs, so the women are afraid to stand vigilance at night now. The only way we will stand vigilance is if we can arm ourselves, since the gangs are going to be armed.

During this period, crime and delinquency were up—dramatically so in comparison with the ideals of stability, security, and safety enumerated by ordinary Nicaraguans as key motives in revolutionary activism (see chapter 2). On the *andén* where I lived, of thirty households, people were victimized by the following crimes in a single four-week period:

- Three or four houses were broken into at night, as the families slept. Thieves crossed over into the backyards of houses to steal clothes hanging on the clotheslines, small pieces of furniture left out of doors, cooking gas cylinders, and assorted small items. People responded by taking most of their possessions indoors every night, securing the doors and windows of their houses with locks, and some families began keeping a rifle in the house.

- A dozen or more minor thefts—pickpocketings—occurred on buses, at busstops, or in crowds at the marketplace. People began to shun bus use except when absolutely necessary.

- Two major muggings transpired: one resident was robbed, at knifepoint, of his two-week salary; another resident, a small merchant, was robbed at gunpoint one day when she happened to be carrying 150,000 córdobas (nearly ten months wages for an ordinary working person).

At this point, the CDS had taken care of one of its problems, replacing unpopular and corrupt *dirigentes* and *comités* with new leadership. Clearly, the organization enjoyed greater prestige after the elections than during the previous six months. But now, another very serious problem demanded attention: resurgent delinquency and street crime, antithetical to the revolution's normative values of domestic order and social tranquility. As of July 1986, a series of CDS *andén* and barrio meetings had failed to revitalize the practice of vigilance: fatigue was cited, and increasingly, people complained that the situation was now too serious for unarmed civilian intervention.

ENVY, LEVELING, AND THE NEW REGIME

While clearly an example of *demobilization*, the case of the CDS and its continuing problems is not at all clearly one of *delegitimation*. The cycle of political mobilization and demobilization, of activism and inertia, is one that lies implicit in the nature of mass political organizations. The CDS organization itself remains intact, retains the bulk of its popular base, and continues to be an effective instrument in certain fields of endeavor. Ordinary members assure me, despite their fatigue, that in the event of an "emergency"—such as impending war with the United States or Honduras, or an escalation of urban counterrevolutionary activity—their vigilance would be immediately resumed. And many of my informants predict that the resumption of vigilance in new forms is inevitable if crime remains at present levels or continues to rise. I trust that they are correct. Popular activism comes in waves, and the troughs between crests are dominated by particularly sharp micro-discourses of complaint and murmur that ultimately serve to propel the next wave of reform and activism.

It is clear, moreover, that economic hardship has been the major stimulant of what we may loosely call "rumor" and "murmuring" and even political demobilization. But this does not mean that Nicaraguans have therefore come to appropriate a "rationalized" and utilitarian concept of legitimacy. The language in which these murmurings are articulated is much more normative than rationalized, and corresponds more closely to the image of "limited good" than to economism. If the popular classes are experiencing shortages and hardships, then it must be because the elites are *hoarding* and *overconsuming*, or because they are abusing their power, or are superexploiting the poor.

"Elites" in the new popular mind may and do correspond to two possibilities: bourgeois elites (*las burguesas, los capitalistas*) and political elites (the Sandinistas). Both provide the subject matter for vituperative complaint, from the same stratum of society, though not necessarily from the same persons. Thus, in Nicaragua's mixed economy, two objects of envy coexist. The one is subject to class conflict, which is directed against Nicaragua's still-significant class of owners, large and small, as well as some professionals. The other envy, treated in detail in this chapter, entails a powerful *status* conflict inherent in postrevolutionary society, between elites and masses. "Envy" provides the continuity between traditional and revolutionary forms: it is the vehicle for class as well as status consciousness, and it provides the model for leveling mechanisms and redistributive policy in the new regime. I refer to envy directed against the political elites as "status" rather than "class" envy because the Sandinistas have no privileged access to property *per se* (or to production more generally defined), although their position does provide significantly greater economic reward, security and opportunities than most non-Sandinistas could expect. While clearly a "hierarchy," then, this is a matter of "prestige," "style of life" or "mode of consumption" rather than of production proper, and should accordingly fall under the rubric of status, not class.[1] And whereas *degrees* of economic interest, even *conflicts* of economic interest, clearly exist between political elites and popular masses, the structure of these interests is constituted differently from those between classes proper. A political elite in the revolutionary or postrevolutionary situation depends on the popular classes for its legitimacy, authority, and ultimately its power in a way that an owning class does not.

In discussing this distinction, we need not imagine that Managua's popular classes have read Weber, or absorbed his content through an obscure process of intellectual osmosis. Distinctions of just this broad sort would seem implicit in the revolutionary and postrevolutionary situation. While for some purposes, my informants blurred the distinction between political and economic elites—for instance, when they spoke of "big men" (*hombres grandes*)—for others they sharply distinguished them. The basic vocabularies for each are quite readily distinguishable: *vanguardia, líder, político* on the one hand, versus *burguesa, capitalista, negocio* on the other.

The case of corruption actually demonstrates this rule: we see the possibility of amassing large enough reserves of wealth that certain officials might rightfully surpass their classification as status elites to emerge as a newly constituted class elite proper. But it is precisely because this accumulation is *illegal* that the political elites remain status, not class, elites. The tension here between two types of hierarchy is the dominant tension in the new society—but it is ultimately a productive tension that serves to both legitimate the new government *and* keep it in check.

Corruption in Nicaragua remains a problem of relatively small scale and relatively petty offenses. The police force, for instance, appears quite uncorrupted, in contrast to the situation in many other Latin American countries. During my extensive interviews with dozens and my informal conversations with hundreds of Nicaraguans, I have never heard of a case of bribery, graft, or corruption involving the Sandinista Police or the military. Barring the eruption of large-scale corruption or its institutionalization in the upper echelons of the regime, one would not expect the Sandinistas to transform themselves into a new "ruling class" proper.

The present political economy with its concomitant status and class conflicts is a problematic formation. Indeed, the present public/private "mix" of the mixed economy seems to produce simultaneously all the problems inherent in both socialism and capitalism. It reduces labor incentive by subsidizing basic necessities; this has ultimately lowered productivity and exacerbated the shortages. At the same time, Nicaragua's productive apparatus remains largely decentralized and even anarchic: artisaniship and petty commodity production still play important roles, and aside from subsidized basic foods, market values still ultimately reign. This leaves available few means of otherwise organizing or increasing production. "Moral incentives" and communal labor mobilizations loom all the more important against such a backdrop.

Nicaragua's present mixed economy is a powerful engine of both status and class conflict, and these ever take the linguistic form of *envy*. The regime controls class conflict by bringing ever larger areas of production under cooperative, collective, or state control. The language of class conflict and class envy is institutionalized as official display as well as private discourse, and one source of the Sandinistas' resilient popularity, despite their poor economic record, is the perception that they weaken and even punish *los ricos* (the rich).

The conflict directed against rulers by the ruled is less susceptible to easy resolution. In some cases, in appropriating the property of private owners into the public domain, nationalization also appropriates a nexus of antagonisms into the new regime. Owners are replaced by state managers, and, in the economy of scarcity, austerity comes to be administered by the state. This strains the sense of identity and continuity between leaders and followers, rulers and ruled, so important in revolutionary states, but here a familiar dialectic develops. On the one hand, the regime will undergo periodic and cyclical renewal of its ranks to maintain its credibility; on the other hand, it may reaffirm its sense of identity with the people by calling their attention to an outside threat. On this latter terrain, revolutionary and postrevolutionary regimes in the Third World have proved far more credible than pre- or nonrevolutionary regimes, and this feature tends to imbue them all with a populist military casting.

In the case of the CDS, we see a particularly revealing example of how the regime functions vis-à-vis such pressures. It is important to note that the FSLN at no time moved to perform a direct purge of its errant lower-ranking members involved, nor even to fully acknowledge the scale of the problem—even though the populace was widely saying that opportunistic and bourgeois elements had taken over the CDS and were running it for their own profit and self-advancement. The exact accuracy of these rumors is unimportant. What is important is the popular impression, which had grown extremely hostile toward CDS directors in a number of barrios across the city. Eventually, the FSLN moved quietly, behind the scenes, in response to such pressures: quietly, so as to avoid public acknowledgment that the ideal (self-abnegation among leaders) was not also the real, and behind the scenes so as not to appear to be orchestrating events in the theoretically independent CDS.

"Fields" or "spaces" of representation to the more visually-oriented, what I have called "macro-" and "micro-discourses" are, of course, more than detached symbol or even communication. They ultimately represent an emergent structure of praxis whose subject is real and material class/status/power relations. Their consequences are real: Ortiz and dozens like him were, effectively, purged; communal labor is either performed or it is not, with whatever consequences that follow; a myriad of power relations are affected on a variety of domains (class, status, organizational, gender) that shape what we mean by "social life" in Nicaragua.

Authority in Nicaragua's emerging system is an ongoing negotiation between macro- and micro-discourses, between official narratives and private rumors. Despite apparent contradictions, both coexist. Many of my informants gossip about alleged abuses by lower- and middle-level individuals in the Sandinista apparatus one day, only to faithfully recite official narratives of sacrifice and self-denial on the next. The language of public display is dominated by the millenarian image, in either its secular form (Sandinismo) or its religious form (liberation theology). The underside of this macro-discourse is the very traditional micro-discourse of envy and leveling, with its myriad forms of gossip, rumor, and murmuring. The resultant totality is a Janus-like system which simultaneously looks backward and forward, whose essential rules of legitimation are normative (both officially and unofficially), and which can successfully reproduce itself, not only *despite*, but *because of*, the pervasiveness of complaint and conflict.

Originally the motivator of revolutionary mobilization and work, the millenarian imagery of sacrifice comes to represent a contract between rulers and ruled in the new regime: the insurance of a society relatively free of instability and stratification. The collective murmurings of the popular classes (as distinct from those of elites) represent the ongoing negotiations between rulers and ruled on various topics. Far from anomalous, the ongoing noise of such murmur should be seen as more constructive than destructive in the elaboration of the shape of postrevolutionary society. How else would masses mediate their relations with political elites where each shares a normative ideal? Key here is that the government of the new state constitutes a "status elite," recognized by the populace as its leadership or political vanguard; the collective fear is that it might also come to represent another *class elite* as well. At this juncture of fact and fear ensues the quibblings over reasonable apportionment of rewards between elites and masses.

The experiences of the revolution, and of the sacrifices made in defense of the revolution, constitute an unusual set of experiences that bind leaders and followers, rulers and ruled, in the new regime. These experiences also underwrite the persistence of a collective myth shared by both vanguards and masses, as expressed in each's endorsement of the flags, anthems, emblems and symbols of the revolution on public occasions. Dependent on the perpetuation of that binding relationship, that shared mythology, is nothing less than the persistence of the new state itself. The popular classes jealously guard that relationship in their private micro-discourses even as the regime itself projects it as the subject of its public macro-discourses.

CHAPTER SIX
Marxism and Religion: A Critique

Though you have all this, you still lack one thing:
God!
—*Rubén Darío (1967: 641), "To Roosevelt"*

Marxism and religion, especially Marxism and Christianity, have long regarded each other with the hostile suspicion of two competing world views, each envious of the other's following, each jealous of its own symbol and myth. Pragmatism has, on occasion, led the two into limited negotiations, as in Italy's historic Christian-Marxist dialogues (see McGovern, 1980:113–115). At the peak of the socialist Second International's influence, various attempts were made to interpret Christianity as socialism and socialism as Christianity. German Social Democratic leader Karl Kautsky (1953) provided the theoretical reasoning for such an equation. In the United States, the Debsian socialist Upton Sinclair (1922) wrote a pamphlet-novel along those lines, treating Christ as the original socialist. And Lincoln Steffens (1926) found in Moses the prototype of Leninist political organization. But in more recent history, and, more consistently, relations between the two might better be typified by Lenin's characterization of religion as "unutterable vileness . . . of the most dangerous kind, 'contagion' of the most abominable kind" (1939b:675–76), or by Cardinal Ratzinger's more recent evaluation of Marxism as "sin" (1984).

Events in Latin America, especially in Nicaragua, have realigned Marxist-Christian relations, perhaps permanently. The spread of liberation theology, the base community movement, and the forms of popular political activism taking shape on that continent have generated a variety of new possibilities: Marxists and Christians working together toward common goals of either a reformist or revolutionary sort; Christians appropriating Marxist texts, or developing

164

parallel analyses out of biblical texts; Christianity and Marxism blending into new, popularly accessible variants of each.

Overviews have been written on this process of Marxist-Christian integration, some more or less secular in orientation, others primarily theological in emphasis. Characteristic shortcomings define most of these statements. The secular analyses can scarcely conceal their breathlessness: something *altogether new* and *unprecedented* is happening in Latin America (or Nicaragua). Thus remaining on the very surface of the conjuncture between politics and religion, and rarely more profound than pop journalism, this literature forecloses the possibility of genuinely comparative analysis. The deep structure of religion/politics is never touched; it is enough to say only that God is officially allowed to exist in the minds of Latin American workers and peasants. Or perhaps, alternatively, the history of Nicaragua is manipulated to "disprove" the history of other Third World countries, other revolutions, which become examples of "dogmatic sectarianism" in contrast to Nicaragua's "pragmatic pluralism." (See O'Brien 1986; Zwerling 1985.)

The theological writings, while typically of a much higher quality than the secular or social science ones on this topic, generally fail to deal with the key theoretical problems involved. The most typical evasion may be paraphrased as follows: "We absorb Marx's critique of religion as it has been appropriated in the service of ruling classes. We offer a new (or, alternatively, the authentic) way of worshipping God, and that way is *faith*, not religion." While satisfying the believer, this approach fails to address the deeper essence of Marx's critique of religion, that it inherently represents a form of "false consciousness" and is the quintessential form of *alienation*.

Marxists, for their part, have also evaded the key questions of their own analysis, namely, "Is theism/religion an inherent form of false consciousness? of alienation?" Instead, they have wrangled with more peripheral issues and have sought to unselfcritically accommodate revolutionary Christian praxis without really (re)considering the essentials of Marxist philosophy. The question, then, becomes the altogether misleading one: "Why have Marxist movements and regimes been so dogmatically atheist in the past, to the point of actively suppressing religion?"

The approach followed here is different. Anthropologically, we should set two tasks. At the level of generalization, we should be able to offer a comparative overview of revolutionary movements in a wide variety of settings; at the level of specificity, we should be prepared to penetrate the deep structures of every such society's particular conjuncture of religion and politics. Seen from a narrow perspective, then, something "new" *is* underway in Nicaragua; seen from a broader angle, events there follow a logic with numerous precedents. Every revolution taps traditional culture as a wellspring against colonialism, capitalism, and anomie. Every revolution devises its own "new religion" based on elements of the old religion. In Nicaragua, the appropriation of religion is open; in other states, it has been covert, concealed behind the facade of official atheism. While the latter fact challenges our understanding of revolution, the former challenges our understanding of Marxism.

For those of us who take Marxism as something more than an academic ornament, this comparative perspective poses an essential question: either religion necessarily and inherently signifies alienation and false consciousness—quite apart from its immediate program on such questions as land reform, health care, popular revolution, social class, and the distribution of wealth—or it does not. If it does signify alienation, as Marx maintains, then the basic texts of Marxism require no substantial revision. If it does not, then the very fundamental texts of Marxism require reexamination in the light of this "new" evidence.

This dilemma is even more profound for "Western" or "critical" Marxism than for any of the numerous variants of state Marxism. State Marxism has maintained an antireligious bias as a matter of party line or official policy, but lines change, policies are periodically adjusted, and, much like the Church, the socialist state may evince remarkable maneuverability—even if it works "dogmatically" out of limited texts. For state Marxism, then, maneuverability is only a matter of nuancing official texts, bringing out their "pluralistic" elements, or shading one's interpretation in favor of one position rather than the other within a single exegetic tradition.[1] Whereas for state Marxism, an antireligious bias is a matter of dogma, for Western Marxism it would appear to be embedded in a deeply reflexive philosophy: atheism is the starting point of Marxist humanism, and lies at the root of its model for human liberation and freedom. Its importance is most crucial *precisely* in those "early" texts that loom so important in the tradition of the Frankfurt school and in Western critical Marxism (and diminishes progressively in the "late" texts that are favored by state Marxisms).

It is our task here, then, to reread the Marxist texts on religion, and to retrace the now open, now hidden history of Christianity and Marxism. Having done so, we are in a position to better understand the emergence of Marxism in the Marxist states, and to postulate a comparative analysis of religion/politics in revolutionary milieus. (This critique, I believe, will also explain the singular failures of critical Marxism to dislodge or significantly modify the state Marxisms.)

THE EARLY MARX

For Marxism, "the *criticism of religion* . . . is the premise of all criticism." Thus begins the sequence of Marx's famous and most sustained critique of religious belief, "Contribution to the Critique of Hegel's Philosophy of Right," penned in 1844, the year Marx began devising his distinct analytic system. The point, for Marx, was to invert the relationship between spirit and matter, idea and reality, as posited by both Christianity and Hegel. The critique of Hegel sustained in this text, then, is identical to the critique of religion, and the one is subsumed into the other.

> *Man makes religion,* religion does not make man. In other words, religion is the self-consciousness and self-feeling of man who has either not yet found himself or has already lost himself again. But *man* is no abstract being squatting outside the world. Man is the *world of man,* the state, society. This state, this society, produce a religion, a *reversed world-consciousness,* because they are a *reversed world.* (Marx and Engels 1964:41)

Following this introduction appears Marx's frequently cited aphorism, which is but a fragment of a much more complicated thought:

> Religious distress is at the same time the expression of real distress and the *protest* against real distress. Religion is the sigh of the oppressed creature, the heart of a heartless world, just as it is the spirit of a spiritless situation. It is the opium of the people. (42)

Marx expresses in these lines an analysis of religion somewhat more complicated than the freely cited "opium of the people" summary would imply: religion both *expresses* and *protests* distress. Working sociologically out of Marx's original framework, it would be altogether possible to trace religion as both an instrument of the status quo and as a popular protest against the status quo. But, sensing a loophole here, some commentators have laid more stress on this than is in fact warranted (Aptheker 1966:33; Kovel 1984:51). The poetics of Marx's construction are unambiguously clear: we are led to the ultimate if unfortunate conclusion that religion *obscures* clear thought much like a potent drug. And the very next paragraph returns us to the opening point. Politically, Marxism demands the critique of religion; philosophically, it demands the dissolution of religion.

> The abolition of religion as the *illusory* happiness of the people is required for their *real* happiness . . . . The criticism of the religion is therefore *in embryo the criticism of the vale of woe, the halo of which is religion.*
>
> . . . The criticism of religion disillusions man to make him think and act and shape his reality like a man who has been disillusioned and has come to reason, so that he will revolve around himself and therefore round his true sun. Religion is only the illusory sun which revolves round man as long as he does not revolve around himself. (42)

These criticisms of religion in "Contribution to the Critique of Hegel's Philosophy of Right" roughly parallel the passages which appear in *The Economic and Philosophical Manuscripts of 1844*, a series of unpublished and sometimes fragmentary notes written the same year. The spirit of these documents is much like the later *Communist Manifesto* (1847–48). As Marshall Berman (1982) has observed in his interpretation of modernism, Marx ruthlessly snatches the halos off persons and things in order to disillusion, and disillusions in order to revolutionize. How could the working class train its sights on its own self-organization, on its battles with capital over wages and unionization, in short, on its *social* interests, if its thoughts were filled with angels, saints, martyrs, and the afterlife? Thus, in *The Economic and Philosophical Manuscripts,* "Communism begins from the outset with atheism" (1964:136).

Ontologically, it is quite clear that communism descended from atheism in Marx's own thought. His doctoral dissertation on Epicurean philosophy, written in the years from 1839–41, begins outlining the themes that will undergo substantial development in the crucial year of 1844: Marx champions the overthrow of the gods through Prometheus' example ("In sooth all gods I hate"), and presents in embryo the notion of religion as restraint on freedom. Similarly, his 1842 article in the *Rheinische Zeitung* attacks religion, religious restraint, and religious authority; it opposes all things religious to science, freedom, and the free press. In neither of these documents was Marx yet a socialist or a materialist. At these early stages, he could best be described as a radical Hegelian. The Marxism of Marx evolved out of the atheism of the early, pre-Marxist writings—and, indeed, if there is a single thread that unites the entire opus of Marx, it is neither the dialectic, nor materialism, but atheism.

These early criticisms of things religious by a doctoral student and newspaper editor continue and are systematized in the writings of 1844, when Marx's conversion to socialism was complete and the evolution of his materialist method was very much underway. Atheism and the vigorous criticism of religion thus lie at the very crux of Marxist humanism because for Marx, as for Nietzsche and Sartre, God must be removed from the scene before man can really be free.

> Since for the socialist man the entire so-called history of the world is nothing but the creation of man through human labor, nothing but the emergence of nature for man, so he has the visible, irrefutable proof of his *birth* through himself, of the process of his creation. Since the *real existence* of man and nature . . . the question about an *alien* being, about a being above nature and man—a question which implies the admission of the unreality of nature and of man—has become impossible in practice. *Atheism*, as the denial of this unreality, has no longer any meaning, for atheism is a *negation of God*, and postulates the *existence of man* through this negation; but socialism as socialism no longer stands in any need of such mediation. It proceeds from the practically and *theoretically sensuous consciousness* of man and of nature as the *essence*. Socialism is man's *positive self-consciousness*, no longer mediated through the annulment of religion . . . (Marx 1964:145–46)

Marx traces out the dialectical progression of his own thought, which he presents as the emergence of socialism: from atheism (the negation of God) to humanism (the affirmation of man) to socialism (the negation of the negation and supercession of such questions: here, man appears as the subject of his own history). The vigorous criticism of religion is a crucial first stage in this process—not an end in itself, perhaps, but a very necessary prerequisite for man's self-consciousness. Man cannot be free as long as God exists; man can only become *real* when God becomes *unreal;* and this reality must be established before man can be a freely acting being. In cadences that resonate with Nietzsche, Marx struggles against "the priest within the self" (in Marx and Engels, 1964: 51) and pathologizes religion in terms of "the diseases of Christianity" (52). "The Holy Family," also written in 1844, again summarizes the essence of the revolutionary critique of religion: religion stands opposed to freedom, and he cannot be free who remains chained to God (59–68).

This critique of religion, crucial to the origins of Marxism, follows several interweaving strands that constitute a fabric: first, God as an obstacle to freedom, and, second, religion as a form of false consciousness. The third and most important strand of this criticism, however, is contained in Marx's theory of alienation. In a sequence of the *Economic and Philosophical Manuscripts of 1844* that anticipated his more mature works on alienation, exploitation, and surplus labor, Marx deduces labor's alienation as its *objectification* and draws two arguments about religion: explicitly, that it is an appropriate master metaphor for alienation, and implicitly, that it is the ontologically original form of alienation.

> Labor produces not only commodities: it produces itself and the worker as a *commodity*—and this in the same general proportion in which it produces commodities.
>
>   This expresses merely that the object which labor produces—labor's product—confronts it as *something alien*, as a *power independent* of the producer.
>
>   . . . The worker is related to the *product of his labor* as to an *alien* object. For on this premise it is clear that the more the worker spends himself, the more powerful becomes the alien world of objects which he creates over and against himself, the poorer he himself—his inner world—becomes, the less belongs to him as his own. *It is the same in religion. The more man puts into God, the less he retains in himself.* [Emphasis here is mine, elsewhere in the original—RNL.] The worker puts his life into the objects; but his life no longer belongs to him but to the object. Hence, the greater this activity, the greater the worker's lack of objects. Whatever the product of his labor is, he is not . . . The *alienation* of the worker in his product means not only that his labor becomes an object, an *external* existence, but that it exists *outside* him, independently, as something alien to him, and that it becomes a power on its own confronting him. It means that the life which he conferred on the object confronts him as something hostile and alien. (Marx 1964:107–18)

Like the alienation of the worker from his *products of labor* (cited above), the alienation of *labor itself* in the process of work (cited below) is also an act of estrangement—and again, reflection on the nature of religion plays a crucial role in Marx's thought.

Just as in religion the spontaneous activity of the human imagination, of the human brain and the human heart, operates independently of the individual—that is, operates on him as an alien, divine or diabolical activity—so is the worker's activity not his own spontaneous activity. It belongs to another; it is the loss of the self. (1964:111)

A minimum of three points may be distinguished in the early Marxian criticism of religion: first, religion stands as an obstacle to the sort of political practice that Marx envisioned and acts as a "conservative," even feudal social force: restriction, inhibition, and censorship are its watchwords—How can man be free if only God is free? How can man be defined as an independent existence if only God's existence is independent? Second, religion may be seen as false consciousness, obfuscation—and this is closely allied to, though not necessarily identical with, the nineteenth-century rational and scientific understanding of religion as superstition and error. Third, and perhaps most importantly, religion is seen as alienation: of man, from his thoughts, feelings, qualities, and actions. While the former two criticisms of religion could easily correspond to any range of liberal, radical, rational, or scientific currents in post-Enlightenment philosophy, the latter criticism is distinctive to Marxism, and it is to Marxism alone that it owes its existence. Indeed, Marxism's particular interest in religion is synthesized into an analysis of alienation; the former two strands only make sense *as Marxism* when seen in the light of the third.

Now Marx's discussion of labor alienation begins on the economic preterrain of a class division between "owners" and "workers" (1964: 106). He proceeds from economic facts "of the present" (107). Seen in this light, alienation and religion may appear as *products* of private property. But at the same time, Marx is attempting to crack open political economy by deriving the *origins* of private property in the process of labor's estrangement, as well. Thus,

though private property appears to be the source, the cause of alienated labor, it is rather its consequence, just as the gods are *originally* not the cause but the effect of man's intellectual confusion. Later this relationship becomes reciprocal. (1964, 117)

The content and significance of this passage is open to dispute, and it appears certain that Marx later reversed the direction of causation. But more importantly, we find the same dialectical tacking between religion and economics, God and labor, spelled out once again: "confusion : God :: alienation : private property." If the essential relationship holds but causality is reversed—as a reading of the later Marx would suggest—then religion would appear as the source and cause of confusion or false consciousness in the same fashion that private property appears as the source and cause of alienation. And this possibility is implicitly hinted at throughout the early and even some of the later texts: that religion constitutes the original phase in the development of alienation and false consciousness.

To summarize, then: religion is the early Marx's master metaphor for both alienation and false consciousness. It is consistently employed to illuminate crucial arguments, and likewise appears as the most powerful example of alienation. That religion sows false consciousness and private property causes alienation—presently if not historically—is observed from "facts of the present." But certainly, Marx was also aware of the existence of religion *before* the stratification of society into classes and the emergence of economic facts of the present. Thus, two possible readings of Marx on the history and anthropology of religion suggest themselves: a stronger case against religion, in which religion is seen as a substantial *source* of false consciousness and alienation, and a weaker case, in which religion is seen as a direct consequence but not a cause of false consciousness and alienation.

In the strong case, religion acts not only as a key metaphor for alienation, but also constitutes the first ontological phase of estrangement or alienation itself. Its supercession would be crucial in the emergence of a free, unalienated humanity because religion embodies that which is primordial and essential in alienation, objectification: it projects onto fantastic creatures qualities that are really human attributes. In the weaker case, religion is still the master metaphor for alienation and false consciousness, but its causative significance in history is undermined: like alienation more generally, it is merely a product of other social and economic forces, and when those relations of production are realigned, its significance would presumably wane and wither away. However, this does not mitigate the responsibility of Marxists to do battle with religious belief, for recall that the relationship has become "reciprocal"; as a key reinforcer of false consciousness, religion acquires an active, reactionary force in fogging men's minds and promoting both alienation and false consciousness.

While some authors have fancied that "Western" Marxism is less hostile to religion than state Marxisms (of, say, the Soviet variety) (McGovern 1980:50, 71, 73, 82; Kovel 1984:54), this conclusion seems altogether unwarranted. To the degree that Western Marxism is deeply committed to the early texts, it is also committed to a particularly strident criticism of religion: as false consciousness, and as the prototype of alienation. No other direct reading of these texts is really possible.

MARX/ENGELS MARXISM: THE LATER MARX

Reading beyond the earliest texts of Marxism, one finds, curiously, not a unified or whole critique of religion, but a scattergun and wide-ranging, sometimes *ad hominem* critique. The parallelisms between religious belief and alienation, so carefully developed in the texts of 1844, all but disappear in the later writings. The criticism of religion is then invariably achieved by counterposing *materialism* to *idealism*, following the strategy of Marx's inversion of Hegel. But the content of the "materialism" juxtaposed to religion varies widely. Why this sudden dissolution of clarity on the topic? If I am correct, Marx's intellectual methods had undergone a revision which, if systematically applied to religion, would have superseded and even reversed his earlier criticism of religion.

Beginning in 1845 with "Theses on Feuerbach," a series of aphoristic sketches, Marx begins filtering out both the crude materialism of an inverted Hegel *and* the remnants of idealism in his own method. We may place the "Theses" at an important juncture in the evolution of Marxism: a mini-revolution within the revolutionary theory. Hidden in the "Theses" is the pivotal development of a reassessment of Marxist materialism. *Praxis* becomes the bridge between idea and matter that forever transcends antiquated philosophical debates about which of the two is "more determinant."

Feuerbach, Marx argues, wanted "sensuous objects really differentiated from the thought-objects," matter really distinguished from our own mental copies of matter. But in this crude materialism, matter itself becomes objectified, reified, *idealized*. Ultimately a transcendent category, matter exists *prior to* and *independent of* our perception, contemplation, or action. Sealed off from man, an eternal and ultimately abstract thing-in-itself resting outside and above history, the reified "matter" of crude materialism inevitably lapses into a disguised form of idealism.

At this crucial juncture in his thought and through this pivotal critique of Feuerbach, Marx decisively breaks with vulgar materialism. Gone here are the facile empiricist assertions that matter is somehow "more real" than thought. In the "Theses," Marx revolutionizes materialism by redefining "matter" as that which is subject to activity, to praxis. Moreover, observation, contemplation, and sensuous perception are themselves forms of *praxis*. Brain, eye, hand, and nature are thus dialectically linked through praxis—and because man is a sensuous, contemplating, signifying and social being, praxis is always *social* praxis. In the end, as Sartre observes, "matter" is not the matter of physical objects, but of *social relations* (1976). The method and the object of inquiry, then, praxis consists of both preexisting social relations *and* the possibility of dissolving and transforming those relations.

In this thoroughly revised materialism developed in the "Theses," the idealistic problems raised in 1844 concerning the "essence of man" are resolved: man is to man and nature linked through and only through his social relations, his social practice. Idea, matter, nature, and other men thus constitute for man a *human* universe whose only key is activity; all other questions are put aside:

> Feuerbach resolves the religious essence into the *human* essence. But the human essence is no abstraction inherent in the single individual. In its reality it is the ensemble of the social relations . . .
>
> Feuerbach, consequently, does not see that the "religious sentiment" is itself a *social product*, and that the abstract individual whom he analyzes belongs in reality to a particular form of society.
>
> Social life is essentially *practical*. All mysteries which mislead theory to mysticism find their rational solution in human practice and in the comprehension of this practice.

In the theory of praxis elaborated here, we may discern both a continuity and a disjuncture between the early, "humanist" Marx and the later "structuralist" Marx (Althusser 1977:32—37). The subjective questions about human existence pondered in the documents of 1844 remain, but are historically situated as social practice. Man, then, is no abstract individual squatting outside his society, but a product and producer of his social relations. The "essence" of man is that he is indeed a *praxical* being, subject to and object of broad systems of practice that constitute social relations. If this is so, then Marx's early humanist interest in "subjectivity" and his later sociological interest in "economic structures" are both comprehensible in terms of this new system of analysis.[2]

While it is clear that Marxism revised its conception of matter, materialism and method—transcending the purely Hegelian opposition between idea and matter—Marx never addressed himself to an explicit reassessment of his critique of religion. Had he done so, he might have continued the thought expressed in the "Theses on Feuerbach": religion is a representational form of social praxis, and, as such, it holds up a certain ensemble of social relations, much like a mirror, to its believers.

—And what sort of praxis would this imply? A social praxis that cements the mutually hostile social classes of capitalist societies together, dousing class conflict and evading disruption? Or something else?

If religion is understood to predate the division of society into classes, then it must be seen to serve the truly *socializing* functions that predate social stratification and without which social life is impossible. Here, Marx could have very reasonably followed the line of analysis later opened up by Durkheim on the subject of religion (1965). And it is clear that Marx was capable of just this sort of acute anthropological insight regarding the cultures of pre- and noncapitalist societies (see Marx's *Pre-Capitalist Economic Formations*).

But it is clear that intellectually and temperamentally, Marx was not inclined to extend his self-revision to the topic of religion. Indeed, if we read beyond the early texts, which do at least yield consistent interweaving analyses, the later texts by Marx and Engels descend into disorganized and *ad hominem* approaches to religion. Religion appears alternately as reflex (Marx and Engels 1964:94, 135–36, 147–48), inversion (*camera obscura*) (74), illusion (79), error (151), neurosis (as in a futile groping after certainty in an uncertain world) (196–98, 203–04), superstition or witchery (77), a ruling class tool (83), and outright deception (176ff). Its opposite, "materialism," is situationally shaded in these passages so as to take many forms, depending on convenience's sake: sometimes it means naturalism, other times empiricism. Rarely is it a "theory of praxis" as outlined in "Theses on Feuerbach," and usually this "materialism" corresponds to the crude materialism Marx himself rejected as disguised idealism.

The conflict between religion and materialism, then, is deployed in an array of disjointed oppositions: the real versus the fantastic, reality versus mere copies of reality, activity versus sublimation, true observation versus error, rational thought versus superstition. Sometimes these remarkable transitions and disjunctures of thought occur within a single text, as in the first book of *Capital*: a string of these associations are conjured, followed by a critique of the very "abstract materialism" (1967:79–80 versus 372–373n.) with which Marx opposed religion!

While Marxism matured beyond crude materialism as an instrument of social and economic analysis, it remained stagnant in its critique of religion and continued to rely on methods which Marx himself had emphatically abandoned. Behind the variety of complex attacks lies a single, simple idea which was never expressly stated in the more mature Marx, but which continued to devil Marx's thought on the topic of religion. If for Hegel the idea "alienates itself by changing into nature" (Engels in Marx and Engels 1964:249), for Marx just the opposite is true: representation alienates matter by transforming it into *idea*. And religion is the worst culprit of all, transforming idea into *abstraction*.

PRE-MARXIST SOCIALISM
(OR, IS A HALO FOR OBSCURING OR
ILLUMINATING THINGS?)

Like Marx himself on the topic of religion, we border on simple-mindedness if we in turn treat Marxism's hostility to religion as a simple *error*. European Marxism is an intellectual product situated in its own cultural and historical milieu, determined under conditions that sustain, alter, or diminish it over time. There are a variety of similarly analyzable milieus that reproduce that ideological formula on other social terrains. The question, then, is not only *how* Marx and Engels opposed religion, and with what stated reasons, but also *why*—and, more significantly, why this assessment was preserved in subsequent Marxisms.

First, Marxism emerged in Europe as a world view competing with established Christianity. Theoretically, this might have been otherwise, but practically, it was not. As an ideology competing with another ideology for the loyalty of the working class, it was incumbent upon Marxism to produce reasons why it was superior to Christian "superstition." This approach blended well with the scientific and rational assumptions that began to flourish in the nineteenth century and with the growing secularism of a Western working class increasingly remote from its peasant origins. Themselves products of economic rationalization and increasingly dislodged from the traditional, religious and culturally conservative outlooks of rural peasant life, Western proletariats developed an increasingly rational outlook that could readily absorb or accommodate the secular and antireligious elements of Marxism in any variety of its forms: communism, socialism, or social democracy.

We would err, then, if we attributed to Marxism alone the conditions of its own theoretical atheism. Atheism, secularism, and an antireligious bias are not at all out of place in the modern industrial society. The machine, the factory, the rule of the market: it was in reality these that proceeded to dissemble the legitimacy of religion in nineteenth century Europe. It was these conditions that permitted Enlightenment doctrines to find a foothold in society at large. Corresponding to the rationalization of the economy: a rationalization of the intellect, in which the notion of God could play only a diminished or auxiliary role at best, and in which the significant attributes of God for precapitalist society could be rationalized out of existence. (This is already quite apparent in the deist notion of "God as Watchmaker," who sets the universe in motion and then retires from activity. This essentially mechanical view of the universe marks a sharp departure from the belief in a God who intervenes daily in human life and the events of the world.)

Lukács defines rationalization as "the sense of being able to predict with ever greater precision all the results to be achieved" by means of "the exact breakdown of every complex into its elements" (1968:88). Thus closely synonymous with predictability and empiricism—and inherently connected with Marx's notion of "objectification"—the rationalization of production posits and requires the infinite and minute manipulation of all known facts. *Indissoluble* complexes, notions like God, that resist analysis by breakdown and could not be productively fed into predictive formulae, were progressively banished from the productive process. The possibility of divine intervention may have a productive meaning in peasant society, but in the modern factory, with its ever-present timeclocks and minutely exact work rhythms, God is the irrational ghost of a previous epoch. He must be exorcised; he is exorcised. At the most, he may represent a *personal* belief, well-secluded in the private sphere, and perhaps even occasionally flaunted in the political or electoral sphere, but God is distinctly archaic in the workplace. It is not, then, that God vanishes from the scene altogether. "Archaic" forms persist, especially where rationalization has proceeded slowly or unevenly, but in the main, religion became either irrelevant to production or an obstacle to it, and God was banished, progressively, from the factory and the marketplace. Corresponding to rationalized production: a taylorism of the psyche, a calculated ethics, a dissemblage of the absolute principles vested in God. And in this sense of rationalization, "the distinction between a worker faced with a particular machine, the entrepreneur faced with a given type of mechanical development, the technologist faced with the state of science and the profitability of its application to technology, is purely quantitative; it does not directly entail *any qualitative difference in the structure of consciousness*" (Lukács 1968:98). To the extent that Marxism articulated atheism, it fell in full stride with the development of modernism out of the mechanical productive apparatus.

Second, this atheistic aspect of Marxism, so at home in the industrial factory, proved particularly exportable. The critique of religion, no matter how unsystematic, provided a handle that could be readily grasped in Third World contexts as well. The wrappings of science made Marxism especially attractive to radicalized and often Western-educated intellectuals. Inclined toward a nationalist ideology stressing modernization, Third World students and intellectuals could very readily appropriate these scientistic and rationalized aspects of Marxism as the kernel of a radical ideology that opposed foreign exploitation, domestic "superstition," and either native or imposed religious practices that might interfere with industrialization and modernization. And to the extent that urban proletariats in such Third World countries are brought under the sway of economic rationalization, the terrain is already set for their appropriation of this secularized and antireligious outlook on a larger social basis as well.

Third, by the time of Marx and Engels, it was no "error" to read the position of the established churches in the West, Catholic and Protestant alike, as essentially "reactionary." Nor would it be amiss to observe in the immediate case that the official church hierarchy in Nicaragua is, on balance, counterrevolutionary. Moreover, religion—even popular religion—may act in many ways, depending on complex social and historical circumstances. Certainly, it is not *unheard* of for (even popular) religion to serve the ends of elite classes, if only circumstantially, temporarily. Neither of these highly qualified cases justifies the unconditional philosophical critique of religion. The one case raises questions about the bureaucratic organization of state religion, not about popular belief: it addresses clergy, not religion proper, and requires us to distinguish *elite* from *popular* religion. The other possibility implies that we situate each political/ religious confluence in its own social and historical milieu. But while neither case proves anything inherent about the nature of religion, the intransigence of religious hierarchies and the intermittently reactionary role of religious belief more broadly speaking *do* provide readily available polemical material, and *appear* to verify Marx's antireligious critique to those already inclined to believe it.

But a fourth and more internally significant factor contributed to the dogged atheism of Marx and Engels, their tireless polemical crusades against Christianity, and to the systematically antireligious outlook of subsequent Marxisms. This largely hidden factor both obscures and nourishes the source of myth and doctrine in the whole corpus of Marxism from its intellectual origins to its subsequent development and in all its subsequent applications. Seen in this context, it was by no accident or error that Marx and Engels labored so vigorously to separate socialism from Christianity, for *pre-Marxist socialism was a largely religious affair with a long intellectual and popular tradition.* The dispute of Marxism with Christianity is much the same as the dispute of a daughter sect with the parent religion, and it is precisely on the point of theoretical atheism that the one distinguishes itself from the other.

Establishing the primacy of secular, scientific or Marxist socialism required rooting out the overtly religious impulse. Marx was not alone in this process, already well underway when both he and Engels arrived on the scene, but it was through their efforts that the final, secularized systematization of socialism was completed, and the *visible* ties of socialism to Christianity severed.

Sometimes, as we have seen, Marx went about this work systematically and single-mindedly; other times, with a loose scattergun approach that fails to sustain close inspection. And sometimes the nature of this work was more or less expressly recognized, as in those sections of the *Communist Manifesto* that treat Marxism's relation to past utopian socialisms: Marx recognizes their utility in the emergence of socialism, but casts them as ultimately retrograde and even reactionary forces in the modern world. But more generally, the nature of this work goes unacknowledged. In Marx's mission, the modernization of socialism, it was crucial to preserve the communal orientation of Christian socialism while ridding it of its appeal to God, divine intervention, the saints, and the like.

One may or may not accept the contention that the early Christian Church of the New Testament was a socialist institution par excellence, but it is undeniable that New Testament doctrine provided the ideological basis for the origins of socialism in Germany during the late middle ages, as Cohn's (1961) historical study carefully documents. Between 1190 and 1195, the Calabrian abbot and hermit Joachim of Fiore emerged as the foremost articulator of this messianic Christian socialism. His prophetic system, which reevoked the latent (and officially suppressed) chiliasm of Christianity, foretold the coming of the Kingdom of God and may well signify the most influential such intellectual system known to Europe "until the appearance of Marxism" (Cohn 1961:99).

Joachim of Fiore's prophecy divided human history into three great world ages, each governed by a different personage of the Holy Trinity, and calculated the arrival of the Third Age in 1260. This Third Age, the Age of the Holy Spirit, deduced from the Book of Revelation, would be typified by the abolition of private property and the universal affirmation of voluntary poverty. Both the state and institutionalized religion as such would disappear in this perfect *communitas*, and "the knowledge of God would be revealed directly in the hearts of men" (Cohn 1961:100). Indeed, in Joachim's egalitarian millennium, man's spiritual nature would come completely to the fore, and work itself would no longer be necessary.

Joachim's prophecy outlived its author. Franciscan abbots shortly set about editing, systematizing, and reworking Joachim's prophecies, and finding new revelations of their own. Similar prophetic movements developed in other parts of Europe, and were absorbed into the general repository of German popular culture. Popular and Franciscan expectations eventually came to center on the reign of Frederick II, who some held to be the spirit of Christ incarnate, and whose reign would establish the Kingdom of God. When Emperor Frederick died in 1250, ten years before the completion of the Joachite prophecy, the movement suffered a setback but was by no means defeated. It was widely rumored that Frederick was in fact still alive and in hiding, or that he would return from the dead, and that he would at any rate return shortly to set things in order. Numerous citings of Frederick confirmed this expectation, and the "Sleeping Emperor" passed into the popular culture as a symbol of future redemption. The *apparent* refutation of Joachim's prophecies—Frederick's death—simply marks their passage "underground" as a subterranean popular cult.

Joachite prophecies freely intermingled with anticlerical, antipapal, and revolutionary sentiments in precapitalist Germany. In this long period of feudalism's decay, various persons emerged claiming to be Frederick II. Such prophets gathered followers and waged campaigns against the rich, the clergy, and the state of affairs in general. One branch of the Flagellant movement that swept Europe along with the Black Death in 1348 appropriated a revolutionary reading of Joachim and foretold the return of Frederick II, who would massacre the clergy and compel the rich to wed the poor in one vast social leveling. In anticipation of the Age of the Holy Spirit, these Flagellants shed their own blood as the sign of penance and incited riots against the established clergy. They confiscated church property and redistributed it to the loose mobs of peasants and artisans that constituted their following.

Another wave of peasant revolts inspired by the messianic imagery of Joachim swept Germany in the fifteenth century. These movements took as their aim the abolition of private property, the leveling of social classes, and the establishment of an egalitarian millennium. The most notable sect of this type, the Taborites, preached a communist doctrine of collective property and communal marriage (Cohn 1961:227). The proliferation of such radical religious sects during the 1400s prefigured both the Protestant Reformation and the emergence of a secularized socialism.

The spirit of Joachim reappeared in Thomas Muntzer's version of the Protestant Reformation and his religious/conspiratorial League of the Elect. Influenced early on by Taborite doctrines, Muntzer foretold the arrival of Christ's millennium by force of arms. It would be the responsibility of a righteous army of the poor to bring about this millennium by defeating the parasitic clergy, licentious princes and unbelievers in general. A former follower of Martin Luther, Muntzer took sides against Luther and with the lower classes in the Great Peasant War of 1525, which Muntzer believed would usher in an egalitarian millennium according to the principles of his League: "a state of affairs in which all would be equal and each would receive according to his need" (Cohn 1961:259). Captured and beheaded the same year, Muntzer's legacy lived on in the Anabaptist movement and in the concept of "class war."

When Marx and Engels arrived on the scene there were still remnants of Christian socialism scattered across Europe, but the main tendencies of socialism were already undergoing various degrees of secularization and systematization in the emerging "materialist" systems of thinkers as diverse as Fourier, Owen, Babeuf, Proudhon, Saint-Simon, Blanqui, and Bakunin. This materialistic and secular trend in socialist thought existed quite independently of Marx and Engels, and corresponded to the new urban and industrial conditions of work for the emerging proletariat in Europe. These conditions of the proletariat, so poignantly captured by the *Communist Mani-*

festo, mandated and propelled this secular, materialist development in socialism: it was, ultimately, not Marx but *capitalism* that stripped halos from the saints and profaned all things holy.

Marx and Engels merely worked more diligently, longer, under more productive conditions and with a greater intellectual repertoire at their disposal than competing trends in socialism, and it is for that reason that most subsequent varieties call themselves "Marxist." But Marxism, like similar socialist doctrines of the period, represents an essentially secular adaptation of Christian socialism.

The major departure of Marxism (and similar varieties of socialism) with its Christian antecedents lay in its emphasis on theoretical atheism. As we have seen, Marx labored at great lengths to show modern socialism emerging in a straight line out of nominalism, empiricism, science and materialism (1977:149–155); he insisted that the intellectual dialectic leading to communism flowed: atheism-humanism-communism (1977:155). While he by no means invented this strategy in the production of knowledge, Marx so thoroughly refined the techniques of materialism in social science that they are still associated with his name. Either deliberately or unconsciously, he worked to obscure the Christian origins of socialism in order to claim it as a *new, revolutionary, contemporary* doctrine accompanying the birth of a new class under new historical conditions.

This insistence on theoretical atheism, reified and projected onto the origins of the socialist idea proper, led to some peculiar intellectual practices by both Marx and Engels. In the *Communist Manifesto,* it is clear that the authors are familiar with the European peasant wars and their socialist ideology, yet they insist that "these first movements . . . had necessarily a reactionary character" (1977: 243). Engels, in *The Peasant War in Germany,* realizes that the "religious wars of the sixteenth century involved primarily positive material class interests; those were class wars." But, having said this, Engels minimizes the role of religion as the binding class ideology; rather, he insists, "demands of the various classes were *hidden* behind a religious screen" (emphasis mine) (in Marx and Engels 1964:98)—when even a cursory reading of his own material would show that the class demands were actually *clarified* by a religious *lens.* In the same work, Engels recognizes and stresses that Muntzer's politics "approached communism," but also feels compelled to argue that his philosophy "approached atheism"—a deduction not at all apparent in Muntzer's words or actions.

While atheism marks the key philosophical break of Marxism with premodern socialism, a number of significant discourses carry over from Christianity into Marxism: the image of apocalyptic change brought about in a single historical moment; an implicit sanctification of the poor as agents of the millennium; much of the biblical language around oppression, exploitation, and usury. As Miranda (1982:1–2) has noted, even the image of communism itself retained by Marx ("From each according to his ability, to each according to his needs") was derived from a description of the early Church in the book of Acts. This self-consciously collectivist passage in the New Testament had long since passed into the political repertoire of both early Christian and later secular socialisms, and had so much entered into the spirit of the secular socialisms then current that Marx perhaps never knew that his own use of the phrase ultimately derived from New Testament sources.

Atheism aside, at least three major doctrinal principles mark the basic continuity between Marxism and the German millenarians: first, a tendency to organize human history into stages that point toward a realizable utopia. For Joachim of Fiore, these were the three world ages of Father, Son, and Holy Spirit; for Marx, they were primitive communism, class society, and classless society. A second continuity was and remains an anticlerical spirit, irreconcilably hostile to the established church. And it was Joachim of Fiore, not Marx, who originally posited the withering away of church and state in the egalitarian millennium. Third, the notion of "class war," the necessity of violence in bringing about the desired goal, and the belief in popular purification through sacrifice: all these have Christian origins and are preseved by Marxism.

MARXISM AS RELIGION

Marxism, despite its denial of God, nonetheless resembles both its millenarian antecedents and present-day liberation theology. All three may be classed, broadly speaking, as refinements and popular rationalizations of Christianity. Marxism likewise ultimately generates a "new religion": secular and atheist in form, perhaps, but very much a "religion" in a number of senses. It establishes a shared sense of the sacred and the profane, things to do and things not to do; it posits the presence of a *will* of sorts in history, resuscitating theology in its atheist form; and it encourages an exegetic method based on a limited number of primary texts.

This realization is in itself nothing new. It has become a standard refrain of scholarship—so common that any sophomore could produce the essential logic of the proposition—that Marxism is a religion. Cohn (1961) and Tucker (1972), for instance, both systematically establish this idea, Cohn working historically, and Tucker textually. This point made, the authors go further to establish the rational nature of their claim against religion: Marxism is religion; religion, especially of a messianic sort, is irrational and ultimately pathological; hence, Marxism is pathology. Having established this tautology, respectable scholarship need no longer concern itself with the *social science* component of Marxism.

But of course, Marxism is *as an intellectual praxis* foremost and primarily a *social science*. Its political principles may be drawn from religious sources, but its analytic principles are no more readily reduced to Judeo-Christianity than are those which flow from the Durkheimian or Freudian traditions. The concept "mode of production," "class" defined as one's relation to the means of production, the inevitability of class conflict springing from a contradiction between labor and capital over wages, the process of commodification: these all rightly belong to social science proper and, in themselves, express scant religious content.

There is, then, a highly productive *tension* in the work of Marx, and in Marxism more generally speaking. Springing from this tension, a curious dialectic has manifested itself in Marxism from the very beginning. A secularized version of Christian socialism, Marxism becomes a social science; the doctrine proceeds as a *mass ideology* to the extent that it reappropriates and becomes *religion*.

This tendency is first strongly evident when Engels, working after Marx's death, sought to inscribe the dialectic *in nature*. Previously a strategy for understanding social relations, historical materialism thus passed into its metaphysical form, dialectical materialism: a monistic theory in which nature and society both give up their secrets in the form of teutonic dialectics. Engels' intention could not be more transparent. Hence forward, nothing could escape the rule of that semi-theological *explanandum*, the dialectic—which, like God, rests *above* man and nature—and Marxism could retrace its journey backward: from social science to metaphysics to theology.

The Russian school quickly asserted this "theological" understanding of Marxism: in the place of a czarist Church-state, the workers' Party-state. Where Russian orthodoxy once governed, Russian orthodox Marxism reigns in its place. The entombing of Lenin's preserved body marks the spot where Marxism consolidated itself as a scientific religion in the Soviet Union, and, by the following logic, whereby an essentially "magical" conception of science fuses with Marxism to generate a *scientistic* religion.

> The Russian Church had claimed that it was a miracle that the saints' bodies endured and were incorruptible. But we have performed a feat unknown to modern science. . . . We worked four months and we used certain chemicals known to science. There is nothing miraculous about it. (Tumarkin 1983:196)

The chemist's statement appears to be a defense of science, but it is a science tinged with the claims and sensibilities of religion. And the intended meaning of the exhibition of Lenin's body is unmistakable. Connected to the principle of the resurrection, Russian Orthodox Christianity maintains that the bodies of saints are incorruptible. Appropriating the style of its Christian predecessor, Soviet Marxism asserts a similar principle with regard to the incorruptible science of Marxism-Leninism.

Most anthropologists would agree that the spirit of cultural relativism is a necessary prerequisite for anthropology. Clifford Geertz, however, sounds more like a Republican banker than an anthropologist when he describes the Indonesian Communist Party as "an aggressive, well-organized totalitarian party hostile to the very conception of democratic, multiparty politics" (1973:281). Clearly, such a biased description can only mystify any attempt at understanding the electoral successes of the party involved. And in much the same spirit as Cohn and Tucker, Geertz forgets his sense of cultural relativism while gazing upon the oddity that in the USSR, the labor theory of value is enshrined as official religion (1984:34–37). But of course, in a genuinely relativistic anthropology, it could be no more peculiar that Lenin should be enshrined than that saints should be similarly displayed, and surplus value would seem as sound a "religious" principle as the transmigration of souls—provided that it embodies at least a minimal social truth.

In Russian orthodoxy, in Mao's yin and yang dialectic, and in the cult of Che—as in dozens of countries with complex multiplicities of symbols—Marxism passes *back into religion*. Mingling with local belief and custom, Marxism passes through the terrain of native spirits and ghosts to produce a curious mixture of the rational with the irrational, a syncretism of the truly social scientific and the genuinely religious. This is the form taken by revolutionary regimes the world over, and, seen from this perspective, their variegated practices appear strikingly similar in a wide variety of contexts.

The attempts of critical Marxism to dislodge, first, the mechanical models of social democracy, and, later, the authoritarian models of communism, have typically shared elements of an approach that attempt to assert Marxism as a *social science*—humanistic, philosophical, even poetic, but a social science nonetheless. Critical Marxism invariably stresses a nontheological, antitheological, "unreceived" mode of inquiry, in the spirit of the early Marxist texts. It is profoundly, theoretically atheist. It asserts the philosophical over the scientific, and the social scientific over the religious. As a strategy, critical Marxism has yielded important discoveries and greatly expanded Marxism's theoretical capacities. But none of these attempts has ever been successfully appropriated as *mass ideology*. Perhaps because thinking is less powerful than believing, no proletariat moves to restore the dialectical unity of the subject-object (Lukács 1971), nor to attain a state of immanence-transcendence (Sartre 1976), nor even to assert the pleasure principle over the performance principle (Marcuse 1966).

On the other hand, the proletariat may be powerfully motivated by a sense of the sacred and the profane that exemplifies its class interests while solidarizing it as a class against elites. The poor invariably gravitate toward precisely those myths where Marxism touches upon their own received traditions—and even if the new doctrine denies the epiphenomenon of religious superstitions, it is most powerful when it rearticulates deep underlying religious structures. Emerging proletariats frequently accept as their own those forms of Marxism that are actually syncretisms of intellectual Marxism with native popular religion. In short, if the rationalizing trend was at work when Marx elaborated scientific socialism, a de-rationalizing trend is most often at work when the popular classes *receive* it.

It is not at all clear, moreover, that dialectical materialism, or a fundamentalist reading of labor value, or any of the other theological variants of Marxism, so distort social practice and governmental policy as to make belief untenable or really impractical. Surely, a common characteristic of socialist systems is the difficulty which any attempt at economic innovation encounters. For instance, realignments in Soviet production, whether of a social or purely technical nature, often meet enormous covert resistance in the form of foot-dragging, underproduction, and noncompliance. The base of such resistance is demonstrably popular, not bureaucratic, and this mandates that such innovations are invariably carried out with great shows of ideological incentive and doctrinal justification. These displays appear quite "wasteful" and inefficient to the managerial point of view.

Belief, then, insofar as it hampers purely instrumental reason, may indeed interfere with the application of cost-benefit analysis. Seen from this point of view, the "unreason" of the marketplace is far more *rational*, for it exerts a cruel, mechanical measure: incompetence, poor performance, or unprofitability are swiftly and severely punished. Reason in socialism is differently constituted. Darwinian principles in the marketplace do not systematically root out unprofitable economic concerns. Workers who are lax are protected by job tenure no less than those who are diligent, and this requires the constant mobilization of ideological incentives, for economic punishments are rarely targeted toward individual workers or enterprises.

Seen thus through the lens of a modern economism, socialism appears a less than efficient system: belief seems to misguide practice. But society is not a gloss on economic efficiency, and there are values that transcend cost-benefit values. Socialism pronounces the values of stablity, security, and equality. Moreover, every religion, while establishing strict rules, also entails rules for breaking rules, rules for evading rules, and careful methods of exegesis that can translate a rule into its opposite. Such are the vagaries of religion and ideology. These are all present in the repertoires of existing socialism, and evince themselves all along the way in its real development.

The point is that the reason constituted in socialist production, unlike that constituted in capitalist production, *need not* and *does not* extinguish that aspect of consciousness we call "religious belief." Indeed, socialism's need for religion manifests itself at two points in socialism's emergence: first, in the simple requirements of social solidarity that are implicit in the nature of proletarian political mobilization *in advance of* and *during* the revolution proper. This moment corresponds to the "millenarian phase" of popular mobilization. When Marxist ideology descends to the masses, it will always be tinged with messianism, and received as an essentially religious purpose.

But after the revolution and developing alongside the revolutionary consolidation is a second requirement for religion. The socialist economy—with its absence of completely rationalized production, its aversion to pure markets, and its concomitant need for ideological incentives—inevitably promotes a consolidated state religion of a sort quite unnecessary, if not counterproductive, to capitalism. Socialism from the beginning *requires* ideological commitment, ideological incentive, and a degree of social control unnecessary to capitalism, because, unlike capitalism, it does not mechanically rely on its markets to distribute goods, nor does it allow its markets to plan production, nor can it ultimately rely on market principles to discipline labor. Capitalism makes use of similar religious incentives — a Calvinist calling, the Protestant work ethic — only at its very beginning; once set in motion, capitalist accumulation proceeds apace, and eventually sheds its religious trappings altogether. The nature of socialist development is different. Essential to socialist production, religion is required by socialism as a permanent motivational system.

In a sense, then, capitalism subordinates man to reason, and reason to profitability, in a series of rationalizations. Socialism inverts this relationship: human need must appear superordinate to reason, and reason to rationalization. This essential structure of real socialism impedes rationalization as an all-destructive force, and it retains a space for "the irrational." And where progressive rationalization fails, religion steps in.

RELIGION AND ALIENATION: A REASSESSMENT

We have seen that (1) Marxism evolved from and out of religion, (2) Marxism, in the work of Marx, is predicated on the criticism of things religious, by way of an analysis that equates religious belief with false consciousness and alienation, and (3) Marxism as political practice evolves *back toward religion,* inevitably and quite apart from any conscious intention. How do we resolve these seemingly contradictory facts with the text of Marxism? How would Marx himself have treated the appearance of these antinomious developments in his own oeuvre?

I will propose a new gloss of the early Marxist texts, a rereading and reinterpretation of the texts on alienation and religion. This reassessment, I believe, is quite in the spirit of Marx's own investigation. Some purists may feel that I am "manhandling" the texts, manipulating them for an immediate purpose, but this in itself is quite in the spirit of Marxist criticism (see Eagleton 1981). Marxism must be kept relevant to the experiences of the popular classes or it becomes a purely academic and hence irrelevant theory. As Walter Benjamin put it, the mission of historical materialism is to "blast a hole through the continuum of history." Here, then, we blast a hole through both history and Marx's own texts. Keeping in mind the emergence of liberation theology and the experience of popular movements in Latin America, suppose we go back to the early material on alienation and religion, and attempt to illuminate the texts with Marx's later theory of praxis. What follows?

In the *Economic and Philosophic Manuscripts of 1844*, Marx divided his theory of alienation into four distinct yet interrelated aspects. The first two we have already seen: (1) estrangement of the worker from his products (the estrangement of things), and (2) estrangement of labor from the worker *in the process of production itself* of the *producing activity itself* (self-estrangement). From these first two, Marx goes on to deduce two more phases in the dialectical development of alienation: (3) estrangement from the species being, and (4) the estrangement of man from man. The estrangement of man from man is evident enough: the imposition of radically different interests estranges workers from owners, and moreover, intraclass competition alienates even workers from other workers and owners from other owners. But what Marx meant by "species being" requires some explanation.

> Man is a species being . . . because he treats himself as a *universal* and therefore free being.
>
> . . . The universality of man appears in practice precisely in the universality which makes all nature his *organic* body—both inasmuch as nature is (1) his direct means of life, and (2) the material, the object and the instrument of his life activity. . . . Man *lives* on nature—means that nature is his *body*, with which he must remain in continuous interchange if he is not to die. That man's physical and spiritual life is linked to nature means that nature is linked to itself, for man is part of nature.
>
> In estranging from man (1) nature, and (2) himself, his own active functions, his life activity, estranged labor estranges the *species* from man. It changes from him the *life of the species* into a means of individual life. (Marx 1964:112)

Universalistic, employing both a quasi-mystical idealism *and* a very crude naturalistic materialism: in these passages we see Marx at his very worst—though not necessarily at his least suggestive. Whence did Marx appropriate this strange hobgoblin, the "species being," and why does he assume humankind to be estranged from it under alienated production?

The term "species being" (*gattungswesen*) is drawn from Feuerbach, whom Marx had not yet definitively critiqued in 1844, and whose notions are still intertwined here with Marx's own. In Feuerbach, the notion of a "species being" is roughly continuous with the problem of "the essence of man." The essence of man, and what separates him from all the other animals, according to Feuerbach, is his capacity to conceptualize himself not only as an individual but also as a *species*, the human race. Thus, man is the only being capable of being simultaneously specific and generic, individual and collective: "consciousness in the strictest sense is present only in a being to whom his species, his essential nature, is an object of thought" (Feuerbach, cited by Struik in Marx 1964:241).

But note Marx's later critique of just this sort of Neoplatonic essentialism. Feuerbach resolves the religious essence into an abstract, universal "human essence," present in every individual, but, for Marx, the human essence is always *social*, defined by a specific configuration of social practices and is therefore always milieu-specific. All the more mature works of Marx flow from this quintessentially anthropological insight. The notion of a species being leads us directly back to a universalistic philosophy of human nature at best, or to a crude materialism that posits *biology* as the "matter" at hand, and likewise obliterates the possibility of real distinctions between societies and epochs.

We have argued earlier that had Marx reworked his conception of religion as a form of representational practice—which is how he clearly defines it in "Theses on Feuerbach"—he might have drawn radically different conclusions about religion's function in cross-cultural settings. In other words, the presence of religious belief in capitalist and precapitalist societies alike would suggest a rather different analogy for religious belief than alienation: it might be seen as rooted in the socializing function shared by all societies. Moreover, had Marx gone back and reworked his earlier writings on alienation in the light of his later development, he might well have reformulated his conception of "alienation from the species being."

In this peculiar concept, Marx is clearly grasping for a collectivist condition that can be opposed to the individuated and lonely existence of man under capitalism. Not only estranged from *man*, man is also estranged from *other men* and from collective humanity in general. But clearly "species being" is an abstraction of the alienated philosopher who has been reading science: there is no reason to fantasize that, once upon a time, humans conceived of themselves as a "species being" before they lost that sense of themselves to social stratification. Indeed, anthropology shows that primitive people always equate "being human" with membership in their own group and knowledge of their own customs, and that the notion of "humanity in the abstract" is quite a modern convention. No one is human in the abstract; one is always human in the !Kung, Navajo, Samoan, North American, or Nicaraguan way.

The state of collectivist consciousness that Marx calls "species being" and that predates the emergence of alienation, then, would have to be rethought in terms of the social solidarity of a given, milieu-specific group—and here we are on anthropologically sound grounds. Thus, the alienation of man from his "social group" (as opposed to his species) would also have to be recast—in terms suggestive of Durkheim's conception of anomie.

For Durkheim, the power of symbols rests on the social integration, the social order, they ultimately represent. Anomie signifies an "absence of regulation" in the social life (Durkheim 1951:258) and a concomitant "loss of meaning" in the spiritual life. The religious implications of this concept are evident in early definitions of the now-archaic English equivalent, "anomy," which signified "disregard for divine law," and, later, "lawlessness" (see Simpson's preface to Durkheim 1933:ix). In the later stages of anomie, meaning itself becomes progressively impoverished and culture is drained of meaning because the social integration on which meaning is based has been dissolved. Thus cut off from the vital sources of shared symbol, divorced from the closed forms of tradition, and estranged from the fixed rules of order and regulation that constitute social solidarity, the "individuated" man experiences *anomie*—or, we might say, "alienation from the social group": a form of disorientation and depression in which symbols lose meaning because the social rules on which they are based have dissolved. We could rephrase Marx's estrangement from the species being, then, as follows:

> Man is a *communal* being because he treats himself as a social and therefore free being.
> . . . The social nature of man appears in practice precisely in the communality which makes all his society his *social* body—both inasmuch as culture is (1) his direct means of life and meaning, and (2) the matter on which he effects his practice, the object and instrument of all his activity. Man *lives* on society—means that society is his *body*, with which he must remain in continuous interchange if he is not to die. That man's physical and spiritual life is linked to culture means that culture is linked to itself, for man is a part of culture.

In estranging from man (1) community, and (2) himself, his own active functions, his life activity, estranged labor thus estranges the *communal* from man. It changes from him the *life of the community* into a means of individual life.

This reworking of Marx's texts is not entirely speculative. Just such a form of analysis manifests itself in a series of notes Marx wrote on precapitalist social formations. Here, Marx stresses the prerationalized aspects of production in primitive and ancient societies and the concomitant stability and regularity of their cultures:

> Thus the ancient conception, in which man always appears (in however narrowly national, religious or political a definition) as the aim of production, seems very much more exalted than the modern world, in which production is the aim of man and wealth the aim of production. . . . In bourgeois political economy—and in the epoch of production to which it corresponds—this complete elaboration of what lies within man, appears as the total alienation, and the destruction of all fixed, one-sided purposes as the sacrifice of the end in itself to a wholly external compulsion. Hence in one way the childlike world of the ancients appears to be superior; and this is so, in so far as we seek for closed shape, form and established limitation. The ancients provide a narrow satisfaction, whereas the modern world leaves us unsatisfied, or, where it appears to be satisfied, is *vulgar* and *mean.* (1965:84–85)

Here we see Marx at his anthropologically most sophisticated—and indeed, the whole passage suggests a correspondence of his theory of alienation with Durkheim's later theory of anomie.

Deriving anomie from alienation is perhaps no great feat, but therein lies the real relevance of religion to alienation. Religious representation, as the "social cement" or "symbolic glue" that holds groups together, resists individuation and perpetually draws men back toward collectivity. As such, it *resists* the estrangement of man from man and from his collective existence, and lays the basis for both a radical resistance to capitalism *and* provides the image for the future collectivist society.

The terms under which Marx equated alienation with religion militate equally against the possibility of anthropology and socialism. Reducing *representation* to *illusion,* and *illusion* to *false consciousness* and *alienation,* is to render not just religion but culture itself an obstacle to human freedom and socialism—for all culture is ultimately representational. Or consider Marx's argument that mere externalization constitutes alienation: by projecting his own attributes onto God, man estranges his own real qualities (1965:107–108). This argument renders not just God but all symbolism and symbolic activity inherently (and equally) alienating, and to the extent that human societies are always symbolizing, all would be equally alienated.

We can immediately see the problem in Marx's reasoning by reproducing his parallelism between religious representation and labor estrangement in the work process:

> Just as in religion the spontaneous activity of the human imagination, of the human brain and the human heart, operates independently of the *individual*—that is, operates on him as an alien, divine or diabolical activity—so is the worker's activity not his own spontaneous activity. It belongs to another; it is the loss of the self. (1965:111; emphasis mine)

The crucial word here, and what leads Marx's analysis astray, is *individual*. Naturally, religious representation appears to operate independently of the individual and exerts a force upon him—as do all forms of collective representation, not excluding socialism. If we recast the whole formulation in terms of the social rather than the individual, however, we can see that the equation of religion with alienation makes no sense—least of all from the point of view of Marxism.

—And what a different approach to alienation this line of reasoning implies! First, it indicates a situational alienation *from* symbols, not universal alienation *by* symbols in the act of symbolizing. Second, this approach allows us to posit not atheism but religion as the working model for human liberation.

Cut off from real historical or anthropological reasoning, Marx thus relied on the peculiar philosophical fetish of a "species being" to present the case for a collectivist consciousness. At the same time, individualist biases were integrated into the theory of alienation at critical junctures, for it was only from the point of view of a reified individual that a critique of religious consciousness could be fused with the theory of alienation. Marx was unable to rectify these errors, even though an application of his later methods would seem to indicate the possibility of a revision. Faced with his own milieu, Marx's analysis was constrained from the outset to show that religion was a form of false consciousness and alienation.

We need not duplicate his error. The body of Christ symbolized for pre-Marxist socialism the corporatist and collectivist aspects of class mobilization, and pointed the way to a future *communitas* free of exploitation and alienation. It signifies the same thing in Latin America today.

CHAPTER SEVEN
Conclusion: Religion, Class Consciousness, and Revolution

The problem of popular religious traditionalism in revolutionary movements—its mobilization, its rationalization—constitutes a special problem in the study of culture and society. When old values are shaken (by capitalist development, by socialist revolution), what values take their place? Who are the carriers of the new values? How are these values really defined in real social groups? And are they really new?

The Nicaraguan popular classes evince a variety of relevant religious phenomena nowadays: the traditional popular religion remains intact, though diminished; it has been joined by liberation theology and, increasingly, evangelical Protestantism. We have traced the composition and logic of these religious and ideological movements in terms of a dialectic between popular traditionalism and popular rationality, and in terms of their specific "fit" with the sublogics of particular types of urban neighborhoods.

The Nicaraguan experience suggests a long overdue theoretical revision of Marxism's thesis on religion. In broad strokes, Nicaragua's popular religion embodies a submerged class consciousness; with its rituals of inversion and reversal, its practices of perpetual leveling, popular traditionalism already outlines the "logic of the poor," and it already imagines a world predicated on equality. These impulses are partially rationalized in the liberation theology of the base community and the Popular Church, where Nicaragua's popular classes read familiar themes of inversion and leveling into the Bible, and ultimately elaborate a self-conscious, systematic world view that is simultaneously an ideology and an analysis. Not even the "escapist" religion of evangelical Protestantism offers an insurmountable obstacle to revolutionary participation; indeed, its very asceticism suggests a popular rationality not at all inimical to the restraint and order of economic collectivism, and it, too, may be seen as a partial rationalization of the tradition. We have drawn out the implications of this Nicaraguan material: in our understanding of postrevolutionary society, and in a new Marxist thesis on religion. But this material shows that it is not only the Marxist theory of religion that stands in need of revision, but its conception of class consciousness as well.

WHAT IS CLASS CONSCIOUSNESS?

> *Not man or men but the struggling oppressed class itself is the depository of historical knowledge. In Marx it appears as the last enslaved class, as the avenger that completes the task of liberation in the name of the downtrodden.*
> *—Walter Benjamin 1968:260*

Many writers working in a Marxist tradition have sharply distinguished between class structure and class consciousness; they emphasize the distinction between categories and groups (see Berreman 1981b:17–19; Bendix and Lipset 1966:5–11; Weber 1966). Itself an analytic concept, a class is always a "category" in that it objectively exists, defined by a given relation to the means of production; a class may become a "group" only if it passes from its inactive state (as an object of history) to the active state of a self-conscious agent organized around a mission—which is to say, the subject of history.

As has often been noted, Marx wrote very little indeed that bears directly and systematically on the topic of class and class consciousness (Hobsbawm 1984:15); one could say instead (concuring with Lenin) that his entire opus is a commentary on social class. But where he did directly discuss the topic, as in crucial passages of *The German Ideology* (1939:48–49) and *The Poverty of Philosophy* (1963:172–75), Marx's own method in describing the ontology of social class and class consciousness is more complicated than a simple category/group dichotomy would suggest. Marx's method is both practical and dialectical. A class passes from an "in-itself" to a "for-itself" state in and through its conflicts, over time, with other classes. A class, then, is never an inert "thing," entirely outside or beneath self-consciousness. To the extent that a real class really exists, a broad range of historical and social experience serves to illuminate its existential dilemmas, its position in the social life, and hence, to willy-nilly produce class consciousness: the conflict of classes built into daily life at a thousand junctures; an ever-present awareness of one's (and one's children's) differential life-chances vis-à-vis the dominant classes; the implicit aggregation of classes into class communities, in continuous communication with each other, and hence already sharing, in Weber's (1966) term, a "style of life" (Marx 1939:48–49). These simultaneously economic and cultural processes speak to the totality of one's life-experience in a given class. Into class, then, are already built resentment, conflict, and awareness, and hence it must also be acknowledged that some reflexivity is built into the existence of class itself.

Two implications follow from Marx's historical conception of class. First, there is a continuity, not rupture, between class consciousness as embodied in formal Marxism and the popular consciousness already present in the populace. Indeed, what gives Marxism its status as something transcending mere sociology is that it represents itself as both discovering and embodying its own subject: Marxism is merely the refinement and systematization of the popular will to working-class power. And second, there is no presumption in the whole corpus of Marx's writings that a working class can ever be wholly and completely without a conception of itself, its dilemma, its relation to superior classes. That is to say, no class is ever only a category; it is also already a group, and, at least implicitly, a project.

Reworked by radical intellectuals, this perspective has vanished from any number of subsequent Marxisms. As E. P. Thompson has put it,

> There is today an ever-present temptation to suppose that class is a thing. . . . "It," the working class, is assumed to have a real existence, which can be defined almost mathematically—so many men who stand in a certain relation to the means of production. Once this is assumed it becomes possible to deduce the class-consciousness which "it" ought to have (but seldom does have) if "it" was properly aware of its own position and real interests. There is a cultural superstructure, through which this recognition dawns in inefficient ways. These cultural "lags" and distortions are a nuisance, so that it is easy to pass from this to some theory of substitution: the party, sect, or theorists, who disclose class-consciousness, not as it is, but as it ought to be. (1963:10)

Lukács (1971:51) develops the perspective critiqued by Thompson most systematically when he distinguishes the "actual" ("empirically given," "psychologically describable") consciousness of the proletariat from the "ascribed" ("rational," "appropriate") class consciousness it might have if it were properly aware of its position in the process of production. Given the possibility of describing a lesser or greater distance between actual and ascribed class consciousness, Lukács opts for a the latter: ascribed "class consciousness has no psychological reality" (1971:51, 75). Indeed, Lukács tends to see "actual" consciousness almost entirely as "a class-conditioned *unconsciousness*" (1971:52), both of which may be safely subsumed under the category, "false consciousness." (How this falseness is mass-produced alongside and within commodities is the subject that occupies the bulk of his treatment.)

This approach is complementary to Lenin's (1929), who distinguished between spontaneous or trade union consciousness and revolutionary class consciousness. The latter represents an analytic and theoretical perspective that cannot naturally develop within the masses; it must be brought to them "from without" by a revolutionary intellectual vanguard.

The same sort of problematic (actual or false versus ascribed class consciousness) is taken up by Gramsci's theory of hegemony. The concept of hegemony transcends the idea of force and that of ideology as instruments of class domination. In practice, it implies the presence of both, in a balance, plus the expiating presence of proper authority. Hegemony, then, implies a consensus of sorts between the dominated and the dominating: a consent imposed on the subaltern by the superaltern classes. More profound and consistent, then, than law, force, and ideology, it progressively approximates the conception of culture encountered in anthropology. As Raymond Williams has put it, at its most profound,

> Hegemony is then not only the articulate upper level of "ideology," nor are its forms of control only those ordinarily seen as "manipulation" or "indoctrination." It is a whole body of practices and expectations, over the whole of living: our senses and assignments of energy, our shaping perceptions of ourselves and our world. It is a lived system of meanings and values—constitutive and constituting—which as they are experienced as practices appear as reciprocally confirming. (1977:10)

Real, effective class consciousness, then, can only be achieved through the construction of a proletarian counter-hegemony.

Yet Gramsci is more generous on this point than either Lukács or Lenin; his approach to the subaltern classes vacillates between what he himself calls an optimism and a pessimism—that is, "an optimism of the will, a pessimism of the intellect" (1971:173–175). On the optimistic side, he affirms that between Marxism and "common sense" there lies a continuity, not a chasm (1971:326); he also recognizes that Marxism must fundamentally base itself in a conception of a popular will to power (346), as revealed in the spontaneous "flashes" of revolutionary philosophy (327) that evince themselves from time to time. But it is also true that Gramsci most frequently poses the issue of everyday consciousness in terms of its deficiencies: it is primarily "incoherent" (325–326), and generally seen as client territory, hegemonized by the directives of the superaltern classes. As a result, Gramsci's disposition toward folkloristic consciousness is almost always a negative one (Eagleton 1986:127). And thus Gramsci's peculiar and balanced rationalistic compromise: Marxism constitutes itself as a critique of common sense originally based in common sense (Gramsci 1971:330). Conceived as a battle to transform the "popular mentality" (348), the mission of Gramsci's Marxism is to imbue the popular classes with "mass coherency" (325).

Freire's (1970) radical pedagogy posits a similarly empty conception of the subaltern classes: the oppressed are submerged (36), silent (35), unreflexive (38), unable to produce signification of their own (47ff), indeed, owing to no fault of their own, they are not quite fully human (27–28), hence unable to act politically on their own behalf without the mediation of affluent radicals whom we might call their *teachers*. For Freire, then, popular culture is essentially a hegemonized "culture of silence." There is no question about restoring it to its full resonance and density, nor even of modulating its already-existing flow of ideas and language, but rather, of rupturing its silence. Lacking the dialectic, the popular masses also lack praxis. Consciousness is not so much false, or even incoherent; Freire really believes it to be *absent*. Despite its methodological pretensions of dialogy and reflexivity (in which the middle class Marxist must enjoin to make praxis *with* and not *for* the oppressed), Freire's pedagogy works over materials that are essentially characterized as inanimate and inert—indeed, it more suggests Moses striking the rock to produce water than it suggests the real give and take of dialogue. And the ultimate insult of all: that the oppressed must be 'taught' to give up their passivity.

Bourdieu's (1977) work takes this rationalistic approach to consciousness one step further. Although it is partly fashioned as a critique of Sartre, his theory of the habitus suggests Sartre's category, the practico-inert, or, practice in accretion: ossified, undialectical practice (Sartre 1976:67, 71, 318–20, 829). The concept of habitus also recalls that of hegemony; it is, roughly, "History turned into Nature" (Bourdieu 1977:78), "habits" trained into the flesh from an early age, and therefore envisioned as residing there (82–83, 87–88, 95). The habitus animates both representation and practice with a logic that is not so much "unconscious" (27–28) as *implicit*. In the end, Bourdieu poses an overdetermination so rigid as to nearly preclude the possibility of conscious reflection. Neither orthodox nor heterodox, the consciousness of the people is *doxic* (159–171): that is, implicit, perpetually below the level of reflection (and hence undebatable) because, inscribed in the body from an early age, it never requires codification as language—except in the form of popular sayings which are the very surface, visible manifestations of the doxa.

Were such predispositions to implicitness so powerful, one would have to ask: How, then, could Bourdieu's theory of the habitus account for its own existence? As was the case with the origins of an "ascribed" class consciousness which could not spontaneously generate itself in the people, the answer lies in the superior rationality of capitalism, and in the intellectual specialization it produces. Popular self-consciousness becomes possible only when capitalism clarifies the real situation of the people by eroding the doxa and exposing the naked self-interest of Homo economicus, which is to say, by disenchanting the world (Bourdieu 1977:176).

What all these currents of Marxism have in common is their systematic extinction of the genius of the people. The net effect of all of these approaches is to elaborate a rationalist paradigm for an "ascribed" class consciousness which is never (or almost never) the natural product of a people's experience, and an "actual" class consciousness that is always inert and in need of direction. And if, as Sartre once put it, "some men are more dialectical than others," then it is their duty to bring that capacity to the undialectical masses. It is in this sense that the bearers of reason—the intelligentsia, the specialist, the vanguard organization–not the proletariat, ultimately become the makers of events, the shapers of politics, and indeed, the subject of history.

We propose instead a method nearer to Marx's own, and more allied to Gramsci's optimism than to his pessimism—a method which might justifiably be called "Marxism-populism." For in the doxa of the people there already preexist the conditions for reflexive self-consciousness. Not silence at all, the consciousness of the people ever erupts in counterhegemonic flashes, in whisperings, in murmurings against the superaltern classes: in the *fiestas patronales*, and in Purísima; in commonplace sayings that perpetually express class envy, like "The rich get richer and the poor get poorer"; in a propensity to find and celebrate those biblical injunctions that condemn differentiating wealth and economic injustice.

This is not to say that the orientation of the people is already rationalistic (nor that it should be), but rather, that in the "irrational" and dialectical pyrotechnics of Santo Domingo there is already an indelibly inscribed class consciousness and a will to power. Nor does this method of Marxist populism contend that the class consciousness of the people is culturally enlightened, broad-minded, or tolerant (it rarely is), or even that there already exists in the people the ability to govern themselves. Our claims are more modest: only that the real conflict of classes (implicit in the composition of those classes) finds its way into the folklore, the doxa, the real culture of the people. Real conflict and real popular will express themselves in the "dialectical images" of folklore and popular culture. The dialectic, then, is not the private reserve of intellectual specialists; it is also the means whereby folk imagine and transform the world.

The issue of "false consciousness" has preoccupied Marxism for a long time, especially the critical Marxism issuing from Lukács' ingenious analysis of commodity fetishism. The work of Adorno, Horkheimer, and Marcuse is largely an elaboration of the problem of reification, mystification and false consciousness opened up by Lukács' *History and Class Consciousness*. At issue: whether it is possible to inculcate masses with 'true' consciousness—or, as Gramsci might put it, with mass coherency. But if Lukács' theory identifies scientific rationalism, objectivism, and empiricism with the commodification of reality that is the real basis for the mass production of false consciousness in advanced capitalist society, if his work shows how capitalism elaborates a new anomic culture, dislodged from tradition, which is basically a reflex on the commodity form, then we must also ask: What, then, is the implicit basis for class consciousness that this line of reasoning suggests? The rational? The measured? The scientific? Clearly, the opposite: the religious, the irrational, the unscientific, the traditional: all those indissoluble complexes which resist the fall of the wheel, the taylorism of the psyche, the drive of the marketplace.

Recent work in anthropology illustrates this very well. Nash's (1979b) ethnography of Bolivian tin miners shows how militant class consciousness is supported by the sense of shared community and tradition. Taussig (1980) untangles the rituals of sugar plantation workers in the Cauca Valley of Colombia and shows how their magical fetishes elaborate a systematic bulwark against the fetishism of commodities. In her study of a South African people, Comaroff (1985) demonstrates the refuge and the resistance constructed by the Tshidi in the Protestant Zionist sects. And Ong's (1987) study shows how the remnants of a traditional moral economy are mobilized by Malay women as a resistance to work discipline in the modern factory.

As we have seen, to be effective, concerted, directed, and to have a chance of winning—that is, to reach what Gramsci might call the "third stage of class consciousness" (Nash 1979b:321) wherein a class becomes roughly synonomous with its political organization (Hobsbawm 1984:20)—the magic of tradition requires at least a partial rationalization to make it consonant with large-scale political or military mobilization. But this partial rationalization implies not a razing of tradition at all, but rather, a variety of appropriate tactics along a range: streamlining, articulation, mobilization. (Many who imagine themselves to be razing the tradition are actually only reproducing it in the confines of a new organizational structure: the disrupted graveyard yields up its very real ghosts.) This poses a distinction, not between actual and ascribed, but between traditional class consciousness and organized class consciousness, with the former providing the material for and the core of the latter.

THE PAST IN THE PRESENT: THE TRADITION IN THE REVOLUTION

It isn't that the past casts its light on the present or the present casts its light on the past: rather, (the dialectical) image is that in which the past and the now flash into a constellation.
—*Walter Benjamin, "N"*

The image of the past, and of tradition, juts up in Nicaraguan consciousness much like the image of the Indian who puts in his appearance at Santo Domingo. Recall that the Indian is fantastically represented in the guise of a stock Hollywood movie Indian. He is also *negro*, and *negro* simultaneously signifies evil, the Devil, and the primitive or pure. Yet, in this case, the primitive black Indian Devil is exalted over the civilized white Spanish God.

In this single image appears a fragment of time in which are embedded other fragments of other times. The image is not faithful to the "reality" of Central American Indians "as they really were" (Benjamin 1968:255), but rather, it is faithful only to itself. And in itself it is awkward, garish, disjointed, and marvelous: it contains within itself a many-seamed and volatile mestizoism of images and times, capable of exploding in any and all directions—or of magically transubstantiating itself into an entirely different image. Seen as an ancient memory, the Indian is also seen from the point of view of a camera lens, a movie screen. Seen as "pure" and "natural," he is also seen as cunning and perhaps evil. And the magic of this image is contagious. Here, the black rubs off to become black youths, running about in mock delinquency. There, horns and color are appropriated, and the thing becomes a black Devil; or, just the horns, and it becomes a female cow.

It is not, then, that the past is a timeless or stable whole, but rather that it is a very dynamic representation of similarly volatile social relations. Likewise, the tradition it embodies and represents is not a static, passive essence, but a dynamic, volatile social practice. But let he who is tempted to imagine the infinite plasticity of such representations take note here. The strength upon which they draw is ambiguous: not so much from their *real* plasticity as from their *impugned* stability and timelessness. That is, people *believe*, at one level, that they are looking at the Central American Indian "the way it really was." They believe *costumbre* is an infinitely long tap root into the past.

Similarly, the strength of the notion of God rests, in part, on a paradox. Its practical historical strength rests on the endless manipulations to which it might be put, the nearly endless projects over whose name He might be invoked. But more significantly, that notion's strength rests on the presumption of a timeless and unchanging God as the moral center of an immoral universe. Like one of Benjamin's aphorisms, these notions—the past, God—contain a dynamic essence concealed within the hull of a very static appearance. The dialectic may be at work, ceaselessly dissolving and reconstituting matter, but it draws its power from self-negation and self-denial. It is in a similar spirit that historical materialism apprehends the lessons of theology: denial of its own activity, concealment of its hand in play, behind the veil of "History."

Previous instantiations of historical materialism have played at this effect implicitly and indirectly. They have declared their atheism to the world, while at the same time reconstituting the idea of God in historical materialism as *History*. Hand behind back, then, revolutions invariably posit a new religion on the ruins of the old one: presenting points of rupture on the surface, concealing points of continuity under the surface. The revolution develops much like a building constructed in a new style on the foundation of an old one. Continuities—the real strength of the edifice—are kept concealed, invisible, underground.

Liberation theology in Nicaragua makes this relationship explicit by *reversing* the approach of previous historical materialisms: it presents its points of continuity on the surface, only to conceal its ruptures within itself. It thus constitutes a marriage of historical materialism with theology which is carried out with *one* hand above the board.

It is in a similar fashion that the Bible—as a voice of tradition and the past, as the principle vehicle for theology—juts up into lower-class consciousness. Shot through with fragments of tradition, the consciousness of base community organizers, political activists, and even ordinary citizens, is likewise shot through with shards of biblical text. But the text has been exploded by the firestorm of capitalist development: fragmented, it has been reconstituted into a meaningful new whole that presents itself as ancient and timeless *because it seeks out those historical parallels which resonate with the present.* The time of the ancient Hebrews and the time of Christ become superimposed: on the time of the Conquest, the time of Sandino, and the immediate present. The poor of small nations stand against the wealthy and powerful of world empires. A series of superimpositions—that we would be disingenuous to deny—thus render the time of the now a richly layered "messianic time" (Benjamin 1968:263) in which suffering and resistance may take many voices, be seen in many lights, express many hopes. The Bible reenchants life, even as life reinvests the Bible with meaning. The mystery here is this: the Bible is both a timeless and a historical document, and the God that animates it both an unchanging essence and a volatile force whose self-disclosure to humanity proceeds through stages as a historical process. Those stages define the history of the poor.

The most invidious role of all is played by the hierarchy of the Church, which actively works to *reverse* the call of God to draw the poor closer to him. Like the Sagisees and Pharisees of yore, the religious bureaucrats posit themselves squarely between the God of the Poor and the people he would redeem, subverting the gospel and enriching themselves in the process. Ecclesiastical authority must be dissolved; it is dissolved. God's *voluntad* in history at the present moment, then, exerts itself in the dissolution of clerical and papal authority: God circumvents the clergy and speaks directly to the people, with the same sweeping historic motion that casts the rich down from their seats. Salvation unfolds for the masses by means of and by measure of their renunciation of clerical for praxical religion.

"When Somoza's guard came through this barrio, they came like all of Herod's army, looking to kill the male youths." "And they are still coming today." "Your country, *gringo*, is today's Roman Empire, and we are but the poor of Palestine, seeking salvation and liberation from the yoke." Or, a fragment from a sermon: "The Babylonians took the Hebrews away as slaves, the Roman guard put Christ to death, the National Guard killed Sandino, and our youths continue to die in the mountains, but we believe in the resurrection of Christ and of his believers. We believe in the judgment day, and in the reign of justice."

It would be an error to read these statements as simple rhetorical devices or empty metaphorical flourishes. No, they are the earnest prayers of a people under the conviction of the Bible, the incantations of a present under the spell of the past.

SOCIAL ORDER AND SOCIALISM

(The messianic idea restores) the ideal content of the past and at the same time delivers the basis for the vision of the future.
——Gershom Scholem, 1971:4

What is the real specter that haunts the bourgeoisie in the *Communist Manifesto*? The specter of *social order*. In a world where "all that is solid melts into air," and "all that is holy is profaned" (1948:12), in a world where radical upheaval and profound dislocation are indispensable instruments of capitalist development, only the image of stability can be truly revolutionary.

Any number of Marxists have *almost* realized the importance of this. Many more, in the mainstream of progressivism, have vigorously denied it. Sorel comes to the very verge of this conclusion in his critique of the myth of progress, and in his predication of traditional virtues (over reason) as the springboard for class consciousness, but then is unwilling to directly counterpose a myth of stability against the myth of progress as its antithesis. Benjamin, who resuscitates the messianic voice implicit in Marxism, perhaps comes closest to this realization when he shows how it is the utopian image of the Kingdom of God that lies beyond and behind the radicalness of the dialectical image.

Marshall Berman's interpretive book, *All That Is Solid Melts Into Air* (1982) exemplifies the problem. Berman almost realizes the import of this antimodernist impulse and its naturally "conservative" image of good, but then reverses the implications of his own reading of Marx by resuscitating an even *more* liberal, more modernist reading of Marx. Modernism becomes sealed off in itself—an impenetrable fact of the unfolding human spirit—and the proletariat, too, must sink or swim in this irresistable current of History. Those who stand opposed to this modernism pit themselves against progress, change, the individual, and liberation; worse yet, against intellectual freedom, artistic expression, and cultural innovation; and, moreover, against inevitability. So goes the all too familiar argument, at the core of Western Marxism, and the source of its lack of appeal as mass, popular ideology.

Our interpretation of comparative society is quite the contrary: wherever the fully modern proletariat has emerged, whenever that proletariat has absorbed and internalized constant flux and constant change, when it has come to accept a thousand miniature "revolutions" in marketing, production, and life-style, it can no longer be revolutionary because it can no longer aspire to a sense of itself distinct from the workings of the market—which appropriates to itself the role of sole arbiter of social good. Abhorring "the irrational," the modernized proletariat no longer retains the tools with which it might fashion a genuine class consciousness, or the material with which it might offer any resistance to the constant revolutionizing of production that typifies capitalism. The modern proletariat thus lives a commodified existence inimical to social revolution: a little work, a little consumption, and the cycle renews itself. Because there is no room for magic in this life, there can be no possibility of *radical transformation*, no vision of a transubstantiated social life. Along with the saints, their magical cures, and the possibility of God's intervention in the world, the possibility of revolution also recedes. Where the marketplace has driven its roots into the very soul through "modernism," there can be no values fully independent of market value.

Bertolt Brecht perhaps came the closest to realizing this very *con-*

servative reading of Marxism in a single aphorism (astutely cited by Eric Wolf (1969:275) to explain how it is precisely the most traditional segment of the peasantry that becomes the most revolutionary): "It is not communism that is radical, it is capitalism." Are we to take this simply to mean that communism is really radical too, but that capitalism initiated the process that leads to the development of communism? This is, essentially, the progressivist reading of Marx: that upheaval has become such a fact of human existence that the longing for stability is pathological. But we may also read in Brecht's statement something both simpler and more profound: that capitalism signifies disorder, chaos, uncertainty, and communism, a humane order. This latter is the only reading of his aphorism that makes any sense. We may also take Brecht's statement as a cogent summary of the *Communist Manifesto*, once shorn of equivocation.

Any Marxism that does not draw its poetics from messianic religion of one variety or another can neither be really revolutionary nor have genuine proletarian appeal. Messianic religion can act as a dynamic force in the social life only by positing two things: a timeless, stable past, disrupted by the sin of exploitation with its concomitant anomie, and a timeless, stable future, defined by the reign of justice and equality. Both Scholem and Benjamin were fully aware of this homology between the Edenic past and the Reign of God.

Thus, my interpretation and my use of Walter Benjamin are quite contrary to Taussig's (1987:441–442), who takes direct issue with the Turners' (1978) paradigm of ritual as a means of affectuating a state of conservative *communitas*—a model which he contends "may fit quite well with certain fantasies of malesness and fascism." (Taussig prefers to draw his own inspiration from the dubious likes of Artaud [442] and Conrad [215–116].) Bending the work of Walter Benjamin to a frankly anarchistic interpretation, Taussig sees the role of ritual, religion, and magic encountered along the Putumayo River of Colombia as providing essentially theatrical displays of the uncertainty and violence of the social life; that is, he finds in the popular dialectic a disorderly and disordering mysticism built up out of the real dislocations of history. For Taussig, in shamanism as in Marxism, it is not so much a matter of restoring order, then, as of "tripping up disorder in its own disorderliness" (390). While we both emphasize the religious aspect of class struggle and consciousness, my interpretation of the *content* of the religion, as I have encountered it in mestizo western Nicaragua, could not be more different than

Taussig's. The strength of the dialectical image expounded by Benjamin, the power of the montage developed in early Soviet aesthetics, lie not in their endless perpetuation of a state of disorder, but in how they point a way out. And the festivities for Santo Domingo, the ritual invocation of María in Purísima, the images of struggle and conflict in liberation theology: these all point past the anomie of the present and toward the Kingdom of God. Which is to say: the popular dialectic is more utopian than nihilistic, more saintly than diabolic.

"And God shall wipe away all tears." If we cannot posit a *timeless time* in the imagination, then we cannot be really radical, for this timeless time is nothing but a simple inversion of the deepest principles of capitalist production and marketing. A *timeless time* is a *normative* time: a touchstone; a promise; a past or future devoid of flux, upheaval, dislocation, and change. This reading of Marx emphasizes the restorative, restitutive, and redemptive powers of socialism as against the disruptive, disordering, and anomic effects of capitalism—and this is the image of socialism most in tune with the utopian dialectics of popular traditionalism. It is indeed a conservative image, one that lends itself to an anti-Epicurean philosophy. But unless we believe in norms of some sort, what can criticism express, other than a purely technocratic or reformist point of view? Or perhaps even an effectively libertarian point of view that falls in full stride with the flow of the capitalist current?

For Nicaraguans, the norms come ready made: they live in religion, and in the rule of tradition. They embody themselves in the leveling mechanisms of the traditional popular religion, and, later, in the popular rationalization of that religion in liberation theology. They already define class consciousness, the self-consciousness of the poor. It only remains to appropriate, streamline, and deploy these norms, these images.

The new society is implicitly shaped by such images, such norms: the language and reality of leveling; the image of stability under socialism; the necessity of martyrdom . . . It is in this spirit that the Giant Woman herself, dizzy from the historic leap but confident of her place in history, projects herself onto the new stage of ritual and public display, and puts in her regular appearance on anniversaries of the revolution: dancing with young men in the parade on the 19th of July, she reminds us of those linkages, those norms.

For others, these norms are hopelessly dissolved. From the messianic point of view, they are lost.

THE ALIENATED TRADITION:
OF POPULISTS, PROGRESSIVES, AND PREACHERS

Let the people take heart and hope everywhere, for the cross is
bending, the midnight is passing, and joy cometh with the morning.
— Eugene Debs in 1918 (Ginger 1949).

The anthropological method implies comparisons, even if they are
of a purely "negative" type, and point up differences in forms of
social life. How things are different is as compelling a study as how
they are the same. We have alluded to how Nicaragua's experience
compares with the histories of similarly situated Third World countries and revolutionary governments. But what do events in Nicaragua
have to say to us, as North Americans? Can the Sandinista revolution throw any light on our own domestic situation?

Comparisons of this type are difficult and fraught with danger. It
is good to recall the foolishness of a group of gringo radicals who
attempted to mechanically import liberation theology from Latin
America to the United States as a formula for successful organizing.
Our traditions are not the same as Theirs. Even our most 'traditional' and practico-magical religious practices are already defined
by the rationalization of a long Protestant history. And our revitalized traditions of class consciousness could only be generated out
of authentic, domestic sources.

We have not seen in the United States a combination of class consciousness, theologically received modes of knowledge, and a normative orientation toward the moral economy—which is to say, in
short, a revolutionary potential—for some time now, and it is necessary to account for its absence. The impulse to make society whole
and normative is weak, formless, and easily deployed along conservative paths to reactionary ends. In some sub-milieus, this impulse
ceases to exist altogether, and rationalized production takes over,
fusing consumerism with labor discipline, to produce a totally modern cage that is both iron-clad and libidinally tinged.

This was not always the case. The great effervescence of American
radicalism that called itself Populism[1] believed deeply in social order and social leveling. It combined a communitarian cultural conservatism with a radical redistributive economic agenda, both of
which must be called normative. It spoke a pietistic and semitheo-

logical language on the struggle between good and evil, the common people and elites. It developed a broad radical agenda and had a genuinely popular base. As our model would predict, its popular base was indeed precisely the most traditional, religious, and culturally conservative segment of the populace: the rural South and Midwest—where Populism crystallized not in spite of but *because of* these characteristics.

The relationship of Populism to religion was occasionally direct: the movement did produce its preachers, and its leaders sometimes made direct appeal to biblical justification. More typically, though, that relationship was indirect: a matter of syntax, vocabulary, style. Who could hear the fire and brimstone oratory of Tom Watson without resonating to religious themes? Who could listen to a speech by William Jennings Bryan without being struck by the language of Christian redemption? What farmers could congregate at the grange without offering a prayer or hymn to invoke God's blessing over their political meeting?

Outmaneuvered and outwitted by Wall Street politicians of both parties, the People's Party ceased to exist as an organized body. For a while its spirit animated the Socialist Party; Eugene Debs understood well what populism was about, although subsequent socialists have not. But in its demise, Populism came to represent whatever was good and just in the Democratic Party. And the spirit of Populism has remained a wellspring for social democratic policies and mass-based reformist politics in the United States ever since.

But the demise of truly radical populism as a viable current in American politics is best illustrated by one theatrical instant. A new sort of radicalism had been nascent for some time, different from and ultimately hostile to the sensibility that defines popular classes when they are about to explode. These two forces had once been intertwined, but had become increasingly differentiated since the Populist electoral debacle of 1896; they came head to head in 1925 in a courtroom in Dayton, Tennessee. What transpired has since been known as the "Scopes Monkey Trial," but we might call it a funeral of sorts.[2]

Now an old man, the great Populist leader William Jennings Bryan acted as people's prosecutor and argued eloquently for the abolition of evolutionism in the schools. Opposite him, Clarence Darrow defended the case for science and free inquiry. Bryan's last campaign was to defend and uphold the normative values implicit in the myth of creation, the mystery that clings to the heart of the myth of order. Darrow's most famous defense forcefully articulated a progressive social doctrine based on scientific humanism. Two opposing versions of social good divided these former allies in the courtroom, and their parting of ways has, in a fashion, divided us ever since.

Bryan won the case, but the cause was ultimately a lost one, and a wedge was permanently driven—or, rather, pointedly symbolized—between progressives and populists. Already weak and on the defensive, populism has never really recovered its footing. A more cosmopolitan country was rapidly growing up around the populist folk of the United States. A new, more pliable proletariat was taking shape, under new conditions.

Populism, and with it the truly revolutionary potential of the American popular classes, retreated into the enclaves of escapist religion. Bouts of prohibitionism alternated with sporadic outbreaks of economic radicalism and leveling/redistribution movements. But the image of order and stability, that utopian myth of the Kingdom of God, the rule of justice, have long since passed into the monopoly of Republican burgher preachers, of whom it may be said that neither their theology nor their social doctrine would be recognized by real populists.

REVOLUTION AND THE END OF HISTORY

> Only the Messiah himself consumates all history, in the sense that he alone redeems, completes, creates its relation to the Messianic. For this reason nothing historical can relate itself on its own account to anything Messianic. Therefore the Kingdom of God is not the telos of the historical dynamic; it cannot be set as a goal. From the standpoint of history it is not the goal, but the end.
> —Walter Benjamin 1978:312

The vision that guides all revolutionaries is an apocalyptic one: a vision of the "end of history" and the resuscitation of man in a timeless time. The beginnings of this vision lie buried in the utopian logic of the traditional popular religion: rituals of inversion and reversal allude to the possibility of a world turned upside down, and the ceaseless functionings of popular leveling mechanisms tie incipient class consciousness to communal norms in a fashion that suggests an ethical subreligion in development.

Revolutionary class consciousness excavates and redeems the subterranean treasures of the traditional popular religion; it takes the form of a partial rationalization of such impulses. The resultant "ethical religion" is still popular, to be sure, but it is a popular religion rationalized on a higher plane than the antecedent, traditional one. In Nicaragua, such ethical trends were originally distinguished into a secular version (*Sandinismo*) and a religious one (liberation theology). These distinctions are now being blurred in practice, although each has its theoretically separate role and place.

Of key importance in this process of redemption is the image of social order and its principle praxis—envy and leveling—for these span the gaps between the traditional popular religion, the millennial religion of the insurrectionary period, and the subsequent post-revolutionary religion. There is no firm locality on which we might fix this image of order, although the *andén* is its irreducible place: an *andén*, a section of *andenes*, a series of overlapping social circles and networks . . . the city, the nation, the world . . . The ideal is to create and maintain a state of equilibrium, and to bring all the parts as near to equality as possible. All parts should remain in their proximate places, all forces in a relative balance. That is the ideal. In practice, one may in fact try to advance oneself and one's own fortunes over one's neighbors, but one will vigorously try to prevent others from doing so—and those very neighbors, likewise, will be acting to maximize themselves while checking everyone else.

Of course, this equilibrium is impossible to maintain absolutely, though it may be achieved relatively. When disturbed in one space, other spaces and forces are mobilized to reassert order. Old alliances are temporarily suspended and new ones generated, as the situation warrants. A flow of surplus money or good fortune into one house, and other houses on the *andén* realign themselves into loose alliances: to siphon off that money, to gossip about the fortunate members of the community, to bring pressure to bear against one household, only to side with it against another as soon as the situation warrants. Real and fictive kin networks, formal and informal alliances: these constitute the balance of forces, which are mobilized across spaces to the end of keeping everything in relative proximity. This traditionalism is a very *dynamic* system of social order.

Tradition, envy, leveling—this ensemble of traits associated with the popular religion represents an irrationality that cuts against the rationality of the capitalist marketplace. Close inspection of events in Nicaragua allows us to formulate a picture of revolution and the proletariat distinct from Marx's predictions, with their reliance on a modern proletariat divorced from religion, and counter to all progressivist philosophy, which politicizes from the critical position of pure reason. What the fully modernized proletariat represents is a weak and ultimately alienated normative impulse, frequently divorced from any sort of class agenda or any sense of itself as a class. Under the reign of fully developed capitalism, the *normlessness* of the marketplace no longer incites envy, a desire to level one's superiors, a need to reclaim the tradition. Unable to mount a normative challenge to the flux and uncertainty of capitalist production, the modernized proletariat can only visualize itself at best as a partly hostile, partly integrated component in the production process. Trade unionism and social democratic reformism, then, are its *highest* forms of class consciousness, and it is quite frequently unable to attain even that level of self-organization.

Revolutionary class consciousness seems virtually impossible for a fully modernized proletariat reproduced in the womb of advanced capitalism. But it is possible in earlier stages of capitalist development, and in regions where advanced capitalism is structurally prevented from fully emerging. That is, revolutionary class consciousness is possible where modernity collides with tradition, and this collision is implicit in the nature of ongoing relations between the West and the Third World. This real revolutionary consciousness draws on rural or peasant traditions in such a manner that it invents a revolutionary proletariat out of vaguely articulated "popular classes," rationalizes its class outlook and agenda, and projects the image of a stable, conservative, *normative* society as its version of the good life. Antithetical to liberalism and progressivism, this class consciousness lies continuous with traditionalism and proximate to conservatism.

Marx was absolutely correct about the conflictive and unstable essence of capitalist production, but he located its "contradictions" in the wrong space and time: mature capitalism in the Western metropoles. Theoretical advances, in Lenin and in subsequent Marxism (Lenin 1939a; Baran 1962; Frank 1971) have somewhat rectified the situation, locating the revolutionary potential primarily in the *peripheries* of the world capitalist economy. But these revisions have largely left unanswered the questions about the cultural and ideological prerequisites for class consciousness and revolutionary mobilization.

I have drawn a somewhat different conclusion—complementary and not diametrically counterposed to Marxist world systems analysis, with its primarily economic emphasis. Why do revolutions occur in Third World countries and not in Western European and North American ones? What predisposes some to insurrection and others to reformism? The answer lies in the nature of *culture*. Where cap-

italism encounters a traditional culture, a traditional moral economy, explosive responses are inevitable. In a myriad complicated
ways, tradition provides the real springboard for revolutionary insurrection. And where capitalist development is complete, there is
no longer any tradition to tap, no revolutionary assault to mount.

Now clearly, the nature of the traditional moral economy of envy
and leveling is not identical to the rationalist calculation that Marx
calls the struggle between labor and capital over wages. In this latter
scenario, class consciousness itself expresses a rationalist tendency
in the proletariat: it knows its relative value on a capitalist labor
market. Traditional envy, on the contrary, is an altogether different
mode of production and distribution. It may well direct itself against
one's neighbors who, from the point of view of class analysis proper,
actually *share* one's own essential position in the class scheme, albeit in a slightly enriched fashion.

This envy, then, is prefigured in precapitalist milieus, where
"riches" (*riqueza*) refers to relative richness, not absolute social class.
Envy levels distinction precisely to the extent that it anticipates significant social distinctions *before* they actually emerge and gel; it
jealously guards against accumulation before it has a chance to reach
stratified proportions. But under conditions of capitalist development, inequality is perpetually giving rise to stratification proper.
The engines of capitalist exchange and development generate not
relative differences within a community of like persons but absolute
differences between *distinct communities* of rich and poor.

And it is here—in the interdigitation of capitalism with traditionalism—that the revolutionary class consciousness of the poor
springs up. Those who do enrich themselves have already estranged
themselves from the commuity. The community, as a body of opinion, nonetheless remains intact and reproduces itself in a hostile
world through its traditions—which are simultaneously cultural and
economic practices. In this sense, then, class strata also correspond
to degrees of traditionalism. And the poor throw up their traditions
as a line of defense against economic innovation, rationalism, and
exploitation.

Thus, the perpetually recurring situation of the poor in the colonized world. Capital cannot completely rationalize and develop
production in those milieus, no matter how long and pronounced
its intercourse with them, for to do so would eliminate the super-
profits that accompany transfers of wealth from periphery to core
(Rey 1982). Capitalism itself, then, paradoxically shores up the very
traditionalism that proves its undoing. The traditional social rela-

tions remain intact—or intact enough—and are reproduced at the heart of the community of the poor. Other, capitalist, relations of exchange infringe upon these, as a powerful irritant and solidarizing force. New objects, new commodities, are received, not in the spirit of capitalist consumption but in the spirit of traditional envy. Ultimately, traditional envy secretes itself into the fissures that lie between classes, and transmutes, by degrees, from community envy, to class envy, to class consciousness. And woe to the ruling class when the popular masses have laid their hands on messianic religion! Thus totalized at the level of capitalist society as a whole, and irrevocably hostile to capitalist production, traditional envy springs into revolutionary class consciousness, guided by a partly rationalized religion, and undertakes a leveling of social classes.

This is the present and future history of the Third World, and will be, as long as capitalism itself exists. And because tradition is ultimately an active *social relation* and not merely a "survival from the past," it will perpetually spring into being wherever capitalism has failed to become self-reproducing and as long as the poor have need of it.

Like Sandino's "army of free men," the example of Nicaragua is a heartening one for Third World revolutionaries, with an importance that extends far beyond its paltry three million inhabitants. In Nicaragua, *Sandinismo* and liberation theology broke a long-standing barrier erected around the cities of the world. If the war cry of revolution was once, "Peasants of the world, overwhelm the cities," this is no longer the case. Urban insurrection was essential in the Sandinista revolution. This fact belongs to culture as well as to economy. The rapid growth of the cities throughout Latin America has produced a phenomenon that is neither truly urban nor rural in the classical sense. Undergirded by their traditional values, disenfranchised peasants migrate to sprawling capital cities. There, this unformed class of urban peasants discovers that the traditional forms no longer work, but are structurally impeded from acquiring truly "modern" ones. The ensuing struggle over *values* impels the new urban dwellers to devise a systematic, rational, ethical religion, based on traditional values, and pointing the way to revolutionary change.

Were an analogous sensibility to somehow emerge once again in a Western proletariat, Western Marxists would be unable to recognize it as class consciousness, because, as a cosmopolitan politics, progressivist leftism confuses the traditional with the reactionary. Its ethos, then, works in concert with the whole apparatus of capitalist production to secure the continual razing of tradition. Ultimately, it degenerates into a politics of cultural radicalism—a perpetual rationalization of the cultural order.

But there are those who can still spring the lock on the cage of history. What lies for them beyond those confines may indeed be called a "non-history"—if we understand history from the outset as a *capitalist* strategy of development, if we understand history as the unfolding of an unfettered rationalism which ceaselessly innovates new productive relations and thereby progressively reorders the totality of human affairs according to the calculations of capitalist reason. The uncircumscribed reason in this "history" is the reason of the marketplace.

Of course, socialist society constitutes its own "reason"—which appears as un-reason from the vantage of market sense: capitalism encounters in socialism the "unreason" of regularities and impositions that suggest the bounded rules of traditional society. These more human environments of postrevolutionary society appear, by turns, idealistic, romantic, awkward, inefficient, and ultimately totalitarian, as seen from the point of view of the utter calculation of free markets in free motion—which is, in turn, exactly what folk the world over experience as the iron cage of capitalist development.

Notes

PROLOGUE

1. After Walter Benjamin's "Theses on the Philosophy of History" (1968:253–264), which excavates the messianic impulse implicit in Marxism. Using similar techniques, I am attempting to throw light on the intertextuality of Marxism, liberation theology, and native experience in Nicaragua. Any clearly first-person phrases or uncited material that appears in quotation marks represents a quote or paraphrase from my informants.

2. Father Antonio de Valdivieso was the first victim of political assassination in Central America, killed by a Spanish soldier in 1550 for defending the rights of Indians in Nicaragua.

3. Scofield informs us that Maktesh refers to the marketplace; literally, "the mortar, a depression in Jerusalem where the bazaars were."

4. See Buck-Morss 1981, especially pp. 58–60; Jameson 1971:60–83; Lowy 1985; and Rabinbach 1985.

INTRODUCTION

1. For examples of this sort of interpretive anthropology, see Geertz (1973) and Rabinow (1977) as well as anthologies compiled by Clifford and Marcus (1986), Ruby (1982), and Rabinow and Haan (1983).

2. Recent interest in the region has promoted the publication of a number of excellent historical and political science books on Nicaragua and Central America: Booth 1985; Burbach and Flynn 1984; Collins, Lappé, Allen, and Rice 1986; Crawley 1984; Dixon and Jonas 1984; Dixon 1985; Harris and Vilas 1985; SCAAN 1983; T. W. Walker 1982; and H. Weber 1981. William Walker's memoirs have also been republished (1985), and the speeches and writings of some FSLN members have become available in English: Borge et al. 1982; Cabezas 1985; and Sandinista Leaders 1985.

3. *Ustedes*, plural, meaning "you North Americans in general."

4. Various attempts at "doing" radical anthropology have revolved around the rather peculiar proposition that anthropology in particular (and social science in general) *can* and *should* play an active, consulting or advisoral role in the radical political transformations of wealth and power going on in the world today (Gough 1968; Huizer and Mannheim, eds. 1979). That an *outside observer*, even a well-intentioned and astute one, has a point of view superior to *inside experience* in the analysis of social problems and the invention of political strategies—this notion rightly deserves our skepticism.

5. I should clarify here: for most, education consists not in a university ed-ucation but in completing high school (*secundaria*), and perhaps receiving special training of a secretarial, mechanical, or electrical sort.

6. See Eric Wolf's *Peasant Wars of the Twentieth Century* (1969) and Sulamith H. Potter and Jack M. Potter's forthcoming *China's Peasants: The Anthropology of a Revolution* (1988).

7. Presumably "short" in two senses: first, in the sense of the impending disaster associated with the World War era, and second, in the sense that its subject matter, primitives, was vanishing.

8. See Barkun 1974; Bruneau 1982; Burridge 1969; Thrupp 1962; Wallace 1956, 1966, 1969, 1970; Wallis 1943; and Worsley 1968.

1. THE RELIGION OF TRADITION: THE POPULAR RELIGION

1. I have used the strong term "schism" here and similar terms throughout. The liberation theology movement clearly has its own organizational structure, formally and informally constituted, both inside and outside of the official church: its own organizational network, officials, organizers, lay activists, newspapers, journals, etc. I should note, however, that at the time of my fieldwork, the Popular Church officially did not represent itself as a split from the Conservative Church. The official position, as stated to Western and North American visitors by var-ious officials, was that the liberation theology movement constitutes itself as a part of the established Church, based on its interpretation of the gospel, and aims to preserve that authentic and original message of Christianity within the es-tablished Catholic Church. This is not at all the version of the movement I re-ceived from base community activists and common people less concerned about ameliorating tense relations with the United States, the West, and the Vatican. Ordinary people speak quite openly in terms of a "schism," and refer to the "Popular Church" as a "parallel church." Following the lead of my informants, I will use the stronger terminology.

2. Apparent debate in Nicaragua is frequently carried out over whether one should draw political lessons from religion; the real debate is actually over *what* lessons one should draw from religion, for quietism or inaction, too, is a form of political practice.

3. Latin American elites are more or less self-conscious and explicit about this. A saying found in affluent families and oligarchies throughout the continent underscores the point: "For a rich family, it is best to have three sons: one to send into the military; another to send into government; the last to send into the Church."

4. See Casas 1972; Hanke 1949; Pendle 1967; and Wagner and Parish 1967.

5. While not the same thing, the *cochón* is the Nicaraguan folk equivalent of the North American homosexual. For a fuller discussion, see Lancaster 1988.

6. Referring to such festivals of "institutionalized disorder," Needham as-serts that "the theme of reversal is itself one of the most pervasive and funda-mental problems in social anthropology" (Introduction to Durkheim and Mauss, *Primitive Classification*, 1963:xxxix). Needham effectively prescribes a function-alist strategy in analyzing these symbolic reversals and inversions of the estab-lished order (xxxvii–xl). See also Gluckman, 1963 and 1965:109, 130; Babcock, ed. 1978: especially 13–36; and Brandes 1980:17–36, especially 30, 32, 34–36.

7. To name only a few: Acheson 1972, 1974; Bennett 1966; Cancian 1972; DeWalt 1975; Gregory 1975; Huizer 1970; Kaplan and Saler 1966; Piker 1966.

8. See Beals 1962:64; Campbell 1963:75; De Gregori and Pi-Sunyer 1969:36–37; Ingham 1970:78; Potter 1974:230; Taussig 1978:393–412.

9. Such mechanisms, which liquidate wealth by turning it into prestige by the logic of gift-exchange (Mauss 1954), have been observed in every type of pre-capitalist social formation, from foraging (Woodburn 1982) and rank societies (Sahlins 1968) to peasant societies (Wolf 1955, 1959:216; Carrasco 1961; see also Brandes 1981). One might gloss this whole range of practices "primitive traditionalism" (Weber 1927:355; Taussig 1980:19).

10. *Pinche* acquires a variety of meanings in various Latin American countries. It usually indicates deviance from socially expected behavior. In Nicaragua, it is consistently used to denote stinginess. *No sea pinche* should translate "Don't be stingy."

2. THE RELIGION OF HOPE: THE POPULAR CHURCH

1. A large body of literature on liberation theology in Latin America has accumulated in recent years. See Berryman 1984; Betto 1985; L. and C. Boff 1984; Brockman 1982; Cabal 1978; Cabestrero 1981, 1985, 1986; Cardenal 1982; Carney 1985; Gibellini 1979; Gutierrez 1973; 1983; Lernoux 1980; Miguez 1984; Miranda 1974, 1980, 1982; Randall 1983; Romero 1985; Segundo 1976; and Sobrino 1978.

2. See "'We are Fighting for a Socialist Future': FSLN Opens Mass Discussion on Goals of the Revolution," *Intercontinental Press* (May 10, 1982), 20(17):388–389; also "Role of Workers in Nicaraguan Revolution: May Day Speech by Commander Tomás Borge," *Intercontinental Press* (May 31, 1982), 20(20):471–479.

3. One of my Sandinista Youth informants, a 13-year-old student and activist in the old Proletarian Tendency of the FSLN at the time of the insurrection, is quite clear about this:

> We worked through the church, we worked with the priests, originally because the church was the only institution in Nicaraguan society that Somoza didn't dare attack. That was before we knew what the revolutionary church was.
> Many priests sympathized with the people and with the movement without being wholly revolutionary, and these provided a measure of safety for our activists and sympathizers. Some have now crossed back over to the side of the reactionary hierarchy—what they wanted all along was capitalism without Somoza, a new government but one without popular power. Other clerics were radicalized by these experiences and have become good revolutionaries. An altogether different group was involved in the base community work early on and was involved in unfolding a proletarian interpretation of Christianity. These were revolutionaries from the beginning, and will be until the end.

4. *Amanacer: Reflexión Christiana en la Nueva Nicaragua* (The Awakening: Christian Reflexion in the New Nicaragua) is the journal of popular liberation theology published by the Antonio Vandivieso Ecumenical Center.

5. These waves of religious ferment met with repression from the Somoza

regime almost from the very beginning. If the *established* churches had been honored as safehouses for political and even revolutionary activity, the Somoza regime was less cautious in its response to the base community movement. For example, one project, "Messengers of the Word," fanned out lay workers into rural Nicaragua in the early 1970s, simultaneously to proselytize the peasants with liberation theology and to organize opposition to the Somoza regime in the countryside. Dozens of these religious lay workers were assassinated by Somoza's national guard. See FSLN Directorate, 1982 (1979):106, 106n.

6. Testimony in the sense of a religious testimony: a profession of one's faith.

7. See Walzer 1985:4.

8. Meaning, to participate in the guerrilla war of the FSLN.

9. See Judges 4–5.

10. And this much is clear: that the present-day religious hierarchy has inherited the legacy of the ancient hierarchy that originally subverted the message of Christ. (Moreover, that earlier hierarchy may likewise be traced to the Jewish priests who both subverted Judaism and resisted the message of Christ in first century Palestine.) Indeed, it is the modification and subversion of authentic (revolutionary) Christianity (or the word of God) that *defines* the hierarchy as such.

11. The *Comités de Defensa Sandinista* (Sandinista Defense Committees) are block committees charged with neighborhood defense and revolutionary vigilance. They are often described in the North American press as neighborhood political surveillance organizations; in standard practice, their community vigilance more typically lends itself to crime prevention, neighborly assistance, street cleaning, and helping drunks home at night.

12. The corruption of the Somoza regime is legendary. Of the $100 million in U.S. foreign aid sent to rebuid Managua after the 1972 earthquake, it is said that $90 million was deposited directly into Somoza's bank account. And at the time of the revolution the Somoza family and its close associates held title to nearly 25 percent of Nicaragua's agricultural land (see Collins et al. 1986:9, 15).

13. Accurate census data on Nicaragua are difficult to obtain. These figures are based on a compilation of existing demographic sources and their plausible projection into the future. Any error in these methods is actually likely to underemphasize the rate of urbanization. The following sources were consulted in my estimates: Richard N. Adams, *Cultural Surveys of Panama-Nicaragua-Guatemala-El Salvador-Honduras* (World Health Organization, 1957); Oficina Ejecutiva de Encuestas y Censos, *Población de Nicaragua, Años 1971–1980* (Republica de Nicaragua, 1977); Richard W. Wilkie, *Latin American Population and Urbanization Analysis: Maps and Statistics, 1950–1982* (Los Angeles: UCLA Latin American Center Publications, 1984); and the *Demographic Yearbook/Annuaire Demographique* (New York: United Nations, 1984).

By employing a narrower definition of what constitutes an urban area (my figures include many small towns), somewhat lower urbanized figures may be derived (although the rate of urbanization remains striking): using 14 urbanized areas, Rudolph (1982:78–80) estimates that in 1960, 71 percent of Nicaragua's population was still rural, but that by the year 2000, 52 percent will be urban.

14. "You are," here and throughout the chorus, is sung neither in the formal *"Usted es"* or the informal *"Tú eres"* forms, but rather in the colloquial informal *Vos sos* form. This *vos* form is used here to indicate friendly informality.

15. The lyrics to all the songs in *Misa Campesina* were written by Carlos Mejía Godoy (1981). The English translations are my own.

3. LIBERATION THEOLOGY AND THE SPIRIT OF SOCIALISM IN NICARAGUA

1. See *U.S. Congressional Record* (Wednesday, April 24, 1985), 131(49):H2472– H2474. Of course, these *ad hominations* are dangerous, not only because they represent bad anthropology or faulty intellectual practice, but because they are formulated in centers of power to justify unjust policy.

2. Bloch and Parry find this general theme of death as a regeneration of life to be widespread across cultures and at least sometimes rooted in the "conservative" vision of life as a "limited good." "Such conceptions imply that death is a source of life. Every death makes available a new potentiality for life, and one creature's loss is another's gain" (1982:8).

3. A very short list includes: Giddens 1976; Green 1973; Marshall 1980, 1982; Poggi 1983; Robertson 1973; Walzer 1965.

4. Thus, citing Marx as his antecedent, Gramsci (1971:377) states that ideology acquires a "material force" in history when it solidly integrates itself into popular beliefs.

4. THE THEOLOGY OF CREATIVE DESPAIR: EVANGELICAL PROTESTANTISM

1. See *Nuevo Diario*, viernes, October 4, 1985: "Daniel Reunido con Religiosas."

2. My method is admittedly informal. This figure was arrived at in close consultation with several key informants (some Catholic, others Protestant) in those barrios. After sampling the religious affiliations of some two dozen households, and also discussing with these households the affiliations of their immediate neighbors, we concluded that 15 percent was an accurate projection.

3. These figures were arrived at through a survey of 30 households, 22 in Sergio Altamirano, and 8 in neighboring Catalonia. The interviews and interpretive material in this chapter are based on extensive work with key informants in 5 households, 4 in Sergio Altamirano, and 1 in Catalonia.

4. This was in December 1985. In June 1986, he was working as a night guard in one of Managua's factories.

5. *Jodiendo*, or screwing.

6. Long (1968:200–236) offers such a view of conversion in Zambia. Roberts (1967) is closer to our paradigm: he documents the appeal of evangelical Protestantism in the marginated neighborhoods of Guatemala City. But whereas Roberts finds evangelical other-worldliness an obstacle to rational political civic activity, I would amend: it may or may not constitute an obstacle, depending on other circumstances. The evangelical "new man" has become indispensible for maintaining order in Managua's *repartos*, and the evangelical churches are being increasingly integrated into the political and civic aspects of the revolutionary process.

7. See Walzer 1965:12–13, 301–302.

5. PRIESTS, SAINTS, MARTYRS, AND GUERRILLEROS: OBSERVATIONS ON THE STRUCTURE OF AUTHORITY IN SANDINISTA NICARAGUA

1. "In contrast to the purely economically determined 'class situation' we wish to define as 'status situation' every typical component of the life fate of men that is determined by a specific, positive or negative, social estimation of *honor*. . . For all practical purposes, stratification by status goes hand in hand with a monopolization of ideal and material goods and opportunities, in a manner we have come to know as typical. . . . 'Status groups' are stratified according to the principles of their *consumption* of goods as represented by special 'styles of life'" (Max Weber 1966:53).

Short of arguing the obvious, that the Sandinistas constitute a "Party" and a power bloc in Weber's "Class, Status and Party" triad, I would argue that they also constitute a "status group," and that emergent hierarchies in postrevolutionary societies constitute status and power, not class, strata.

6. MARXISM AND RELIGION: A CRITIQUE

1. For instance, in one place Marx chides his (Lasallian) opponents for not getting beyond "bourgeois pluralism" on the issue of religion; in another, Engels warns against Blanquist and Bakuninist extremes in the promulgation of atheism (see Marx and Engels 1964:144, 142–143, and also 149). Ambiguity and contradiction in Marxist texts, like ambiguity and contradiction in the Bible, render compilations of texts susceptible to a broad range of interpretations.

2. My reading of Marx and the force given materialism in my argument as a matter of *praxis* is much influenced by the praxis theorists (Markovic 1974; Markovic and Petrovic, eds. 1979; Petrovic 1967) who emanate from Lukács (1971), and by Sartre's interpretation of Marxism in *Critique of Dialectical Reason* (1976).

7. CONCLUSION: RELIGION, CLASS CONSCIOUSNESS, AND REVOLUTION

1. See Woodward (1978) and Goodwyn (1978).

2. Ginger (1958) gives a detailed account of this confrontation, but his telling is deeply colored by strong sympathies with Darrow. Unfortunately, his liberal-progressivist approach produces little valuable insight into Bryan and his supporters. Pretending to delve into the psychological origins of what is seen as Bryan's (and his followers') authoritarianism, Ginger's overall polemical strategy is to pathologize Southern and Midwestern populism as a form of mental illness.

References

Acheson, James M. 1972. "Limited Good or Limited Goods? Response to Economic Opportunity in a Tarascan Pueblo." *American Anthropologist* 74:1152–1169.

Alberle, David F. 1962. "A Note on Relative Deprivation Theory as Applied to Millenarian and Other Cult Movements." Sylvia Thrupp, ed., *Comparative Studies of Society and History*, Supplement II: *Millennial Dreams in Action*, pp. 209–214. The Hague: Mouton.

Althusser, Louis. 1977. *For Marx*. London: NLB.

Aptheker, Herbert. 1966. *Marxism and Christianity*. New York: Humanities Press.

Babcock, Barbara A., ed. 1978. *The Reversible World: Symbolic Inversion in Art and Society*. Ithaca, N.Y.: Cornell University Press.

Bakhtin, Mikhail. 1984. *Rabelais and His World*. Translated by Helene Iswolsky. Bloomington: Indiana University Press.

Banfield, Edward C. 1958. *The Moral Basis of a Backward Society*. New York: Free Press.

Baran, Paul. 1957 (1962). *The Political Economy of Growth*. New York: Monthly Review Press.

Barkun, Michael. 1974. *Disaster and the Millennium*. New Haven: Yale University Press.

Beals, Alan R. 1962. *Golalpur: A South Indian Village*. New York: Holt, Rinehart and Winston.

Bendix, Reinhard. 1962. *Max Weber: An Intellectual Portrait*. New York: Doubleday Anchor Books.

Bendix, Reinhard and Seymour Martin Lipset. 1966. *Class, Status, and Power: Social Stratification in Comparative Perspective*. New York: Free Press.

Benjamin, Walter. 1968. *Illuminations*. Edited with introduction by Hannah Arendt. New York: Schocken Books.

——1968. "Theses on the Philosophy of History." In *Illuminations*, pp. 253–264. New York: Schocken Books.

——1977. *The Origins of the German Tragic Drama*. London: Verso-New Left Books.

——1978. *Reflections: Essays, Aphorisms, Autobiographical Writings*. Edited with an introduction by Peter Demetz. New York: Schocken Books.

——1979. *One-Way Street, and Other Writings*. London: Verso-New Left Books.

———1983. "N [Theoretics of Knowledge: Theory of Progress]." *The Philosophical Forum*, 15(1–2):1–40.

Bennet, John W. 1966. "Further Remarks on Foster's 'Image of Limited Good.'" *American Anthropologist* 68:206–210.

Berman, Marshall. 1982. *All That Is Solid Melts Into Air*. New York: Simon and Schuster.

Berreman, Gerald D. 1968. "Is Anthropology Alive? Social Responsibility in Social Anthropology." *Current Anthropology* 9(5):391–396.

———1981a. *The Politics of Truth: Essays in Critical Anthropology*. New Delhi: South Asian Publishers PVT LTD.

Berreman, Gerald D., ed. 1981b. *Social Inequality: Comparative and Developmental Approaches*. New York: Academic Press.

Berryman, Phillip. 1984. *The Religious Roots of Rebellion: Christians in the Central American Revolutions*. Maryknoll, N.Y.: Orbis Books.

———1987. *Liberation Theology: The Essential Facts About the Revolutionary Movement in Latin America and Beyond*. New York: Pantheon Books.

Betto, Frei (y Fidel Castro). 1985. *Fidel y la Religión: Conversaciones con Frei Betto*. Havana: Oficina de Publicaciones del Consejo de Estado.

Bloch, Maurice and Jonathan Parry, eds. 1982. *Death and the Regeneration of Life*. Cambridge: Cambridge University Press.

Boff, Leonardo and Clodovis Boff. 1984. *Salvation and Liberation: In Search of a Balance Between Faith and Politics*. Maryknoll, N.Y.: Orbis Books.

Booth, John A. 1985. *The End and the Beginning: The Nicaraguan Revolution*. Boulder: Westview Press.

Borge, Tomás. n.d. *La Revolución Combate Contra la Teología de la Muerte: Discursos "Cristianos" de un Comandante Sandinista*. Managua: no publisher given.

Borge, Tomás, Carlos Fonseca, Daniel Ortega, et al. 1982. *Sandinistas Speak: Speeches, Writings and Interviews with the Leaders of Nicaragua's Revolution*. New York: Pathfinder Press.

Bourdieu, Pierre. 1977. *Outline of a Theory of Practice*. Translated by Richard Nice. Cambridge: Cambridge University Press.

Brandes, Stanley. 1980. *Metaphors of Masculinity: Sex and Status in Andalusian Folklore*. Philadelphia: University of Pennsylvania Prss.

———1981. "Cargo Versus Cost Sharing in Mesoamerican Fiestas, with Special Reference to Tzintzuntzan." *Journal of Anthropological Research*. 37(3):209–225.

Brenner, Anita. 1929. *Idols Behind Altars*. New York: Harcourt, Brace.

Brockman, James R. 1982. *The World Remains: A Life of Oscar Romero*. Maryknoll, N.Y.: Orbis.

Bruneau, Thomas C. 1982. *The Church in Brazil: The Politics of Religion*. Austin: University of Texas Press.

Buck-Morss, Susan. 1981. "Walter Benjamin—Revolutionary Writer (I). *New Left Review* 128:50–75.

Burbach, Roger and Patricia Flynn. 1984. *The Politics of Intervention: The United States in Central America*. New York: Monthly Review Press.

Burridge, Kenelm. 1969. *New Heaven, New Earth: A Study of Millenarian Activities*. New York: Schocken Books.

Cabal, Latorre. 1978. *The Revolution of the Latin American Church*. Norman: University of Oklahoma Press.

Cabestrero, Teofilo. 1981. *Mystic of Liberation: A Portrait of Pedro Casaldáliga*. Prefatory poem by Ernesto Cardenal. Maryknoll, N.Y.: Orbis Books.

——1985. *Blood of the Innocent: Victims of the Contras' War in Nicaragua*. Maryknoll, N.Y.: Orbis Books.

——1986. *Revolutions for the Gospel: Testimonies of Fifteen Christians in the Nicaraguan Government*. Maryknoll, N.Y.: Orbis Books.

Cabezas, Omar. 1985. *Fire from the Mountain: The Making of a Sandinista*. Foreword by Carlos Fuentes, afterword by Walter LaFeber. New York: New American Library, Plume Books.

Campbell, J. K. 1963. "The Kindred in a Greek Mountain Community." In Julian Pitt-Rivers, ed., *Mediterranean Countrymen: Essays in the Social Anthropology of the Mediterranean*. pp. 73–96. Paris: Mouton.

Cancian, Frank. 1972. *Change and Uncertainty in a Peasant Society: The Maya Corn Farmers of Zinacantan*. Stanford: Stanford University Press.

Cardenal, Ernesto. 1982 (1975). *The Gospel in Solentiname*. Vols. 1–4. Maryknoll, N.Y.: Orbis Books.

Carney, Padre J. Guadalupe. 1985. *To Be A Revolutionary: An Autobiography*. San Francisco: Harper and Row.

Carrasco, Philip. 1961. "The Civil-Religious Hierarchy in Mesoamerican Communities: Pre-Spanish Background and Colonial Development." *American Anthropologist* 63:483–497.

de las Casas, Bartolomé. 1972 (1656). *The Tears of the Indians*. New York: Oriole Chapbooks.

Cleary, Edward L. 1985. *Crisis and Change: The Church in Latin America Today*. Maryknoll, N.Y.: Orbis Books.

Clifford, James and George E. Marcus. 1986. *Writing Culture: The Poetics and Politics of Ethnography*. A School of American Research Advanced Seminar. Berkeley: University of California Press.

Cohen, Abner. 1969. *Custom and Politics in Urban Africa: A Study of Hausa Migrants in Yoruba Towns*. London: Routledge and K. Paul.

Cohn, Norman. 1961 (1957). *The Pursuit of the Millennium: Revolutionary Messianism in Medieval and Reformation Europe and Its Bearings on Modern Totalitarian Movements*. 2d ed. New York: Harper and Row.

Colburn, Forrest D. 1986. *Post-Revolutionary Nicaragua: State, Class, and the Dilemmas of Agrarian Policy*. Berkeley: University of California Press.

Collins, Joseph with Frances Moore Lappé et al. 1986 (1982). *Nicaragua: What Difference Could A Revolution Make? Food and Farming in the New Nicaragua*. Third Edition. New York: Food First/Grove Press.

Comaroff, Jean. 1985. *Body of Power, Spirit of Resistance: The Culture and History of a South African People*. Chicago: University of Chicago Press.

Condominas, Georges. 1973. "Ethics and Comfort: An Ethnographer's View of His Profession." 1972 Distinguished Lecture, American Anthropological Association Annual Report, 1972, pp. 1–17. Washington, D.C.: AAA.

Crawley, Eduardo. 1984 (1979). *Nicaragua in Perspective*. New York: St. Martin's Press.

Darío, Rubén. 1967. *Poesías Completas*. Vol. 2. Madrid: Aguilar.

Davis, Natalie Zemon. 1978. "Women on Top: Symbolic Sexual Inversion and Political Disorder in Early Modern Europe." In B.A. Babcock, ed., *The Reversible World*, pp. 147–190.

De Grazia, Sebastian. 1948. *The Political Community: A Study of Anomie.* Chicago: University of Chicago Press.

DeGregori, Thomas R. and Oriol Pi-Sunyer. 1969. *Economic Development: The Cultural Context.* New York: John Wiley and Sons, Inc.

DeWalt, Billie R. 1975. "Inequalities in Wealth, Adoption of Technology, and Production in a Mexican Ejido. *American Ethnologist.* 2:149–168.

Dixon, Marlene and Susan Jonas, eds. 1984. *Nicaragua Under Siege.* San Francisco: Synthesis Publications.

Dixon, Marlene, ed. 1985. *On Trial: Reagan's War Against Nicaragua, Testimony of the Permanent People's Tribunal.* San Francisco: Synthesis Publications.

Dodson, Michael and T. S. Montgomery. 1982. "The Churches in the Nicaraguan Revolution." In T. W. Walker, ed., *Nicaragua in Revolution,* pp. 161–180.

Donahue, John M. 1986. "The Profession and the People: Primary Health Care in Nicaragua." *Human Organization,* 45(2):96–103.

Douglas, Mary. 1966. *Purity and Danger: An Analysis of Concepts of Pollution and Taboo.* New York: Praeger.

Du Bois, Cora. 1944 (1960). *The People of Alor.* 2d ed. Cambridge: Cambridge University Press.

Durkheim, Emile. 1933. *The Division of Labor in Society.* Preface by G. S. Simpson. New York: Free Press.

——1951. *Suicide: A Study in Sociology.* Edited with introduction by George Simpson. Glencoe, Ill.: Free Press.

——1965 (1915). *The Elementary Forms of Religious Life.* New York: Free Press.

Durkheim, Emile and Marcel Mauss. 1963 (1903). *Primitive Classification.* Edited with introduction by Rodney Needham. Chicago: University of Chicago Press.

Eagleton, Terry. 1981. *Walter Benjamin, or, Towards a Revolutionary Criticism.* London: Verso-New Left Books.

——1986. *Against the Grain: Essays 1975–1985.* London: Verso-New Left Books.

Erasmus, Charles J. 1961. *Man Takes Control: Cultural Development and American Aid.* Minneapolis: University of Minnesota Press.

——1968. "Community Development and the Encogido Syndrome." *Human Organization,* 27:65–74.

Escorcia, Rev. Carlos. 1985. "Las Asambleas de Dios en Nicaragua." *Amanecer: Reflexion Cristiana en la Nueva Nicaragua.* (December), 38–39:22–25.

Evans-Pritchard, E. E. 1952. *Social Anthropology.* Glencoe, Ill.: Free Press.

Fabian, Johannes. 1983. *Time and the Other: How Anthropology Makes Its Object.* New York: Columbia University Press.

Forman, Shepard. 1975. *The Brazilian Peasantry.* New York: Columbia University Press.

Foster, George M. 1965. "Peasant Society and the Image of Limited Good." *American Anthropologist,* 67:293–315.

——1972. "The Anatomy of Envy: A Study in Symbolic Behavior." *Current Anthropology,* 13(2):164–202.

Foucault, Michel. 1979. *Discipline and Punish: The Birth of the Prison.* New York: Vintage Books.

Frank, Andre Gunder. 1971. *Capitalism and Underdevelopment in Latin America.* 2d ed. New York: Monthly Review Press.

Frank, André Gunder. 1972. *Lumpenbourgeoisie: Lumpendevelopment; Dependence, Class and Politics in Latin America.* New York: Monthly Review Press.

Freire, Paulo. 1970. *Pedagogy of the Oppressed.* New York: Seabury Press.

FSLN Directorate. 1982 (1979). "The Role of Religion in the New Nicaragua." In Borge et al., *Sandinistas Speak*, pp. 105–111.

Geertz, Clifford. 1973. *The Interpretation of Cultures: Selected Essays*. New York: Basic Books.

———1980. *Negara: The Theatre State in Nineteenth Century Bali*. Princeton, N.J.: Princeton University Press.

———1984. "Socialism in Siberia." A book review. *The New Republic* (Aug. 6), 191(6):34–37.

Geertz, Hildred. 1975. "An Anthropology of Religion and Magic, I." *Journal of Interdisciplinary History*, 8:14–32.

Gibellini, Rosino, ed. 1979. *Frontiers of Theology in Latin America*. Maryknoll, N.Y.: Orbis Books.

Giddens, Anthony. 1967. "Introduction" to *The Protestant Ethic and the Spirit of Capitalism*, by Max Weber, pp. 1–12. New York: Scribner's.

Ginger, Ray. 1949. *Eugene V. Debs: The Making of an American Radical*. New York: Collier Books.

———1958. *Six Days or Forever? Tennessee v. John Thomas Scopes*. Boston: Beacon Press.

Girardi, Giulio. 1985. "La Teosofía de la Liberación de Sandino." *Amanecer: Reflección Cristiana en la Nueva Nicaragua* (enero-febrero), 32–33:30–35.

———1986. *Sandinismo, Marxismo, Cristianismo en la Nueva Nicaragua, volumen I: La Confluencia*. Mexico, D.F.: Ediciones Nuevomar.

Glazer, Nathan and Daniel P. Moynihan. 1963. *Beyond the Melting Pot: The Negroes, Puerto Ricans, Jews, Italians, and Irish of New York City*. Cambridge: MIT Press and Harvard University Press.

Gluckman, Max. 1963. *Order and Rebellion in Tribal Africa*. New York: Free Press.

———1965. *Custom and Conflict in Africa*. Glencoe, Ill.: Free Press.

Goodwyn, Lawrence. 1978. *The Populist Movement: A Short History of the Agrarian Revolt in America*. New York: Oxford Univesity Press.

Gough, Kathleen. 1968. "World Revolution and the Science of Man." In T. Roszak, ed., *The Dissenting Academy*. New York: Random House.

Gramsci, Antonio. 1971. *Selections from the Prison Notebooks*. Edited and translated by Quinton Hoare and Geoffrey Nowell Smith. New York: International.

Green, Robert, ed. 1973. *Protestantism, Capitalism and Social Science: The Weber Thesis Controversy*. Lexington, Mass.: Heath.

Gregory, James R. 1975. "Image of Limited Good, or Expectation of Reciprocity?" *Current Anthropology* 16:73–84.

Gutierrez, Gustavo. 1973. *A Theology of Liberation: History, Politics and Salvation*. Maryknoll, N.Y.: Orbis Books.

———1983 (1979). *The Power of the Poor in History*. Maryknoll, N.Y.: Orbis Books.

Habermas, Jurgen. 1970. *Toward a Rational Society, Student Protest, Science, and Politics*. Boston: Beacon Press.

———1975. *Legitimation Crisis*. Boston: Beacon Press.

Hanke, Lewis. 1949. *The Spanish Struggle for Justice in the Conquest of America*. Philadelphia: University of Pennsylvania Press.

Harris, Richard and Carlos M. Vilas. 1985. *Nicaragua: A Revolution Under Siege*. London: Zed Books.

Hobsbawm, E. J. 1959. *Primitive Rebels: Studies in Archaic Forms of Social Movement in the 19th and 20th Centuries.* New York: Norton.
——1984. *Workers: Worlds of Labor.* New York: Pantheon Books.
Holy Bible. 1909. Edited by Rev. C. I. Scofield, D. D. Authorized King James Version. New York: Oxford University Press.
Horkheimer, Max. 1974. *Critique of Instrumental Reason: Lectures and Essays Since the End of World War Two.* New York: Seabury Press.
Horowitz, Irving Louis, ed. 1967. *The Rise and Fall of Project Camelot: Studies in the Relationship Between Social Science and Practical Politics.* Cambridge: MIT Press.
Hubert, Henri and Marcel Mauss. 1964 (1898). *Sacrifice: Its Nature and Function.* Foreword by E. E. Evans-Pritchard. Chicago: University of Chicago Press.
Huizer, Gerrit. 1970. " 'Resistance to Change' and Radical Peasant Mobilization: Foster and Erasmus Reconsidered." *Human Organization* 29:303–313.
Huizer, Gerrit and Bruce Mannheim, eds. 1979. *The Politics of Anthropology: From Colonialism and Sexism Toward a View from Below.* The Hague: Mouton.
Iglesia Guatemalteca en el Exilio (I.G.E.). 1983. *Cristianos: Por Qué Temen a la Revolución?* Mexico, D.F.: no publisher given.
Ingham, John M. 1970. "On Mexican Folk Medicine." *American Anthropolgist* 72:76–87.
Instituto de Estudio del Sandinismo. 1983. *El Sandinismo: Documentos Básicos.* Managua: Editorial Nueva Nicaragua.
Jameson, Fredric. 1971. *Marxism and Form: Twentieth Century Dialectical Theories of Literature.* Princeton: Princeton University Prss.
Kaplan, David and Benson Saler. 1966. "Foster's 'Image of Limited Good': An Example of Anthropological Explanation." *American Anthropologist* 68:202–206.
Kautsky, Karl. 1953 (1908). *Foundations of Christianity.* New York: S. A. Russell.
Kovel, Joel. 1984. "Marxism and Christianity." *Monthly Review* (June), pp. 49–57.
Kroeber, A. L. 1948. *Anthropology.* New York: Harcourt, Brace.
Lancaster, Roger N. 1986a. "Comment on Arguelles and Rich's 'Homosexuality, Homophobia and Revolution: Notes Toward an Understanding of the Cuban Lesbian and Gay Male Experience.' " *Signs,* 12(1):188–192.
——1986b. "Festival of Disguises." *The Progressive* (Nov), 50(11):50.
——1988. "Subject Honor and Object Shame: The Construction of Male Homosexuality and Stigma in Nicaragua." *Ethnology,* (April), vol. 27, no. 2.
Leacock, Eleanor. 1971. *The Culture of Poverty: A Critique.* New York: Simon and Schuster.
Leiken, Robert S. 1984. "Sins of the Sandinistas: Nicaragua's Untold Stories." *The New Republic* (October 8), 191(15):16–22.
Lenin, V. I. 1929. *What Is to Be Done? Burning Questions of Our Movement.* New York: International Publishers.
——1939a. *Imperialism: The Highest Stage of Capitalism.* New York: International Publishers.
——1939b. *Selected Works.* Vol. XI. London: Lawrence and Wishart.
Lernoux, Penny. 1980. *Cry of the People: United States Involvement in the Rise of Fascism, Torture, and Murder and the Persecution of the Catholic Church in Latin America.* New York: Doubleday.

———1986. "Polarization, Confusion Ravage Nicaragua: Partisan Priorities Eclipse Religious." *National Catholic Reporter* (May 16), Vol. 22, no. 29.

Levine, Daniel H., ed. 1986. *Religion and Political Conflict in Latin America.* Chapel Hill: University of North Carolina Press.

Lewis, Oscar. 1961. *The Children of Sánchez: Autobiography of a Mexican Family.* New York: Random House.

———1966. "The Culture of Poverty." *Scientific American* (Oct.), 215(4):3–10.

Lewis, Oscar with Ruth M. Lewis and Susan M. Rigdon. 1977, 1978. *Living with the Revolution: An Oral History of Contemporary Cuba,* 3 vols. Urbana: University of Illinois Press.

Long, Norman. 1968. *Social Change and the Individual: A Study of the Social and Religious Responses to Innovation in a Zambian Rural Community.* Manchester: Manchester University Press.

Lowy, Michael. 1985. "Revolution Against Progress: Walter Benjamin's Romantic Anarchism." *New Left Review* (August), 152:42–59.

Lukács, Georg. 1968. *History and Class Consciousness: Studies in Marxist Dialectics.* London: Merlin Press.

McFadden, Thomas M. 1975. *Liberation, Revolution, and Freedom: Theological Perspectives, Proceedings of the College Theological Society.* New York: Seabury Press.

McGovern, Arthur F. 1980. *Marxism: An American Christian Perspective.* Maryknoll, N.Y.: Orbis Books.

Malinowski, Bronislaw. 1947. *The Dynamics of Culture Change.* New Haven: Yale University Press.

———1961. *Argonauts of the Western Pacific.* New York: Dutton.

Mannheim, Karl. 1936. *Ideology and Utopia: An Introduction to the Sociology of Knowledge.* Preface by Louis Wirth. New York: Harcourt, Brace and World.

Marcuse, Herbert. 1966. *Eros and Civilization: A Philosophical Inquiry Into Freud.* Boston: Beacon Press.

Markovic, Mihailo. 1974. *From Affluence to Praxis: Philosophy and Social Criticism.* Ann Arbor: University of Michigan Press.

Markovic, Mihailo and Gajo Petrovic, eds. 1979. *Praxis: Yugoslav Essays in the Philosophy and Methodology of the Social Sciences.* Boston: D. Reidel.

Marshall, Gordon. 1980. *Prebyterians and Profits: Calvinism and the Development of Capitalism in Scotland, 1560–1707.* Oxford: Oxford University Press (Clarendon Books).

———1982. *In Search of the Spirit of Capitalism: An Essay on Max Weber's Protestant Thesis.* New York: Columbia University Press.

Marx, Karl. 1939. *The German Ideology (Parts I and III).* New York: International Publishers.

———1963a. *The Eighteenth Brumaire of Louis Bonaparte.* New York: International Publishers.

———1963b. *The Poverty of Philosophy.* New York: International Publishers.

———1964. *Economic and Philosophical Manuscripts of 1844.* Edited with introduction by Dirk J. Struik. New York: International Publishers.

———1965. *Pre-Capitalist Economic Formations.* Edited with introduction by E. J. Hobsbawm. New York: International Publishers.

———1967. *Capital: A Critique of Political Economy.* Vol. I. New York: International Publishers.

———1977. *Selected Writings.* Edited by David McLellan. Oxford: Oxford University Press.

Marx, Karl and Friedrich Engels. 1948. *The Communist Manifesto.* New York: International Publishers.

———1964. *On Religion.* Edited with introduction by R. Niebuhr. New York: Schocken Books.

———1968. *Selected Works.* New York: International Publishers.

Mauss, Marcel. 1954. *The Gift: Forms and Functions of Exchange in Archaic Societies.* Glencoe, Ill.: Free Press.

Mead, Margaret. 1963 (1939). *Sex and Temperament in Three Primitive Societies.* New York: Morrow.

Mejía Godoy, Carlos y Pablo Martinez. 1981. *La Misa Campesina Nicaragüense.* Managua: Ministerio de Cultura.

Miguez Bonino, José, ed. 1984 (1977). *Faces of Jesus: Latin American Christologies.* Maryknoll, N.Y.: Orbis Books.

Mills, C. Wright. 1959. *The Sociological Imagination.* New York: Oxford University Press.

Mintz, Sidney. 1953. "The Folk-Urban Continuum and the Rural Proletarian Community." *American Journal of Sociology,* 59(2):136–143.

———1973. "A Note on the Definition of Peasantry." *Journal of Peasant Studies,* 1:91–106.

Miranda, José Porfirio. 1974. *Marx and the Bible: A Critique of the Philosophy of Oppression.* Maryknoll, N.Y.: Orbis Books.

———1980. *Marx Against the Marxists: The Christian Humanism of Karl Marx.* Maryknoll, N.Y.: Orbis Books.

———1982. *Communism and the Bible.* Maryknoll, N.Y.: Orbis Books.

Moynihan, Daniel P. 1965. *The Negro Family: The Case for National Action.* Washington: U.S. Department of Labor.

———1967. "The President and the Negro: The Moment Lost." *Commentary* 43:31–45.

Nash, June. 1979a. "Ethnology in a Revolutionary Setting." In Huizer and Mannheim, eds. *The Politics of Anthropology,* pp. 353–370.

———1979b. *We Eat the Mines and the Mines Eat Us: Dependency and Exploitation in Bolivian Tin Mines.* New York: Columbia University Press.

Needham, Rodney. 1963. "Introduction." In Durkheim and Mauss, *Primitive Classification,* pp. vii–xlviii.

Nelson, Susan Rosales. 1986. "Bolivia: Continuity and Conflict in Religious Discourse." In Daniel H. Levine, ed., *Religion and Political Conflict in Latin America,* pp. 218–235. Chapel Hill: University of North Carolina.

O'Brien, Conor Cruise. 1986. "God and Man in Nicargua." *The Atlantic* 258(2):50–72.

Ong, Aihwa. 1987. *Spirits of Resistance and Capitalist Discipline: Factory Women in Malaysia.* Albany State University Press.

Orwell, George. 1952. *Homage to Catalonia.* New York: Harvest Books.

———1968. *The Collected Essays, Journalism and Letters of Goerge Orwell. Vol. I: An Age Like This, 1920–1940.* Edited by Sonia Orwell and Ian Angus. New York: Harcourt, Brace and World.

Palma, Milagros. 1985. La Rebelión de la Mujer: Los Personajes en las Danzas de Santo Domingo." *Ventana (Barricada Cultural),* sábado, 10 de augusto.

Pendle, George. 1967 (1963). *A History of Latin America.* Baltimore: Penguin Books.

Petras, James. 1980. "Whither the Nicaraguan Revolution?" Somerville, Mass.: New England Free Press Pamphlet.

Petrovic, Gajo. 1967. *Marx in the Mid-Twentieth Century*. Garden City, N.Y.: Anchor Books.

Piker, Steven. 1966. "'The Image of Limited Good'": Comments on an Exercise in Description and Interpretation." *American Anthropologist* 68:1202–1211.

Poggi, Gianfraco. 1983. *Calvinism and the Capitalist Spirit: Max Weber's Protestant Ethic*. Amherst: University of Massachusetts Press.

Potter, Jack M. 1974. "Cantonese Shamanism." In Arthur Worl, ed., *Religion and Ritual in Chinese Society*, pp. 207–231. Stanford: Stanford University Press.

Potter, Sulamith and Jack Potter. 1988. *China's Peasants: The Anthropology of a Revolution*. Cambridge: Cambridge University Press.

Rabinbach, Anson. 1985. "Between Enlightenment and Apocalypse: Benjamin, Bloch and Modern German Jewish Messianism." *New German Critique* (Winter), 34:78–124.

Rabinow, Paul. 1977. *Reflections on Fieldwork in Morocco*. Foreword by Robert N. Bellah. Berkeley: University of California Press.

Rabinow, Paul and Norma Haan, eds. 1983. *Social Science as Moral Inquiry*. New York: Columbia University Press.

Randall, Margaret. 1983. *Christians in the Nicaraguan Revolution*. Vancouver, B.C.: New Star Books.

Ratzinger, Joseph Cardinal. 1984. *Instructions on Certain Aspects of the "Theology of Liberation."* Dublin: Veritas Publications.

Redfield, Robert. 1930. *Tepoztlán: A Mexican Village*. Chicago: University of Chicago Press.

—— 1941. *Folk Cultures of Yucatán*. Chicago: University of Chicago Press.

—— 1955. "The Social Organization of Tradition." *Far Eastern Quarterly* (Nov), 15(1):13–21.

—— 1960. *The Little Community, and Peasant Society and Culture*. Chicago: University of Chicago Press.

Rey, Pierre-Philippe. 1982. "Class Alliances." *International Journal of Sociology* 12(2):1–120.

Roberts, Bryan R. 1967. "El Protestantismo en Dos Barrios Marginales de Guatemala. *Seminario de Educación: Estudios Centroamericanos*, no. 2, pp. 7–22.

—— 1978. *Cities of Peasants: The Political Economy of Urbanization in the Third World*. Beverly Hills: Sage.

Robertson, Hector M. 1973. *Aspects of Economic Individualism: A Criticism of Max Weber and His School*. Clifton, N.J.: A. M. Kelley.

Robinson, James M. 1968. *The Beginnings of Dialectic Theology*. Vol. I. Richmond, Va.: John Knox Press.

Romero, Archbishop Oscar. 1985 (1980). *Voice of the Voiceless: The Four Pastoral Letters and Other Statements*. Introductory essays by I. Martin-Baro and J. Sobrino. Maryknoll, N.Y.: Orbis Books.

—— n.d. *Bienaventuranzas*. (El Salvador?): Coordinación Nacional de la Iglesia Popular (CONIP).

Rosset, Peter and John Vandernaeer, eds. 1983. *The Nicaragua Reader: Documents of a Revolution Under Fire*. 2d ed. New York: Grove Press.

Roth, Robert Paul. 1985. *The Theatre of God: Story in Christian Doctrines*. Philadelphia: Fortress Press.

Ruby, Jay. 1982. *A Crack in the Mirror: Reflexive Perspectives in Anthropology.* Berkeley: University of California Press.

Rudolph, James D. 1982. *Nicaragua: A Country Study.* Foreign Area Studies, American University. Washington, D.C.: GPO.

Sahlins, Marshall. 1968. *Tribesmen.* Englewood Cliffs, N.J.: Prentice-Hall.

Sandinista Leaders. 1985. *Nicaragua: The Sandinista People's Revolution: Speeches by Sandinista Leaders.* New York: Pathfinder Press.

Sartre, Jean-Paul. 1976 (1960). *Critique of Dialectical Reason: Theory of Practical Ensembles.* Atlantic Highlands, N.J.: Humanities Press.

SCAAN (Stanford Central America Action Network). 1983. *Revolution in Central America.* Boulder: Westview Press.

Scholem, Gershom. 1971. *The Messianic Idea in Judaism and Other Essays on Jewish Spirituality.* New York: Schocken Books.

Segundo, Juan Luis. 1976. *The Liberation of Theology.* Maryknoll, N.Y.: Orbis Books.

Sinclair, Upton. 1922. *They Call Me Carpenter: A Tale of the Second Coming.* New York: Boni and Liveright.

Smith, Waldeman R. 1977. *The Fiesta System and Economic Change.* New York: Columbia University Press.

Sobrino, Jon. 1978 (1976). *Christology at the Crossroads: A Latin American Approach.* Maryknoll, N.Y.: Orbis Books.

Sorel, Georges. 1950. *Reflections on Violence.* Introduction by E. Shils. New York: Collier Books.

——1976. *From Georges Sorel: Essays in Socialism and Philosophy.* Edited with introduction by J. L. Stanley. New York: Oxford University Press.

Steffens, Lincoln. 1926. *Moses in Red: The Revolt of Israel as a Typical Revolution.* Philadelphia: Dorrance.

Stoll, David. 1986. "Headache of the Revolution: Evangelical Protestants in the Sandinista-Contra War." Manuscript.

Strathern, Andrew. 1979. "Anthropology, 'Snooping,' and Commitment: A View from Papua New Guinea." In Huizer and Mannheim, eds., *The Politics of Anthropology,* pp. 269–273.

Sweezy, Paul. 1980. *Post-Revolutionary Society.* New York: Monthly Review Press.

Tamez, Elsa. 1979. *La Biblia de los Oprimidos: La Opresión en la Teología Bíblica.* San José, Costa Rica: Departamento Ecuménico de Investigaciones (DEI).

Taussig, Michael. 1978. "Nutrition, Development, and Foreign Aid: A Case Study in a Colombian Plantation Zone." *International Journal of Health Services,* 8(1):101–121.

——1980. *The Devil and Commodity Fetishism in South America.* Chapel Hill: University of North Carolina Press.

——1987. *Shamanism, Colonialism, and the Wild Man: A Study in Terror and Healing.* Chicago: University of Chicago Press.

Thompson, E. P. 1963. *The Making of the English Working Class.* New York: Vintage Books.

Thrupp, Sylvia L., ed. 1962. *Millennial Dreams in Action: Essays in Comparative Study.* The Hague: Mouton.

Tucker, Robert. 1972. *Philosophy and Myth in Karl Marx.* Second edition. Cambridge: Cambridge University Press.

Tumarkin, Nina. 1983. *Lenin Lives! The Lenin Cult in Soviet Russia.* Cambridge, Mass.: Harvard University Press.

Turner, Victor and Edith Turner. 1978. *Image and Pilgrimage in Christian Culture: Anthropological Perspectives.* New York: Columbia University Press.

Valentine, Charles A. 1968. *Culture and Poverty: Critique and Counter-Proposals.* Chicago: University of Chicago Press.

Vilas, Carlos M. 1986. *The Sandinista Revolution: National Liberation and Social Transformation in Central America.* New York: Monthly Review Press and Center for the Studies of the Americas.

Vogt, Evon Z. 1976. *Tortillas for the Gods: A Symbolic Analysis of Zinacanteco Rituals.* Cambridge: Harvard University Press.

Wagner, Henry Ramp with Helen Rand Parish. 1967. *The Life and Writings of Bartolomé de las Casas.* Albequerque: University of New Mexico Press.

Walker, Thomas W., ed. 1982. *Nicaragua in Revolution.* New York: Praeger Publishers.

Walker, General William. 1985 (1860). *The War in Nicaragua.* Foreword by R. Houston. Tucson: University of Arizona Press.

Wallace, Anthony F. C. 1956. "Revitalization Movements." *American Anthropological Association* (April), 58(2):264–281.

——1966. *Religion: An Anthropological View.* New York: Random House.

——1969. *The Death and Rebirth of the Seneca.* New York: Knopf.

——1970. "Religious Revitalization: A Function of Religion in Human History and Evolution." In E. Hammell and W. S. Simmons, ed., *Man Makes Sense: A Reader in Modern Cultural Anthropology,* pp. 370–383. Boston: Little, Brown.

Wallis, Wilson D. 1943. *Messiahs: Their Role in Civilization.* Washington, D.C.: American Council on Public Affairs.

Walzer, Michael. 1965. *The Revolution of the Saints: A Study in the Origins of Radical Politics.* Cambridge: Harvard University Press.

——1985. *Exodus and Revolution.* New York: Basic Books.

Weber, Henri. 1981. *Nicaragua: The Sandinista Revolution.* London: Verso Editions and NLB.

Weber, Max. 1927. *General Economic History.* Translated by Frank H. Knight. New York: Greenberg.

——1947. *The Theory of Social and Economic Organization.* Edited with introduction by T. Parsons. New York: Free Press of Glencoe.

——1958. *The Protestant Ethic and the Spirit of Capitalism.* Introduction by A. Giddens (1976). New York: Scribner's.

——1963. *The Sociology of Religion.* Introduction by T. Parsons. Boston: Beacon Press.

——1966. "Class, Status and Party." In R. Bendix and S. M. Lipset, *Class, Status and Power.*

——1971. *The Interpretation of Social Reality.* Edited with introduction by J. E. T. Eldridge. New York: Schocken Books.

——1978. *Economy and Society: An Outline of Interpretive Sociology.* Edited by Guenther Roth and Claus Wittich. Berkeley: University of California.

Williams, Raymond. 1977. *Marxism and Literature.* New York: Oxford University Press.

Wolf, Eric R. 1955. "Types of Latin American Peasantry." *American Anthropologist,* 57:452–459.

——1957. "Closed Corporate Communities in Mesoamerica and Central Java." *Southwestern Journal of Anthropology,* 13:1–18.

——1959. *Sons of the Shaking Earth.* Chicago: University of Chicago Prss.

REFERENCES

——1969. *Peasant Wars of the Twentieth Century*. New York: Harper and Row.
Wolf, Eric R. and Joseph Jorgensen. 1970. "Anthropology on the Warpath in Thailand." *The New York Review of Books* (November 19), vol. 15, no. 9.
Woodburn, James. 1982. "Egalitarian Societies." *Man* 17(3):431–451.
Woodward, C. Vann. 1978 (1938). *Tom Watson: Agrarian Rebel*. New York: Oxford University Press.
Worsley, Peter. 1968. *The Trumpet Shall Sound: A Study of "Cargo" Cults in Melanesia*. New York: Schocken Books.
Zwerling, Philip and Connie Martin. 1985. *Nicaragua: A New Kind of Revolution*. Westport, Conn.: Lawrence Hill.

Index